The Rites of Rulers

The
Rites of Rulers

Ritual in Industrial Society –
The Soviet Case

CHRISTEL LANE

Lecturer in Sociology
University of Aston in Birmingham

CAMBRIDGE UNIVERSITY PRESS

Cambridge
London   New York   New Rochelle
Melbourne   Sydney

Published by the Press Syndicate of the University of Cambridge
The Pitt Building, Trumpington Street, Cambridge CB2 1RP
32 East 57th Street, New York, NY 10022, USA
296 Beaconsfield Parade, Middle Park, Melbourne 3206, Australia

First published 1981

Printed in Great Britain at
The Pitman Press, Bath

British Library Cataloguing in Publication Data

Lane, Christel
The rites of rulers.
1. Rites and ceremonies – Russia
2. Russia – Social life and customs
– 20th century
I. Title
301.2'1 DK32 80-41747

ISBN 0 521 22608 2
ISBN 0 521 28347 7 Pbk

Contents

Contents

Contents

Illustrations

Acknowledgements

I am indebted to the SSRC, whose research grant made this work possible, and to Geoffrey Hawthorn of the University of Cambridge who made valuable comments on the whole manuscript. I would like to thank those Soviet professionals and friends who helped me in various ways with my work on a visit in 1978. Lastly, I am grateful to Novosti Press Agency for permission to include the illustrations of rituals.

University of Aston in Birmingham   C.L.

ABBREVIATIONS

ASSR   Autonomous Soviet Socialist Republic
CPSU   Communist Party of the Soviet Union
RSFSR   Russian Soviet Federated Socialist Republic

Introduction

The culture of every society is in part spontaneously generated by its members and in part consciously shaped and directed by its political elites. By "culture" I mean both the formalized ideological constructs, such as art, law or religion, and the more informal way in which members of a society perceive themselves, their society and their relations to the material, social and intellectual products of that society. The balance between spontaneous creation and conscious management of culture, however, varies between different types of society and within a society during different stages of historical development. A process of cultural management is more pronounced in societies with a one-party system, sustaining a single ruling elite unified by the urgent pursuit of a number of clearly defined general goals for their society, such as modernization, industrialization, social and economic reconstruction after a military defeat or the emergence from colonial domination, or the building of socialism. It is less pervasive in a pluralist society with less general, permanent and urgent social and political objectives and more piecemeal approaches to their implementation. Cultural management becomes an overriding concern when the first type of society has been newly formed. During the early formative period, when old societies have to be radically transformed in all spheres, cultural management may be so extensive and drastic that it becomes a cultural revolution.

Both cultural management and cultural revolution utilize a large variety of means to achieve the desired changes in the consciousness of individual members of society. Besides reconstructing culture by changing actual social relations in that society, that is, changing relations of production and the economic and occupational structure, breaking up status hierarchies and formal or informal social groupings, the agents of cultural management or revolution may press into service education, political ideology, religion or a new "revolutionary" art.

1

Thus cultural revolution differs from cultural management only in the extent of change effected and in the range of tools employed to this end. Most studies have focussed on those cultural revolutions which have been accompanied by fundamental social upheaval and repercussions on nearly every aspect of society; where wide-ranging changes have been wrought either in social relations and forms of ideology, for example the Soviet Cultural Revolution of between 1928–32 (see Tucker 1977 and Fitzpatrick 1978), or in the ideological dimension of a belief system and in the political and social hierarchy derived from it, for example the Chinese Cultural Revolution of the 1960s.

Hardly any attention has been paid to the less spectacular silent revolutions which have left the existing social structure intact and have instead focussed on the behavioural dimension of ideology (in the widest sense), that is, cult and ritual, as a means to change deep-seated moral orientations, fixed by habit, custom and, often, by an older form of ritual. The neglect is due in part to the fact that this form of partial cultural revolutuon is less obtrusive and in part to the fact that the analysis of ritual is widely believed to be irrelevant to the dynamics of a modern society.

The present work, in contrast, is concerned with ritual as a tool of partial cultural revolution or, better, cultural management, namely with the ritual derived from Soviet Marxism–Leninism in the contemporary Soviet Union. Cultural management and cultural revolution are by no means new phenomena in Soviet society and have been endemic there ever since the Revolution. The means used to this end and the scope of revolution have varied between different historical periods (see pp. 153ff), but a direct, rather than derivative, assault on outmoded value orientations through ritual and cult has always played some part among them. Soviet political elites have realized from the very beginning that they will not succeed in creating a new type of society unless political change is accompanied by efforts which, to quote Marriott (1963: 29), "educate their citizens to this newly chosen way of life and mobilize them in support of deliberately cultivated values" and modes of social behaviour. Most of the Bolshevik leaders were convinced of the urgent necessity of this task. Thus for Trotsky the Revolution meant essentially "the people's final break with the Asiatic, with the Seventeenth Century, with Holy Russia, with icons and cockroaches" (Trotsky 1960: 94). Lenin was particularly aware of the fact that the socio-political changes wrought by the October Revolution had to be followed by a less violent transformation of basic attitudes if the Revolution was to succeed. But for the early Soviet political leaders cultural revolution always went hand in hand with social revolution, with the former consolidating or preparing for the latter. Since the middle thirties, however, cultural revolution or, more properly, cultural management has become a substitute for social revolution and has thus assumed a conservative character. Consequently it has achieved a position of great importance in the arsenal of means to exert social control employed by political elites, although the degree of importance and the approach to tools of cultural management have varied significantly during different stages of Soviet social development. Up to the early sixties, ritual as a tool of cultural management has only been utilized selectively and has never been part of a sustained and general campaign. It is the universal introduction of a *system* of rituals from the early sixties onwards that express the values and norms of Soviet socialism which forms the subject of the present study.

My analysis of ritual thus focusses on the way in which ritual has become an important means to structure and maintain power relations in Soviet society. Whereas most recent books on aspects of the Soviet political process have concentrated on the distribution of, and struggle for, power within or between political elites, this study attempts to shed light on power relations between the political elites and the masses. I try to show that this aspect of the distribution of power – which has become neglected by political sociologists as a consequence of the discrediting of the "totalitarian" approach to Soviet society – is still vital to our understanding of Soviet society.

This process of creating and introducing such a complex of rituals has gone largely unnoticed in the West, and of those few scholars who have become aware of its existence, many have not realized the full implications of it. These lacunae of knowledge and understanding can be found in the writing both of specialists on ritual in industrial society and of authors who have made a special study of the value system and the methods of its inculcation in contemporary Soviet society. Thus Shils in an article on ritual in modern society (1969) maintains that contemporary Soviet rulers are deliberately anti-ritualistic. Hollander (1973), in the sections of his book that deal with values and political socialization in Soviet society, shows not only imperfect knowledge but also inadequate understanding of the new system of rituals. He devotes only a few lines to the new ritual which, basing his information on a very inadequate Western source, he writes off as "not having taken root" in Soviet society (*ibid.*: 192). He is unaware of the very

3

important propaganda function of ritual, and the very special way in which ritual inculcates political norms and values, when he claims that "Soviet propaganda tries to affect its audience primarily on a conscious rather than sub- or semi-conscious level . . . The effort to prompt people to act on the basis of motives and impulses of which they have little or no awareness has no easily identifiable Soviet equivalent [to American practice in the field of advertising]" (*ibid.*: 127). And a more recent study of political culture by White (1979) that has as one of its chief aims the study of the formation of political attitudes, omits discussion of the system of socialist rituals.

A fuller and more informed discussion of the new system of rituals can be found in a few, relatively unknown, articles on the subject (see McDowell 1974; Unger 1974; Powell 1975; Binns 1979).

Little, therefore, is known by Western readers about either the rituals themselves or about the many theoretical implications of their utilization, and a few introductory remarks are in order. These rituals span a wide spectrum. They range from mass political ritual, such as that contained in the celebrations of the Anniversary of the October Revolution, through rituals of initiation into various social and political collectives, such as the Pioneers, the Army, the working class, to such individual *rites de passage* as the Festive Registration of the New-Born Child and the socialist wedding and funeral rites. In addition, there is much ritual in the holidays of the calendric cycle, such as a summer solstice, a Harvest Festival or a winter carnival. While some of the holidays and rituals have their origin either in Russian or earlier Soviet times, many have been newly devised or adapted during the sixties and seventies. It is only from this period onwards that one can speak of a system of Soviet rituals which, although highly diverse in form, have been unified by their common value content.

The theoretical and empirical study of this system of Soviet rituals will cover the following aspects. The book starts with a definition and theoretical analysis of ritual and related concepts, drawing on recent Western work in this field. A short critical overview of the theoretical and practical approach to ritual by Soviet social scientists and workers in the field of ideology, comparing their work with that of Western students of ritual, will throw light on its nature and function in Soviet society. This is followed in chapter 2 by a theoretical discussion of ritual in contemporary Soviet society, which will deal with the question of *why* ritualization of social relations has come to predominate as a means of maintaining social control at the present time and, by comparison, has had relatively little importance in earlier periods. It will present a historical analysis of Soviet ritual in relation to other strategies of maintaining social control adopted at different stages of Soviet social development. Chapter 3 is concerned with the problem of whether the Soviet system of rituals is sacred or secular or whether it holds an ambiguous mixture of the two attitudes, and discusses whether the beliefs and rituals of Soviet Marxism–Leninism are best viewed as ideology, religion or as political religion. Chapter 4 covers the problems surrounding the organization of the Soviet system of ritual. It provides information about how individual rites or holidays are actually created or adapted and introduced into Soviet life, looks at the work of ritual specialists and masters of ceremony, at financial and political support for this work and at the relations between ritual specialists and those who actually perform the rites.

This general theoretical introduction of the new Soviet system of ritual is followed by a long and detailed (as detailed as existing sources permit) description and analysis of all the major rituals and holidays performed at the present time. Besides describing the actual scenario of various versions of each ritual, a short outline of their social context and historical background is given to help the reader to see them in perspective. While most of the rituals and holidays are fairly recent creations or revivals, two of the mass political holidays have long and eventful histories. The concluding chapter of this descriptive section will therefore be given over to a historical analysis of these holidays and their ritual from 1918 up to the present time, showing how changed social and political conditions and concerns are reflected in the changing ritual form and content of these holidays.

Having familiarized the reader with the actual rituals and holidays, the next chapters give a theoretical interpretation of them from various angles. Chapter 11 presents an analysis of the ritual symbolism employed, and chapter 12 deals with the nature of syncretism in Soviet ritual. Chapter 13 offers an evaluation of the impact of this ritual, assessing it in terms of the number of participants and in terms of its effects on attitudes and on behaviour.

The concluding chapter presents a comparative study of political ritual in modern society. Besides looking at some contemporary societies it examines the ritual systems of the two modern historical societies which reveal the most striking parallels with the Soviet system. Short descriptions, based on available secondary sources, of such ritual in the USA and Britain, in some developing African countries, in

France after the 1789 Revolution and in Nazi Germany are given, which relate each system of ritual to the notions of civil and political religion. Comparisons between the ritual of each of these different societies and that of the USSR will establish what is general to ritual in modern society and what is unique about ritual in contemporary Soviet society, and some explanations for these patterns are suggested.

The preceding outline of the contents of this book indicates that it tries to fill serious gaps existing both in the field of Soviet area studies and in the sociological/anthropological study of ritual in modern industrial society. In addition, it has something to offer also to sociologists of religion. For Soviet area specialists, the book is particularly relevant to those interested in problems of ideology and political socialization. But it should also be of interest to a much wider circle of students of Soviet society, since a study of a society's ritual sheds much light on the general problem areas found in that society and on the strategies adopted by political elites to deal with them. Sociologists and anthropologists involved in the study of ritual should find in this work many insights both of a substantive and a theoretical nature about areas as yet insufficiently or not at all explored. I am referring to such areas as ritual in an industrial and state socialist society; ritual with an avowedly secular orientation; ritual sponsored "from above" rather than spontaneously generated by those performing it; ritual still in the process of creation and implantation into social life. In addition, the amount of descriptive material on a large variety of rituals, as yet chiefly unknown in the West, will be valuable to students of ritual for comparative purposes. Sociologists of religion will be interested in learning about the efforts of Soviet political elites to replace conventional religious rites with the new rites of Soviet Marxism–Leninism. They may also gain something from the application of the notion of political religion to the beliefs and practice of Soviet Marxism–Leninism.

Finally, a few comments have to be made on the methods employed to collect the data presented in this book. The first and most extensively used source has been the written accounts of the various rituals presented by Soviet ritual specialists, that is those actively involved in the creation and the introduction of the rites, by Soviet social scientists and by newspaper correspondents. The second source of information has been my observation of various rituals during two study visits to the Soviet Union in 1977 and 1978. The third method has entailed having informal talks with Soviet citizens from different walks of life who have been participants in these rituals, as well as with Soviet people who are professionally involved either in the study or the practical organization of some or all of these rituals.

Unlike most anthropological studies of ritual, which base themselves mainly on sources two and three, this work has had to rely more on the first source of information. This is for two reasons. First, the greater impersonality and reliance on written communication in industrial society makes written sources more widely available and direct oral communication more difficult for the student of ritual. Secondly, the greater degree of closedness of Soviet society in comparison with most other societies makes access to something even as public as ritual a problem for a foreign outsider. Although some of the rituals are relatively easily observed others are more inaccessible. They may be difficult to locate, or they may be performed by selected collectives in non-public buildings or admission to public spaces is reserved for selected people and by ticket only, as is the case with the culminating events of some of the mass political holidays. While observation of rites can thus be difficult, systematic interviewing of participants in the rites is impossible for the foreign researcher.

The implications of these restrictions on direct access to the topic of research and the consequent greater reliance on secondary data are not as serious as it may appear at first sight. It must be remembered that most of the written accounts of rituals utilized have been rendered by ritual specialists, that is by people deeply involved in the subject matter, whose accounts are usually written for methodological purposes and are meant to guide and advise other people in the field of ritual on the basis of practical experience; they are thus relatively free of bias. They have been written at a time when the process of devising and introducing the new ritual is still under constant examination and more often than not are composed in a critical rather than self-congratulatory or advertisement-type manner. A more serious limitation on this study is the non-availability of direct information from participants in the ritual, as this makes an evaluation of the effect of the rituals very difficult. It must be remembered, though, that adequate information on this aspect of ritual is very difficult to obtain even in societies where the researcher has easy access to information.

Part I

The theory and organization of ritual

1

Ritual and related concepts

A THEORETICAL PERSPECTIVE

The task of clarifying the concept of ritual presents an unusually large problem. Although anthropologists and, to a lesser extent, sociologists and political scientists have been grappling with this problem since the very beginnings of their disciplines there is still, in the words of Leach (1968: 526), "the widest possible disagreement as to how the word ritual should be understood". This particular study is not intended to be a theoretical treatise on the concept of ritual. It neither reviews the extensive literature on the subject up to date nor does it claim to establish a new definitive answer to the problem of ritual in general. It merely takes up those aspects of the general debate which seem relevant to the study of a system of rituals as a tool of cultural management and political socialization in modern industrial society and throws new light on the debate on ritual from its own perspective.

Ritual, I suggest in this preliminary definition, is a stylized, repetitive social activity which, through the use of symbolism, expresses and defines social relations. Ritual activity occurs in a social context where there is ambiguity or conflict about social relations, and it is performed to resolve or disguise them. Ritual can be religious or secular.

The symbolic nature of ritual lies in the fact that it is significant not for its ostensible meaning but that it stands for, and has to be interpreted by reference to, a transcendent principle outside the means–goal relationship. The "transcendent principle" is constituted by those beliefs and values at the top of a hierarchy of meaning which order and structure those at the lower levels. The activity can be entirely symbolic, or it can have both a symbolic and an instrumental or expressive aspect. Ritual activity is distinguished from the other two, to quote Myerhoff (1974: 3), in that "it always goes beyond them, endowing some larger meaning to activities it is associated with". The distinction

11

is, however, not always easy to make and careful contextual analysis is often necessary. While most students of ritual have emphasized the difficulty of separating ritual from instrumental activity, the Soviet social context also makes the distinction between drama and ritual problematic. This is the case because much of Soviet ritual is representative ritual, that is a ritual reconstruction and celebration of the revolutionary or patriotic past in a dramatic form, while much of the drama is historical and ideologically charged.

In so far as ritual always entails the enactment of a social relationship between an individual or a group of individuals and another, more inclusive, group, the relationship is shown in such a way that it both portrays and subtly alters the relationship framed in the ritual act. Ritual, in the words of Geertz (1968: 7), provides both "a model of" and "a model for" that relationship. I would extend Geertz's insight by suggesting that the emphasis given to these two properties of ritual will vary according to the social context in which the relationship is set. If the social context has merely blurred, weakened or temporarily disturbed that relationship and the resulting ambiguity has to be removed, the "model of" aspect will predominate. If, however, the social context is also one of conflict, that is there is a great discrepancy between the ideological definition of the relationship and the relationship as it actually affects the actors, then the "model for" aspect will be more prominent, asserting the ideological definition with varying degrees of consciousness. To rephrase this idea in the words of Terence Turner (1974: 19): "ritual, as a controllable and orderly pattern of action, constitutes an effective mechanism for manipulating or reordering the ambiguous aspects of the situation in relation to which it is defined".

In the social context of the small, internally relatively homogeneous group, such as the family, *Gemeinschaft* type of group, or societies of the "primitive" type, the interests of the individual and that of the group will have considerable overlap. In this context *all* members of the group have an active interest in removing ambiguity and in keeping conflict at bay. The performance of ritual is motivated by this general interest, and its function is to reaffirm and strengthen a pre-existing value consensus. Consequently, social anthropologists studying simple societies usually adopt a functionalist approach to ritual and are disinclined to explain ritual in terms of conflict management, although there are several notable exceptions among them. But groups of the *Gemeinschaft* type are not only the province of social anthropologists. They are also formed in large internally differentiated societies as a result of an awareness of some common conflictual political or ideological relation (e.g. political and religious sects), and their ritual is usually of the protest kind.

The social context in which conflict is pervasive is that of complex, internally differentiated social units, such as *Gesellschaft* type groups and all types of society other than the "primitive" one. If both parties of a social relationship are aware of a conflict in interests and have become openly divided by it, its ritual enactment is not practised. If, however, the conflict is only latent, one precondition for ritual enactment of the relationship is given. Participants in the ritual must not have a full awareness of *all* the social implications of the ritual. Therefore conflict is not necessarily acted out in the ritual but may be merely implied by it, in that the assertion of one principle of social organization necessarily precludes the expression of another. Two further conditions have to be fulfilled for ritualization of a social relationship to take place. First, the social relationship has to be perceived as significant by both parties, though not necessarily for the same reasons. Secondly, the individuals involved, although not perceiving conflict, need to be aware of some ambiguity, temporary disturbance or weakening in that relationship (usually a turning-point in the life of an individual or of a group is involved).

Thus, to summarize, in a conflictual social context a ritual can successfully be derived from a social relation if the conflict is latent and if the relation is valued by both political elites and non-elites, though not necessarily for the same reasons. (For example, a family rite may be rescripted to define the relations of the individual to the state.) The role of ritual in such a social context is thus to bring about a consensus in values (expressed in ritual action and symbols) which, at best, were only weakly affirmed prior to the ritual and, at worst, were viewed indifferently. The greater the aspiration for value consensus on the part of the political elites, the greater will be the deliberation with which the "model for" aspect of ritual will be developed. Ritual will be adopted as a tool of cultural management.

As the foregoing discussion implies, ritual action can take place in a variety of social contexts and is not confined to a conventional religious milieu. Whether or not a ritual act is to be called religious or not cannot be settled *a priori*; the answer depends on an analysis of the beliefs and the attitude towards the ritual object embodied in the ritual action. While the question is easily answered if we define religion in the conventional exclusive sense, it is more problematic if we operate with more inclusive definitions in the Durkheimian tradition (for a detailed discussion of these points, see pp. 35–6).

Two related terms used in this book – ritualization and ritual specialists – also need to be defined. Ritualization is used in the sense Gluckman (1962: 24) defined it, meaning simply a highly developed tendency to act out social relationships in ritual form in order to express and alter them. Ritual specialists I call all those who devise new, or adapt old, rituals in order to uphold their definition of social relationships. They are thus distinct from mere "masters of ceremony", although in practice both functions may be performed by the same person. In a social context where relationships have become merely weakened or temporarily disturbed, such specialization in ritual function is not highly developed, and rituals may be generated by those who perform them. In conflictual social contexts, in contrast, a division between those who devise and those who perform rituals is strongly developed. The creation of ritual becomes a conscious effort, although the very nature of ritual puts limits on the *independent* creativity of ritual specialists. The foregoing does not, however, imply that, given the right social context, *any* social activity can be turned into a ritual at the whim of ritual specialists. As pointed out above, ritualization will only occur if both parties value the relationship (although they may value different aspects of it) and view the change in that relationship as a significant one (for an elaboration of this argument see chapter 13).

Many anthropologists have distinguished ritual from ceremony. This distinction has been made either on the grounds that the former is religious and the latter is secular symbolic activity: see Leach's (1968: 521) discussion of it. Alternatively, it has been more persuasively argued that ceremony does not involve the acting out of a conflictual social relationship, but that a single mood of social harmony is signalled (Gluckman and Gluckman 1974: 12ff). When I adopted the latter distinction and tried to analyse Soviet data with these dichotomous concepts of ritual and ceremony I found it impossible to maintain such a distinction with consistency. Although some of the complexes of festive activity I reviewed required more passive participation and conveyed their messages fairly obviously and directly, they also defined relationships. Also, the dividing line between symbol and sign was difficult to maintain, given our lack of access to the psychic processes of their assimilation by participants. Furthermore, some of

the long-established configurations of Soviet festive activity displayed
the characteristics specified by Gluckman's definition of ceremony
more distinctly at some periods of time and in some parts of the
complex than in others, so that a frequent and confusing switching of
terms would have been required. All these problems have moved me
to abandon a consistent analytical distinction between ritual and ceremony and instead to use the two interchangeably. The word "ritual" is
used both to refer to a single act and as a collective noun referring to the
whole genre. "Rite" is used interchangeably with "ritual" in its singular meaning.

A final concept which needs definition is the word "holiday", an
inadequate translation of the Russian, *prazdnik*, derived from *prazd-
novat'* – to celebrate. In Russian, therefore, it does not have the con-
notation of being a holy day, in the sense of being associated solely
with conventional religion. It is merely a festive day on which an
important event is celebrated. The mode of celebration may include
ritual, but it will also include various forms of recreational activity,
such as entertainment, sport and a festive table at home, bringing
together family and/or friends. "Holiday" is thus a much wider concept than ritual and contains a complex of festive activities of which
the latter is only one. But usually ritual is the central activity determin-
ing the holiday's special character. In this context it is interesting to
note that some recent Soviet literature on the subject strenuously
avoids or plays down the use of the term "ritual" and instead talks of
"holidays". A prime example is the semi-official publication *Nashi
prazdniki* (Our holidays) (1977). The word "festival", an alternative
translation of *prazdnik*, I would like to confine to those festive events
which do not recur annually but are either unique or episodic occasions, such as the Soviet Youth Festival or the French revolutionary
Festival of the Supreme Being.

The theoretical orientation to ritual and related concepts adopted in
this book has the advantage of combining two major approaches to the
study of ritual that are usually thought to be mutually exclusive,
namely the functionalist and the Marxist approach. The functionalist
approach is implied in the emphasis on the "model of" aspect of ritual
in social contexts where value consensus is strong and where all
members of the group have a major interest in keeping conflicts at bay.
Ritual thus strengthens or restores the pre-existing value integration.
A Marxist orientation is entailed in the emphasis on the "model
for" aspect of ritual in *Gesellschaft*-type social units, where a marked

15

discrepancy between the ideological definition of social relations and their actual state has not yet led to *open* conflict. Ritual, in such a context, is a tool of political elites in their effort to perpetuate the political *status quo*. Which of the approaches becomes dominant in an analysis depends not only on the social context in which the ritual is being performed but also, in the conflictual context, on whether the researcher is focussing on the motivations of ritual participants or ritual specialists.

In addition, the analysis of ritual undertaken is also informed by a structuralist approach that derives the properties and implied functions of ritual from its internal structure. Such an approach implies answers to the perennial question of what role ritual plays in society. Therefore questions like "Does ritual lie?" or "Does ritual inhibit change?", posed in a recent study of political rites (Goodin 1978: 291ff), appear at best superfluous and, at worst, ridiculous. Although the analysis of ritual employed in this book shares elements with other approaches, it differs from them in its overall interpretation in that it combines them into a new synthesis. In its conclusions this study is very near to the work of Steven Lukes (1975), although a different road has been followed to reach them.

While the definition of ritual implied in this approach is thus wide and flexible in one respect, it is narrow and confined in another. The fact that my definition emphasizes the stylized and repetitive nature of ritual means that it excludes all those symbolic actions which are less consistently formalized or occur too spasmodically to become recorded sociological data. Instead the focus is mainly, though not solely, on ritual already institutionalized and, more importantly, on officially sanctioned ritual. This course has been necessitated by the constraints in the Soviet Union on independent sociological research by Western investigators. They make an anthropological-type immersion into the studied culture impossible and instead dictate a concentration on "approved", public and institutionalized ritual, that is ritual of affirmation of societal values. The study therefore neglects any ritual by *Gemeinschaft*-type groups which serves to express and maintain their identity and thus, consciously or not, marks them off from, and puts them in opposition to, the wider total society. (An example of the latter would be the ritual of Human Rights groups, such as their illegal demonstration on Human Rights' Day on 10 December.) Consequently the subsequent analysis and evaluation of Soviet ritual centres only on the cultural management function rather than on the reinforcement role of ritual as outlined above. Information on the latter kind of ritual is not available, as one might expect. A partial exception to this rule is conventional religious ritual. I have consciously omitted its consideration in this book but have dealt with aspects of it previously (Lane 1978).

Although the analysis of ritual offered so far is based on a consideration of its internal structure (its "model for" and "model of" aspects), a more detailed examination of the properties of ritual is necessary to determine the mechanisms which allow ritual to fulfil the functions attributed to it. Such an analysis, congruent with my own approach, has been cogently made by several recent studies (Munn 1973; Terence Turner 1974; and, in relation to symbolism, by Victor Turner 1967 and Ortner 1973). I therefore need do no more here than briefly summarize their arguments as they are relevant to this study.

A recognition of the "modelling" capacity of ritual as an essential component of its structure, first found in the work of Geertz (1968), is also central to the work of Munn and Terence Turner and has received further useful elaboration by them. According to Munn's (1973: 593) very succinct formulation: "Symbolic acts operate through their capacity to map changed or adjusted perceptions of the possibilities inherent in a situation onto the actor's orientation to it . . . Ritual action influences the actor's experience of immediate aspects of this situation by creating messages that reconstruct them in a manner modelling the problem and/or the desired ends." The two properties of ritual which enable it to act in this way are:
(1) the iconicity of ritual, that is the capacity to present things in direct sensual form rather than in statements about things, and
(2) the capacity for objectification, that is the endowment with authority of shared meaning, through presentation in forms external to the subjective experience of the individual.

Unlike myself, Munn and other structuralists concentrate only on the special features of the modelling process. They ignore such problems as the possible existence among social actors of conflicting ideas about how a social relationship is to be modelled, and whose model prevails over others and why. Ortner (1975: 134) is the only one among these authors who recognizes group interest as a conscious source of strategic bias in the modelling process. Turning to the analysis of the structure of ritual symbolism, both Munn and Victor Turner (1967) emphasize the highly economic nature of communication through ritual, due to the capacity of ritual symbolism to synthesize a great variety of meanings in a condensed form. Victor Turner's third property

17

of ritual symbolism, the polarization of meaning, and his and Ortner's (1973) work on distinguishing different types of symbols on the basis of these properties, will be considered in a later chapter that deals with the analysis of Soviet ritual symbolism.

A last theoretical problem in need of clarification is the relationship between ritual and ideology. Ritual, I said, expresses the norms and values of those who created it. Ritual performed at the societal rather than the small group level consequently expresses the values of the political elite, that is the dominant ideology. But this does not mean that there is necessarily a one-to-one correspondence between the two. Ritual may embody the tenets of this ideology in a selective way, as well as changing the emphasis put on different components of the ideology. The elements chosen or omitted and the relative emphases given to them are very good indicators of what interpretation of the official ideology is made by current political elites. A study of ritual can thus tell us which values are emphasized above all and which have been relegated to the background, as well as indicating the concrete interpretation given by ritual specialists to the more abstract tenets of the official ideology. Such a comparison between the value content of ideology and ritual is particularly pertinent in the case of a well-established ideology elaborated into long-term political programmes, but is difficult where a highly abstract, vague and uncodified ideology is concerned.

THE SOVIET ANALYSIS OF RITUAL

To understand ritual in Soviet society it is instructive to consider how Soviet scholars and ritual specialists themselves approach the subject, both in general and in Soviet society in particular, and to reflect what the social implications of their theoretical analyses are. As might be expected, Soviet scholars conduct their discussion of ritual in a Marxist theoretical framework. In the large majority of cases this avowedly Marxist approach is not consistently maintained. Although this is rarely acknowledged (exceptions are found in the work of Korchagina (1970a) and Ugrinovich (1975)), their theoretical work is heavily influenced by functionalist theory. Significantly, those few scholars who do not vacillate between the two paradigms in this way conclude that the introduction into Soviet life of a system of socialist ritual is incompatible with the spirit of Marxism–Leninism (for details see below).

Those scholars and workers in the field of ideology who shift be-

18

tween theoretical orientations, although developing their argument in different ways, implicitly or explicitly take the following general approach. They start out with the question of what function ritual plays in society, suggesting that ritual transmits social knowledge and traditions and has thus a communicatory function. Because ritual transmits knowledge in the form of social norms or, in other words, as models of behaviour, they conclude that it performs at the same time another more crucial function. This is variously called the ideological, regulatory, normative or social control function. Ritual performs the control function particularly effectively for three reasons. First, the norms embodied in the action are said to be clearer and less ambiguous than the notions they symbolize. They provide a distinctive graphic example of conduct and have, therefore, more impact on both consciousness and conduct of participants. Second, the norms embodied in the actions appear to be those of the collective and thus possess added authority. Third, the conventional form of ritual gives it great stability and thus ensures lasting control. Ritual, then, is seen primarily as a form of political socialization, as a way of inculcating the norms and values of the dominant ideology. By implication, ritual is also regarded as a means of increasing group solidarity. The common performance of ritual, it is assumed, can transform a collective of the associational kind into a political community which is able to mobilize individual members on its behalf.

This social control function of ritual is the one which receives the most attention in the literature on the subject. Other seemingly subsidiary functions, which enhance the success of the former, are also discussed and can be compressed into two general roles. These are the capacities of ritual, first, to express and canalize individual emotions and, secondly, to satisfy aesthetic needs through utilizing and uniting the creative arts in ritual form.

Soviet scholars posit the ideological or social control function of ritual for all societies, independent of their mode of production and ideology. They point out that socialist ritual shares its core functions with religious ritual. An evaluation of ritual, they argue, cannot be based on an analysis of its functions but must be derived from an evaluation of the ideological system which sanctions the norms embodied in ritual. Just as they consider their ideology progressive, socialist ritual is, by derivation, seen as assisting social progress towards communism. For them, the conviction that "the new Soviet system of rituals shapes and strengthens the most humane modes of

19

communication and serves the goal of reproducing the most just form of life – the socialist one" (Zots and Poluk 1978: 191) is ample justification for the introduction of such a system of rituals. Thus they conclude that while religious ritual in Soviet society and/or in capitalist society, because of its harmful ideological content, serves to prevent the development of class consciousness, ritual in Soviet society serves to increase social solidarity and thus furthers the construction of a communist society.

Soviet scholars and ritual specialists are aware of the fact that internalization of the goals and norms of Soviet Marxism–Leninism through ritual action occurs in a habitual and uncritical way (Fursin 1972: 179). They suggest that even at the present stage of socialist development there are still people who cannot easily grasp abstract general ideas and norms and who, therefore, need to internalize them through the simplified form of ritual (*ibid.*: 178; Ugrinovich 1975: 136). They see no contradiction between this and the fact that Soviet society is trying to create a new, rational man as well as to eliminate the gap between social strata engaged in mental and physical labour. It is not iniquitous to them that one group of Soviet citizens applies its intellect to devise and disperse ideological notions, while another group is induced to dispense with rational judgment in favour of an uncritical emotional approach. Nowhere is there a suggestion that the new ritual is a necessary evil which will be abandoned as soon as the gap between mental and physical labour has been eliminated. It is assumed that the new ritual will become a permanent element of Soviet society. Indeed, it is frequently suggested that the new ritual is of great benefit to the people because it satisfies their emotional and aesthetic needs. One author even goes as far as seeing ritual as an important means to form artistic taste, as a counter-measure "to the soulless mass culture as known in the West" (Sukhanov 1973: 240f). This is not to say that there are no critics of this development. But those who are critical of the creation of a system of socialist rituals have been given very little, and usually rather obscure, space to publicize their criticism. While books and articles devoted solely to a positive analysis of the new ritual abound, critiques are only to be found in book reviews or discreetly tucked away in books devoted to a different topic.

My exposition of the Soviet theoretical approach to ritual has shown that it combines several basic theoretical orientations into a distinctive approach of its own, though it shares some of the component elements with Western anthropological and sociological work. The Soviet work reflects the same endeavour as that made by recent Western anthropological work, for example Munn (1973) and T. Turner (1974), of explaining the social efficacy of ritual by laying bare its internal structure. The more important elements of the Soviet approach are an explicit Marxist frame of reference and an implicit functionalist orientation. But in contrast to my use of these two approaches, Soviet work in the field has not derived them from the internal structure of ritual and has thus failed to integrate them into one new unified approach. Instead, Soviet analysis of ritual is informed by a rather divided theoretical allegiance, with each of the two approaches being confined to the analysis of a different type of society.

A functionalist orientation, stressing the eufunctional effects of ritual and being concerned with the achievement of value consensus and social solidarity, comes to the forefront when Soviet ritual is under discussion. A Marxist approach, stressing the role of ritual in mystifying class relations and assisting domination of one class by another, prevails when religious ritual or any form of ritual in capitalist society is at issue. Therefore, much of the Soviet work on ritual in socialist society has a lot in common with Western work in the neo-Durkheimian functionalist tradition, such as that of Shils and Young (1953) and Warner (1965). Although Shils and Young and Soviet "Party sociologists" make very strange bedfellows in most respects, the formers' analysis of the British coronation (1953), replete with references to value consensus and the sacred nature of society and political authority, is uncannily similar to scores of Soviet "sociological" descriptions of such mass political holidays as the Anniversary of the October Revolution or May Day, excepting only the absence of a reference to a transcendental power in the work of the latter.

In their theoretical analysis of the relation between ritual and value integration, Soviet scholars show the same indetermination and ambiguity as Western functionalists (see Lukes 1975: 296 on the many inconsistent interpretations offered by the latter on this). Thus while several Soviet scholars insist that ritual must be regarded as an expression of existing value integration (e.g. Sukhanov 1973: 43 and 1976: 38; Fursin 1977: 3), they also state ambiguously that ritual can channel feeling in *new* directions (Sukhanov 1976: 48), that ritual makes the individuals realize and appropriate ideas and resolutions long ago found by the collective (Ugrinovich 1975: 120) or that ritual develops or inculcates certain value orientations (*Nashi prazdniki* 1977: 2). When dealing with this point in relation to religious ritual a different

21

interpretation is put forward. It is then claimed either that ritual participants are largely unaware of the values involved (Korchagina 1970:
171), or that there is a conflict between emotions actually experienced
by people and emotions created by ritual (Sukhanov 1976: 55).

The confusion is heightened by the fact that in the Soviet work there
is often a discrepancy between the theoretical analysis and the practical
recommendations for the creation of ritual derived from it. When
recommendations are made by ritual specialists for the development of
new rituals, or when discussion centres on the desired effects of
already existing rituals, it is usually implied that ritual is regarded as a
mechanism *to bring about* value integration. This is also realized by one
rather exceptional Soviet critic of the new ritual when he says that "the
impression is given that for some authors [on the subject of new
rituals] the holidays and rituals appear an almost universal means of
solving the most complex social problems" (Petukhov 1969: 273). Such
an interpretation is implied in the advocacy of wedding and engagement rituals in order to strengthen the nuclear family (Gerandokov
1970: 32), or of the Ritual of the First Wage to combat the drunkenness
usually associated with this occasion. It is more explicit in the suggestion to increase the quantity and quality of ritual for social and occupational groups showing a low level of ideological consciousness, such as
collective farmers or construction workers (Lisavtsev 1966: 76).

The capacity of the new ritual to bring about a more general and
fundamental change in value orientations is implicitly asserted in
nearly all the Soviet literature in the field when the belief is expressed
that the new ritual will eliminate not only religious traditions but
generally rid people's consciousness of all harmful survivals of the past.
It must be stressed that the very creation of the new ritual in the late
fifties/early sixties was prompted by the hope, expressed by the
Komsomol organization, that the new rites might help to reduce the
number of offenders against the public order (Binns 1979: 20) and by
the efforts of the atheist Knowledge Society which saw the "secular"
rites as a weapon against the churches. This actual function of Soviet
ritual, as opposed to those vaguely posited in Soviet theoretical analysis,
is also underlined by the wide use of the term "inculcation" (*vnedrenie*)
of ritual, suggesting that the values and norms thus imparted are not
presumed to be firmly established among ritual participants.

Such a view of ritual as a mechanism to bring about value integration
is consistent with an emphasis on the social control function of ritual, a
notion alien to Western functionalists. While the latter rarely relate

ritual to political socialization, Soviet writers are very explicit about the connection, as the quotation shows: "The basic social significance of Soviet rituals and holidays is the affirmation and reproduction in the consciousness, feeling and conduct of members of our society standards of the socialist way of life" (Fursin 1977: 3).

Another contrast between Western and Soviet work on ritual which springs to mind is the very narrow focus on one basic type of ritual among Soviet specialists. In the West, ritual is studied both in its integrative role and in its roles of expressing protest or releasing aggression (see Lukes 1975). Soviet ritual specialists are so concerned with affirming and strengthening the social order that they are preoccupied only with rituals which reinforce existing rules and social roles. This type of ritual, it is often suggested (e.g. Da Matta 1974: 19), predominates in a totalitarian social system, that is a system which has abandoned multiplex visions of the social structure in favour of a total view. It follows that in the contemporary Soviet Union little escape ritual has been developed. The more perceptive Soviet writers in the field express concern about the fact that opportunities for emotional release are not given by rituals themselves but are tagged on to them by providing "fun and games" after the ritual proper (Kampars and Zakovich 1967; Brudnyi 1968: 136). But they do not probe into the reasons for such a state of affairs.

Rituals of Rebellion in Gluckman's sense (1962), that is rituals which mock or question the social order, are even more alien to the Soviet approach to ritual. In Soviet society, where the existing social order is sacred, rebellion even in ritual form is out of the question. Rituals of Protest by politically oppositional minorities are, of course, never even considered.

This unpreparedness to relinquish control even in ritual is also expressed in the structure of the new ritual. When we analyse it with the help of Van Gennep's (1960) and V. Turner's (1969a) ideas about the tripartition of all ritual into the stages of separation, transition or limen and incorporation, it becomes obvious that incorporation is stressed above all and that the potentially dangerous liminal stage is minimized and made almost non-existent. Such an exaggeration of structure at the expense of "liminal communitas", according to V. Turner and others, may lead to pathological efforts to attain "freedom from structure" outside or against the law (e.g. Hell's Angels). As yet this has not occurred in the Soviet Union on a mass scale, unless we regard immersion in traditional religious ritual as coming close to it.

23

2

Ritual in Soviet society: a theoretical analysis

The analysis of ritual in Soviet society can give us insights into the following problems: first, what elements of the official ideology have become embodied in the system of ritual? Second, what role does ritual play in Soviet society? Third, why has ritual come to be so important at the present stage of Soviet social development?

Ritual in Soviet society, according to Soviet writers on the subject, embodies the norms and values of Soviet Marxism–Leninism. A more precise statement would be to say that ritual expresses a version of Soviet Marxism–Leninism which is seen by political elites to be congruent with current political goals and strategies. I would contend that the version revealed by a study of ritual differs in important respects not only from the ideology which inspired the foundation and guided the early years of Soviet society, but also from that given concrete expression in the last Party Programme in 1961. The official ideology of Soviet Marxism–Leninism which emerges in this study is clearly no longer a revolutionary ideology mobilizing people for fundamental social change. It has become a very conservative set of rationalizations which support and legitimate the existing order. The association of this ideology with a revolutionary past is utilized to mask the conservative policies of the present. Many of the more detailed deviations will be pointed out in the description and analysis of the actual rites in chapters 5 to 10. Some of the more far-reaching divergencies deserve immediate attention. The most fundamental is that ritual in no way reflects the important goal of Marxism–Leninism to gradually effect "a withering away of the State" and the facilitation of a greater political participation by all citizens at every level of government. On the contrary, ritual has as one of its foremost tasks the legitimation or even sacralization of the present political structure. The cult of the leader, too, can only be described as completely antithetical to the essence of

24

this original goal of Soviet Marxism–Leninism. Another central idea of the ideology, the importance of labour in the progression of society and man towards the communist stage, has suffered a basic reinterpretation in ritual. Soviet labour ritual is exclusively about the increase in the quantity and quality of labour effort on the part of the workers and is silent about a transformation of the nature of labour which furthers the emancipation from its constraints by those who perform it. Another departure from the original ideology is the neglect in ritual of an internationalist orientation and an adoption, in its place, of a nationalist one. (Although the holiday of internationalism, May Day, is still vigorously celebrated, its ritual does no more than pay lipservice to this once-central value of Soviet socialism; for greater detail, see chapter 10.) Not only has a nationalist focus replaced an internationalist one in the performance of ritual but the values of the military–patriotic tradition, once non-existent in Soviet Marxism–Leninism, have also been given such prominence in the new ritual that they have overshadowed those of the revolutionary tradition.

The system of Soviet rituals is seen as an instrument of cultural management enabling political elites (through their ideological cadres) to gain acceptance for a general system of norms and values congruent with their interpretation of Marxism–Leninism. It is thus one important strategy utilized to maintain social control. Ideological cadres are able to do this by consciously asserting, through ritual, definitions of significant social relations which, first and foremost, offer a "model for" those relations to shape or restructure participants' perceptions of them. Only secondarily, and to a much lesser extent, do these definitions contain a "model of" actual relations that permits ritual participants to express or clarify their feelings about these relations. Relationships seized upon for conveying Soviet values and norms in ritual form are those which, because they represent important turningpoints in individuals' lives, generate emotions which can be directed in a politically acceptable direction. The following quotation from a Soviet source confirms this strategy: "Rituals are conducted at important turning-points of a man's life. Owing to psychic mood he is particularly receptive to external influences. These opportunities to exert effective influence we must utilize in the interests of communist education" (*Kommunist Estonii*, 7, 1968: 32). Such ritualization of social relationships is very prolific in contemporary Soviet society for the following reasons: first, because Soviet political elites are highly committed to the achievement of value consensus, that is of definitions of social reality shared by leaders and led; secondly, and related to the first, because up to now the discrepancy between the ideological definition of social relations and the relations as they actually affect actors has not yet been consciously perceived by a large part of the Soviet population; and thirdly, because attempts to define social relationships in accordance with the tenets of Soviet Marxism–Leninism – a philosophy of life or total ideology – will necessarily be extended over a wide range of such relationships. Given these characteristics of the Soviet social context, a large-scale ritualization of social relationships has resulted. This has necessitated the evolution of a group of ritual specialists entrusted with the following tasks: to identify relationships suitable for ritualization; to devise new or adapt old ritual scenarios in such a way that the officially sanctioned definition of the social relationship prevails and the conflictual aspect remains obscured; to propagandize and introduce into Soviet life the new or adapted rituals. A division into (1) a politically influential group of ideologues who package and distribute ideological notions in the form of rituals and (2) a politically powerless group of consumers of such notions in the form of ritual becomes very obvious when one considers who are the creators and who are the recipients of this new socialist ritual.

The ritual specialists are almost exclusively local organizers and administrators of the Party, the Komsomol, the trades unions and the local soviet (a local government organization), who receive backing from the highest Party circles. They draw in as advisers and helpers members of the intelligentsia, but have been unable to mobilize sufficiently the creative intelligentsia, that is composers, artists, poets and cultural workers (for greater detail on ritual specialists see chapter 4). The recipients of ritual are mainly those who, because of age or social position, have been unable *fully* to develop their critical faculties: children, youths, manual workers and collective farmers. Very notable is the absence of regularly recurring ritual specifically for members of the intelligentsia or the Communist Party. While rites such as initiation into the working class, Day of the Miner, Day of the Metal Worker abound, there is no Initiation into the Intelligentsia, Day of the Nuclear Physicist or Day of the Poet. Similarly, while initiation into the Pioneers or the Komsomol is widespread I have encountered only one mention of an initiation rite into the Communist Party, and my enquiries about a possible extension of this latter rite were usually met with a mixture of amusement and amazement.

My association of Soviet ritual with such attributes as "consciously

26

created" and "new" may appear a contradiction in terms to many who, like Monica Wilson (1971: 129), tend rather to connect ritual with the notions of antiquity and spontaneity. If my emphasis on a conscious elaboration of the "model for" aspect of ritual appears to be too strong, it is necessary to remark that we are dealing with a system of ritual which is distinctive in several ways. First, it is the ritual of a society whose rulers believe in the possibility and desirability of extensive and carefully planned cultural management. Secondly, this ritual is still in the process of being created or adapted and of being implanted into Soviet society. Therefore conscious purpose becomes more obvious than is usually the case in the study of ritual, especially as most of the Soviet literature on the subject is written by people actively involved in the processes of creation and implementation.

To understand why ritual has become such an important means of maintaining social control at this particular stage of Soviet social development and why Soviet practice in this respect differs in such a striking way from approaches adopted in Western societies we need to view ritual in a wider theoretical context. Rulers can resort to three basic strategies to induce the ruled to accept their definitions of social reality. They can change social conditions to bring them closer to their ideological definition, they can change the consciousness of the ruled to bring perceptions of social reality into line with their ideological definition or they can influence the ruled, by various means, to accept the discrepancy between the ideological definition and the reality of social relations. In other words, rulers can initiate social revolution, or cultural revolution, or they can maintain social control through coercion or remuneration.

Ritual in Soviet society, I said earlier, is regarded by political elites as one means to gain acceptance for their definitions of crucial social relations and must therefore be viewed as an instrument of cultural revolution or, to indicate less spectacular cultural changes, of cultural management. To establish why this development has become important in Soviet and not in Western society, especially at this particular stage in its history, we must relate ritual to the other means of gaining or maintaining control that have been employed by Soviet rulers at different stages of Soviet social development. First, we must compare ritual with other means of cultural management employed at various times. Secondly, we must bring to bear on our analysis of the changing relations between rulers and ruled all three concepts of strategies used to maintain social control – social revolution, cultural revolution and influence through coercion and/or remuneration. Although these three basic strategies are commonly used in various combinations, rulers of different types of society gave a different emphasis to each; furthermore, within a given society one strategy may come to predominate over the others at certain stages in social development.

In Soviet society cultural management in general and ritual in particular are much more important as the means to maintain social control than they are in Western society. The Soviet regime continues to derive its legitimacy from the claim that it is implementing the goals of Marxism–Leninism, even when it has long abandoned the idea of social revolution that is necessary to achieve these goals. Therefore it is continually forced to cover up this discrepancy between ideology and reality by structuring citizens' perception of the latter. In the West, in contrast, political leaders do not claim to be striving for the realization of some ideal end-state, and legitimacy is not derived from such far-reaching claims. Consequently, political performance that is directed towards the satisfaction of more limited and short-term goals is much more important than cultural management as a means of maintaining social control.

Although cultural revolution or management has always been an important strategy in Soviet society it has by no means always been the foremost approach of political elites, nor has cultural revolution or management always taken the same form. In the early post-revolutionary years and through most of the twenties, when political elites still sought voluntary and conscious acceptance for their new blueprint of social relations, cultural revolution was held to be a crucial means to this end. In the early years it went hand in hand with social revolution, and the two reinforced each other. With the assumption of the New Economic Policy only cultural revolution remained. But in both periods cultural revolution tried to persuade the Soviet people by appealing predominantly to their rational faculties, and education and *agitprop* (agitation and propaganda) were its chief methods. The failure on the part of a small group of enthusiasts to gain acceptance for a system of socialist *rites de passage* during this period was due, to a large extent, to widespread feelings in the Party that cultural revolution through ritual could not be reconciled with either the revolutionary nature of Soviet Marxism–Leninism or with its emphasis on rationalism (for a description of these rites see Veresaev 1926). For the same reasons a leader cult was at first strongly repudiated and then, after Lenin's death, developed only slowly and in a relatively moderate

28

form (see pp. 210ff). But ritual as a form of cultural management was not completely eschewed during this period. The mass political holidays were keenly cultivated. The ritual of these holidays, however, was much more balanced in the development of its "model for" and "model of" aspects. It was as much a means for the masses to express their relation to the new social order as it was a tool of political socialization.

With the beginning of industrialization, collectivization and the firm establishment of Stalin's leadership from 1929 onwards, ideological persuasion greatly receded in importance and maintained only a marginal position all through the Stalinist era. Although the period from 1928–31 came to be called the Cultural Revolution this transformation of culture did not occur by a direct ideological onslaught but was a derivative of social revolution from above.

Remuneration and coercion were additional means to elicit support. Although there were no immediate rewards for the masses there was enough economic success to make manipulation with future rewards credible. During the period of the so-called Cultural Revolution, when social and cultural transformation still coincided for a significant part of the Soviet population and compliance was often inspired by revolutionary enthusiasm and altruism, coercion was only selectively applied. Later on in the Stalinist period, when revolution from above had been abandoned, coercion was applied indiscriminately. Also, the immediate material and symbolic reward of a few selected occupational and functional groups, particularly indispensable to the economic and military development of the country, became a distinguishing feature of this time.

As long as cultural management continued, it did so in drastically changed form. Instead of appealing to the intellect and to the moral sentiments of people in order to gain acceptance for Stalin's interpretation of Marxism–Leninism, a leader cult was built around the person of Stalin and, to a lesser extent, of Lenin, to play on people's emotions and instincts.

With the assumption of power by Khrushchev in 1957 the means of maintaining social control were subjected to a conscious and radical change. The cult of the personality and, more importantly, the use of coercion to gain compliance were publicly repudiated by Khrushchev. (The political violence of the Stalinist period had threatened political elites as much as the masses.) Further social revolution from above was ruled out, as it was by now regarded as a threat to the privileges of the bureaucratic stratum, although more modest social engineering, such as the Educational Reform, was still being carried out. Instead Khrushchev advocated a much stronger reliance on remuneration and a new approach to normative control. The following claim regarding remuneration, made by him in his memoirs, well sums up his intentions in the late fifties:

It is time for us to realize that the teaching of Marx, Engels and Lenin cannot be hammered into people's heads only in the classroom and newspapers and at political rallies; agitation and propaganda on behalf of Soviet power must also be carried out in our restaurants and cafeterias. Our people must be able to use their wages to buy high-quality products manufactured under socialism, if they are ultimately to accept our system and reject capitalism. (Quoted by McAuley 1977: 213)

But Khrushchev's promises of greater material rewards were based on an over-optimistic appraisal of both Soviet economic capabilities and of his own ability to effect a reallocation of resources within the economy from the production of producer goods and military hardware (heavy industry) to that of consumer goods and agricultural products.

During the close of the fifties, economic development slowed down considerably, and the state of emergency engendered by the rapid industrialization process came to an end. This meant a slow-down of economic growth and of rapid upward social mobility. Although the country had reached an economic level which ensured a satisfactory level of material well-being and social welfare, demands for greater *immediate* rewards for *all* the population could not yet be satisfied. Also Khrushchev's efforts to give a major impetus to the development of consumer industries (including agriculture) were relatively unsuccessful. In this situation, the political leadership was obliged to have much greater recourse to the second strategy of maintaining social control advocated earlier, in order to prevent the surfacing of long-submerged conflicts in Soviet society. Cultural management had to come once more to the fore to assert the definitions of social reality favoured by the current leadership. Thus the period of Khrushchev's rule became distinguished by a general revival of ideology and by a great ideological onslaught on the minds and hearts of the Soviet population. The advocacy, for various reasons, of a system of socialist ritual, made around this time by Young Communists, seemed to provide the answer to this problem, and the idea was soon generally accepted.

Although most of Khrushchev's policy innovations were discontinued after his ousting, the establishment of a system of socialist rituals was continued and has since been expanded and strengthened. Like Khrushchev, Brezhnev and Kosygin came in as reformers but, as McAuley (1977: 264) points out, "the battles over reform have almost always been won by the conservatives". Brezhnev's regime consequently faced the same dilemma *vis-à-vis* strategies of maintaining social control. Like Khrushchev's regime, Brezhnev's tried to perpetuate a political system created in the thirties but without resorting to the coercion that was an important element in Stalin's rule. Furthermore, it was clear that the problem of securing the population's ideological commitment had in no way diminished.

Large-scale sociological surveys conducted in the late fifties/early sixties had established that Marxism–Leninism had not yet become a philosophy of life for the majority of the population and that religion was still a serious ideological competitor. An insufficiently developed normative commitment among the population in general was made more disquieting by the fact that during the sixties, there had come to maturity the first generation of Soviet citizens who had no personal memories either of the periods of social revolution or of the time of unified struggle against an eternal enemy of the Soviet past. The young people of this generation have been brought up by a generation of parents who have tried to shelter them from the deprivations they themselves had endured. These two factors together, says Sukhanov (1973: 223), have created a generation which is materialistic and has a low ideological commitment. Seeking their compliance by remunerative influence, even if possible, would have rendered the regime dangerously dependent on economic performance. The only way to tie them closer to society and to prevent them from becoming a harmful influence in the future, suggests the same Soviet author, is to find a way to increase their ideological commitment.

All these developments together therefore made it imperative from the early sixties onwards to greatly strengthen cultural management. There was a widespread realization that ideological commitment is not easily gained by mere appeal to the intellect or to the moral sentiments of individuals and that conventional means of persuasion had not had the necessary success. There is ample evidence (see White 1979: 113ff, 142) that the traditional means of inculcating the values of Soviet ideology, agitation and propaganda, have had only little impact and a limited appeal. Some strata of the population, such as non-working women, old and young people and the rural population, have proved difficult to reach with these media. All this made the political elites

31

open to ideas about new approaches. The conviction that an appeal to the emotions must be utilized, particularly among the culturally immature strata of the population, made ritual appear to be the ideal tool for this purpose. The capacity of ritual to convert individual emotion into collectivity oriented moral sentiment, it was thought, would make it a powerful means to revive the dried-up flow of normative commitment. It would be able to evoke the powerful revolutionary and patriotic impetus of the past. Moreover, ritual particularly recommended itself as a tool of cultural revolution because the ensuing revolution would be silent and unobtrusive. Ritual could thus effectively be utilized to obscure basic conflicts in Soviet society which, up to then, had become apparent only to the more perceptive of its members.

In Soviet society such basic conflicts ensue from a lack of the ideologically posited fit between the individual and the collective good. They are therefore about the unequal distribution of material, social and cultural values as well as of power. While the first three affect mainly the manual working class and the peasantry, the unequal distribution of power is more widely effective. In Soviet official ideology only some of these conflicts are acknowledged in such phrases as "non-antagonistic contradictions between mental and physical labour, and between town and country", which will be overcome gradually. It is significant that a ritual overcoming of conflict is only practised in relation to the culturally more backward or immature social strata who do not perceive of inequality as a basic conflict in their society. There is no attempt to ritualize conflictual relations which have been brought into the open, such as the unequal access to influence and power by certain sections of the intelligentsia, familiar to us as "dissident intellectuals". Ritual, I said earlier, can only successfully gloss over conflicts (or resolve ambiguities) in societies, or sectors of society, which accept their social order uncritically. I would contend that up to now Soviet society, once safely established, has been distinguished from Western societies by the fact that, for various reasons, the legitimacy of the regime and the system have not been questioned in any basic manner except by a small section of the intelligentsia. I would suggest that only when a society aspires to a common value system does ritualization of conflictual social relations on a societal scale gain wider currency. Ritual, in the words of Moore (1974: 29), "communicates the non-negotiability (the unquestionability), the sacredness of certain interpretations of social life".

In this respect Soviet society is different from Western capitalist society, where the open questioning of basic social values and goals makes extensive ritualization both futile and unacceptable. Ritualization is also more imperative in Soviet than in Western society because its conflicts are potentially more explosive and therefore more threatening. The reason for this is that socialist ideology has all-pervasive influence, and conflicts cannot be dispersed through different social relationships, but gain accumulative force. Just as all social relations are governed by the same norms, the same basic expectations of being treated according to these norms are engendered in such different sub-systems as, say, the family and the economy. In the West, in contrast, there is a stronger distinction between public and private morality.

To sum up, ritual in Soviet society has become one important means of glossing over conflictual social relationships. The greater currency of ritual in Soviet, as opposed to Western, society does not necessarily indicate a higher level of conflict. It merely points to a more developed tendency among Soviet political leaders to aspire to value integration and to an ideologically conditioned failure to face up to conflict threatening such integration.

Although the emergence of a system of ritual in the late fifties/early sixties has been explained as part of a strategy, adopted by the political elites, to maintain the social and political *status quo* it would be wrong to view it exclusively in this way. First, it would be misleading to imply that a system of rituals was consciously created for this purpose. Although the first steps in the process of introducing this system of rites are now shrouded in the mists of history it is certain that the first impetus came from lower political cadres rather than from the top of the political apparatus. It is quite likely that, as these groups claim, the initiative was taken partly in response to suggestions from below, from ordinary Soviet citizens. (It is important to remember that initially only new life-cycle rites were contemplated.) It is certain, however, that the introduction of the new system of rites would not have proceeded the way it did if it had not been for the recognition of its great potential as a tool of cultural management on the part of the political elites.

Secondly, it would be an oversimplification to suggest that the only role taken by this ritual is that of ideological mystification to preserve the political *status quo*. Ritual, I have repeatedly made clear, can only succeed if it responds to some degree to the emotional requirements of those who are meant to perform it. Therefore the acceptance of the new ritual by a substantial part of the Soviet population must mean

33

that the rites in some way answer the needs of those who enact them. The problem of analysing *what* exactly these needs are is a very difficult one and is dealt with in detail elsewhere. Here it is sufficient to say that the new ritual fulfilled to some extent the urgent demands for more colour, beauty, heightened significance and dignity in personal life. As is well documented by Dunham's study (1976) of popular literature, these demands arose once the struggle for economic survival and the deprivations of the early post-war period had eased up, and more time and money for personal concerns were available. There is no doubt, to give only one example, that the beauty and solemnity of the wedding palace and all the festive attributes provided for the young couple and their guests are a great improvement on the stultifying drabness and impersonality of the registry office which, for the majority of couples, was the only option. It needs to be emphasized, too, that these popular demands to spend leisure time in a more elevated manner in no way conflict with the aims of political elites who, as Dunham (*ibid.*) states, have long been concerned to introduce *kul'turnost'* (a cultured manner) into the lives of Soviet citizens.

But for many Soviet critics of the new ritual these are modest gains which have been bought at too high a price. The description given to me by one Soviet intellectual of the new ritual "as a means to buy the people's souls" aptly sums up this estimation. It expresses a disillusioned recognition of the fact, highlighted by me, that the system of Soviet socialist rituals will facilitate the efforts of political elites to use the ideology of Marxism–Leninism as a set of rationalizations to support and legitimate dominant interests. Such a use of the new system of rituals makes even more remote the chance that the original conception of the ideology of Marxism–Leninism as a blue-print for social revolution and human liberation will make any significant impact on Soviet society.

3

The beliefs and ritual of Soviet Marxism–Leninism as political religion

It is now necessary to explore the precise nature of the new Soviet ritual as manifested in the attitude taken towards the ritual object. Soviet writers on the subject call it variously civic, secular, socialist or just new ritual, agreeing only on the fact that it is not religious in the sense of embodying beliefs in the existence of supernatural forces. "New" is analytically useless to determine either the object of the ritual activity or the attitude towards that object. "Civic" is both too narrow to encompass the wide range of rituals included in the system and too vague to indicate the attitude towards the ritual object. To characterize this ritual more precisely involves identifying the transcendent principle which the ritual action embodies and the object it refers to. In the case of the Soviet ritual this transcendent principle is given by the (socialist or) communist ideology of Marxism–Leninism as interpreted by political leaders and recorded in such "holy" documents as the current Party Programme (including the Moral Code of the Builder of Communism), and the Constitution. Given the fact that the Soviet order created on this basis is still at the socialist stage of development, "socialist" (in the Soviet sense) will be the qualifying adjective I shall adopt in my anlysis of Soviet ritual. In this I concur with one Soviet author, namely Brudnyi (1968: 187).

This adjective, however, tells us nothing about the attitude towards the ritual object and the transcendent principles realized in it. I would agree with the Soviet authors that the new ritual is not religious, given a conventional exclusive definition of religion, and it cannot *simply* be regarded as a substitute religious activity. But if we depart from the conventional exclusive definition of religion and consider a wider definition based on a sacred–secular dichotomy, such as that developed by T. Turner (1974: 34ff) from Durkheimian beginnings, it

35

turns out that the new Soviet ritual is not completely secular either. According to Turner, an object and the related beliefs and acts become sacred when the subjects develop a fetishistic attitude (in the Marxian sense) to the transcendent principle it embodies. This means that something which is a product of social relations is no longer accepted as such, but is perceived to be a principle beyond human or social control. Conversely, the ritual object is secular if it is regarded as humanly created and thus changeable. Now the transcendent principle inspiring ritual behaviour in Soviet society is, of course, constituted by the norms and values embodied in Soviet Marxism–Leninism. The order created on its basis is regarded as humanly created and, in principle, changeable. Is its ritual therefore secular? My answer would be an ambiguous yes and no. Although theoretically changeable, in practice the social order is regarded as unchangeable, except in an evolutionary direction towards full communism. A suggestion of any basic change in any other direction is regarded as sacrilegious. The ritual resulting from such an ambiguous relation to the transcendent principle and the ritual object is, consequently, also ambiguous. It is both secular and religious, the basic secular orientation having become sacralized. I shall point out below the ways in which a predominantly secular focus is developed. Here I would like to show how this religious orientation manifests itself in practice.

There is a notable tendency in the new ritual to create its own holy scripture, traditions, ritual attributes, saints and its holy places of pilgrimage. They are holy or sacred in the sense that they are given a timeless importance and are considered as part of the unalterable order of things. Often Soviet writers will themselves use the word "holy" to describe them (Rudnev 1974: 43, 60; Shevelev 1976: 50). Revolutionary traditions, for example, are described by one team of writers as follows: "Revolutionary traditions are our 'holy of holies' . . . a living spring from which we may draw life-giving strength and emotional health" (Kampars and Zakovich 1967: 182). The existence of saints is suggested by the excessive amount of hero-worship in most rituals. These are heroes representing the three "holy" traditions of the Revolution and the Civil War, of the Great Patriotic War and of Labour. Above all the minor saints stands Lenin. The slogan "Lenin lived, Lenin lives, Lenin shall live" meets the eyes in many locations and well sums up the place he occupies in the public consciousness (for details of hero-worship and the cult of Lenin see pp. 210–19). National holy places of pilgrimage associated with Lenin and with the big events in

Soviet history are Lenin's mausoleum, the Smolny Institute, the Finland Station, the area around where the *Aurora* is anchored and some
of the war cemeteries and war memorials in the "hero towns". One
such place is described by a Soviet author as "the holy ground every
Soviet citizen longs to tread once" (Rudnev 1974: 47). Besides these
national places of pilgrimage there is, in the words of another Soviet
writer, "in every town, in every village . . . a memorial of Glory, and it
has already become a tradition to go there both on the day of a
nation-wide holiday and on a day of family celebrations, to put down
flowers, stand in silence, to reach out with one's heart to the memory
of those who gave their life for us" (Shevelev 1976: 50).

Among the many symbolic objects utilized in the new socialist ritual
a few stand out as having a sacred character and may be described as
holy ritual attributes. Examples are the Red Banner of an enterprise or
organization, in front of which people kneel and which they kiss
during a ritual performance, and the Eternal Flame of war memorials
(for details see p. 197).

A sacred orientation also comes out in the effort to achieve through
ritual action permanence and timelessness. This manifests itself in the
widely used symbolism of the relay race and the baton. The symbolic
relay race is between three generations of builders of communism and
the three holy traditions of Soviet society are represented by the baton,
which is symbolically handed on from generation to generation and
thus relates the past to the future and transcends individual mortality.
It is also expressed in such diverse activities as the ritual planting of
young trees, the projection into the sky of lit-up sacred names or
objects and the pronounced tendency to erect monuments to out-last
their designers. The tendency in recent years to create special buildings where life-cycle rites can be performed separately and apart from
everyday utilitarian activity and be given an extraordinary character
strongly suggests the idea of a church in the Christian sense. At least
one author (Kampars 1969: 21) acknowledges this similarity.

Soviet Marxism–Leninism not only claims to provide a socialist belief
system but also a secular one, and Soviet ritual specialists naturally
insist that the new socialist ritual is also secular. I have already pointed
out that the attitude towards the ritual object is ambiguous, being both
secular and sacred, and I have shown how the sacred orientation
manifests itself in practice. Now it is necessary to clarify how far the
Soviet claim to secularism receives support from the facts and by what
means such a secular attitude is maintained. I said above that ritual can

be described as secular if the ritual object referred to – in our case the Soviet social system – is regarded as humanly created and changeable. Earlier I stressed that in as far as the possibility of change was acknowledged it was strictly circumscribed as to direction (towards full communism) and nature (gradual). (Naturally these restrictions do not apply to pre-Soviet times and to other societies.) Within these narrow limits, however, change by human agency is not only tolerated but strongly encouraged. One of the most striking differences of Soviet Marxism–Leninism from religion, conventionally defined, lies in the former's insistence that man is the master of his own fate and that social progress will be achieved solely by active human effort towards this end. In other words, a religious attitude prevails only in relation to the fundamentals of the system. Within the immutable parameters, however, a secular stance is encouraged. Therefore, instrumental orientations and diversity of opinion on matters not impinging on these fundamentals is in no way irreconcilable with political religion.

Secular beliefs are not only maintained at the general and abstract level of ideology but are also concretized and made socially effective through a number of norms and sanctions and the practical policies based on them. Thus the most important of the negative norms and policies is the complex of anti-religious injunctions and practical measures. Among the many positive norms and policies embodying them are the connection made between conscientious labour of *any* kind and social progress, the emphasis on the social benefits of work for the collective and the important role attributed to scientific and technological advance in moving towards communist society. Although this vigorous advocacy of human action to effect social progress most certainly contains an element of cynical pragmatism directed towards achieving a highly disciplined and productive labour force in initially extremely adverse conditions, it must also be credited with being motivated by the secular strand in the belief system.

How then does this secular orientation manifest itself in the system of socialist rituals? Although ritual specialists have been relatively unsuccessful in creating new secular symbolic forms, this orientation is conveyed explicitly or implicitly in many of the rituals. It receives the most explicit, though mainly verbal, expression in the new funeral rite. It is implied in the many rituals celebrating collectivism in general or labour and educational improvement for the good of society in particular. To sum up, the ambiguity involved in extolling the power of human agencies to change society and, at the same time, setting strict limits as to the extent and nature of the change is expressed in the dual nature of Soviet socialist ritual, which tries to inspire both a sacred and a secular orientation towards the ritual object. Therefore it does not make sense in the case of Soviet ritual to view the "sacred" and the "secular" as dichotomous, mutually exclusive categories, but instead it is appropriate to envisage a continuum between the sacred and the secular, with Soviet ritual occupying an ambiguous middle position.

This apparently contradictory duality of orientation in Soviet social-ist ritual and in the belief system embodied in it is, I suggest, due to the fact that the two do not form a political ideology, as the Soviets themselves claim, nor a religion, as some Western critics of the Soviet system infer, but a political religion. To develop this claim it is neces-sary to state what I mean both by religion and by political ideology. One feature of religion, which I identified earlier when analysing the Soviet attitude to their belief system and society as expressed in social-ist ritual, is its ability to make beliefs and the social structures derived from them appear to be part of the unalterable order of things and immune to change by human agency. A general definition of religion which concurs with this partial characterization (see points (2), (4) and (5) below) and is both lucid and persuasive is that of Geertz. Defi-nitions of ideology in the sociological literature are either too general (including religion) or too narrow (e.g. the Marxist definition) to be suitable for the purpose of this analysis. Instead I shall develop my own definition in the course of discussing Geertz's description of religion. Religion, according to Geertz (1968: 4ff), is:

(1) a system of symbols which acts to
(2) establish powerful, pervasive and long-lasting moods and motivations in men by
(3) formulating conceptions of a general order of existence and
(4) clothing these conceptions with such an aura of factuality that
(5) the moods and motivations seem uniquely realistic.

While (1) is a statement which can be said to apply to many belief systems, (2), (4) and (5) are related points referring to ritual, which have already been discussed above. While political ideology also pur-sues these ends it does not, and need not, normally rely on ritual to the same extent as religion does to achieve these ends. The reason for this lies in the different range of application of the beliefs basic to the two systems. Political ideology has a narrower and more clearly defined field of reference. Consequently, Geertz's point (3), stating the content and range of application of beliefs, is decisive in making a distinction

39

between religion and political ideology and needs further examination before it is applied to the Soviet belief system of Marxism–Leninism. According to Geertz's definition, religious beliefs contain conceptions of a general order of existence. What then are these conceptions? First, religion provides explanations of anomalous events and experiences, such as death or other natural catastrophes, and generally helps man to comprehend confusing aspects of nature, self and society. Secondly, religion deals with the problem of suffering by helping man to endure the world. Thirdly, religion helps to deal with the problem of evil, that is undeserved suffering, with moral anxiety and with confusion by establishing moral coherence (Geertz 1968: 13ff). Although Geertz presents them as three separate conceptions, they are in fact closely related. The explanations offered by religion do not just help comprehension (1) but also acceptance of the world as a meaningful, morally coherent place (3) and thus foster endurance of suffering (2). (For an interesting analysis of Soviet Marxism–Leninism with the aid of a different definition of religion, see Zeldin 1969.)

Political ideology, in contrast, offers less comprehensive conceptions of order applying only to the social and political realm and, if such ideology is of a normative nature, may also regulate individual action within these parameters. Because of this concern with more finite and clear-cut dilemmas, which can, at least in theory, be solved here and now, political ideology, unlike religion, encourages social action rather than acceptance and endurance, although the two are not necessarily mutually exclusive. Also of course religion encourages individualism, while political ideology tries to relate the individual to the collectivity.

What then is the nature of the conceptions contained in Marxism–Leninism? Although the Soviet belief system addresses itself to a much wider area of human concerns than is usually the case for self-styled political ideologies, it does not claim to offer explanations of anomalous events which lead to their acceptance. Instead it concentrates on explaining the relation of self to nature or matter and to society in such a way that individuals feel their lives to be meaningful and purposeful. Although this latter explanation encourages individual suffering for the greater social cause (the "work now, live later" injunction during Stalinist industrialization), the Marxist belief that the suffering caused by human agency can also be eliminated by the same means and will be fully overcome in a future perfect society (full communism) sets strong limits on the extent to which suffering can be justified, if the belief system is to maintain its credibility. (This explains the great reluctance

40

of the present Soviet political elites to go the whole way in exposing the suffering imposed during the Stalin period.) More importantly, because the Soviet value system offers only social explanations, which may give meaning to life but, unlike religion, not to death, it cannot and does not claim to offer a comprehensive answer to existential problems. Although the utopian aspect of the Marxist–Leninist belief system does put forward a picture of an ideal future under full communism, likened by some commentators to the heaven of conventional religion, one cannot truly liken this prospective utopia to the preoccupation with a life beyond death of conventional religion. Thus there is in the content of the Marxist–Leninist belief system the same dual orientation as already identified in the ritual. On the one hand, the former assumes a religious function in that it offers explanations which not only help individuals to comprehend but also induce them to accept and endure life's sufferings for the sake of some greater good. On the other hand, however, the emphasis in the belief system on human and social agencies sets severe limits to the amount of acceptance and endurance as well as precluding explanations reconciling man to suffering caused by non-social events. It condemns individualistic solutions to human problems and seeks to develop collectivism. Soviet Marxism–Leninism is therefore part religion and part political ideology and is best described by the term "political religion". The many critics of Soviet society, particularly those of a religious (in the conventional sense) persuasion, who claim that Soviet society is completely unable to make its citizens' lives meaningful and morally coherent, are therefore only half right. Although the Soviet political religion is inherently incapable of providing answers to *some* existential problems it can and does provide a philosophy of life and a related ethic.

It must by now have become clear that political religion differs in fundamental ways from civil religion. Although the concept of "civil religion" first entered social scientific discourse through the work of Rousseau, the subject has become topical again only during the sixties through the work of R. N. Bellah on American civil religion. Whereas Bellah's early work on the subject (1967; 1969) has been widely interpreted as putting forward a concept of civil religion as a belief system which has both shaped and legitimized the historical experience of the American people, Bellah's later book (1975) corrected this interpretation by presenting American civil religion as an absolute and independent truth, by the standards of which present American society and

41

politics are to be judged. Rather than legitimizing the present social and political system American civil religion, for the later Bellah, could become a lever for social transformation in a vaguely defined socialist direction. It is Bellah's earlier sociological approach rather than his later theological concepts concerning civil religion that I shall refer to in the following discussion. According to this former approach (Bellah 1969: 346), "civil religion at its best is a genuine apprehension of a universal and transcendent religious reality as seen in or, one could almost say, as revealed through the experience of the American people". Although in the case of both political and civil religion a religious dimension has been introduced into the realm of politics in order to enhance its legitimacy, the nature of that religious element differs significantly between the two. First, whereas in political religion the religious element is contained in the sacralization of the existing political order, in civil religion it is provided by a linking of that order with a transcendent power which is derived from the traditional religion forming the basis of the various religious creeds professed in that society. Secondly, while political religion claims authority not only over the political affairs of a society but over all of social life, civil religion confines itself to the former. Consequently, political religion has a system of specific values and norms, while the content of civil religion is at such a high level of generality that it conflicts neither with conventional religious nor with political norms and values (see the findings on this of Wimberley *et al.* 1976).

Unlike both conventional and civil religion, political religion has to solve some human dilemmas here and now and thus contains in itself the seeds of its eventual decline. As Apter (1963: 81) correctly points out, "to the extent that development (in a new society) becomes successful it becomes possible to consider the decline of political religion and in its place the rise of a constitutional order". This threat to political religion is of three different kinds. First, although the economic development of a backward country is often facilitated by the existence of a centralized authoritarian political rule, the operation of a highly developed society becomes incompatible with such a rule. It requires that economic and, by implication, political authority becomes decentralized and that efficiency becomes increased. This undermines centralized charismatic leadership and requires a switch from "wert-rational" to "zweck-rational" orientations. Secondly, political religion loses its potency to the extent that the gap between the postulated ideal end-state and the actual development of society narrows. Although Soviet society has by no means achieved the goals set by its ideology it has reached a state where the urgency for further struggle has become considerably reduced. The third threat to political religion is given by a change of generation. The present rising generation in Soviet society was born into a society where the revolutionary achievement was already consolidated and had therefore become remote to this generation. As Apter (*ibid*.: 95) makes clear, such a loss of function on the part of political religion is at the same time a threat to political leaders whose authority is derived from it. This stage, I would argue, has now been reached in the Soviet Union, and the institution of a system of socialist rituals has to be seen as an attempt by the leaders to halt the decline of political religion.

The above attempts to identify both religious and secular or political strands in the Soviet Marxist–Leninist belief system and its ritual, and to distinguish what I termed as "political religion" from civil religion, have brought out the complexity of the problem and the difficulty of reaching easy conclusions in this area. This recognition is in strong contrast to the conclusions of two recent studies of ritual in modern industrial society. Bocock's study of ritual in contemporary Britain (1974) devotes some space to the exercise of distinguishing religious from political (he calls it "civic") ritual (*ibid*.: 60ff). He suggests that, although both are actions oriented to sacred or charismatic objects, only in the case of conventional religious ritual is the object holy. He concludes that it is a relatively straightforward exercise to distinguish between the two kinds and proposes three criteria on which to base the distinction. This exercise does, however, remain very unsatisfactory because his view of both the religious and the political remains very tied to conventional definitions. Although he sees political (or civic) ritual as being oriented towards sacred objects he never makes it clear what he means by this and so fails to explore the ideas implied by either civil or political religion.

The second study to explore the relation between the religious and the political is Goodin's (1978), an attempt to create a typology of political ritual and to re-examine its nature and functions in the light of such a typology. Goodin, unlike Bocock, is aware of the fact that you cannot neatly separate the political and religious into tidy boxes. He points out that the magico-religious rite (as he calls it) still has a role to play in contemporary politics. But, similar to Bocock, he works with a narrow, exclusive definition of religion and so only identifies the conjunction of religious and political orientations in "civil religion".

He is unable to deal with "political religion" which, given his evaluation of the nature and functions of magico-religious political rites (*ibid.*: 291ff), ought to have been subsumed under this category. The neglect in the writings of both Bocock and Goodin of the specific conjunction of the religious and the political that is found in political religion is owing to the fact that they have studied ritual only in the context of Western industrial society. The very important differences in institutionalized ritual (outside the churches) between Western and state socialist societies will be explored in chapter 14.

A more sophisticated theoretical sociological discussion of the concept of civil religion by Robertson (1978: 180ff) poses the problem within the context of the relationship between individuation and societalization. He attempts to show what types of culturally perceived relationships between the individual and society are more likely than others to lead to the emergence of civil religion. Robertson concludes that civil religion is most likely to be advocated when society is primary and that it will assume its greatest intensity when the efficacy of the societal entity is at risk. This conclusion is difficult to reconcile with the prominence of civil religion in American society in which, according to Robertson's own interpretation (*ibid.*: 181), "the differentiation of individual life from societal functioning is most acute". Robertson might have avoided this impasse if he had distinguished between political and civil religion. Casting my own argument in Robertson's terms, both these forms of religion come to the forefront when the societal entity is at risk, either because of internal change or because of the impact of an external threat. Civil religion is celebrated in societies where the individual is dominant, and political religion evolves where society is primary.

4

vvvvvvvvvvvvvvvvvvvvvvvvvvvvvvvvvvvvvvvvvvvvvvvvvvvvvvvvvvvvvvvvvvvvvvvvvv

The organization of Soviet ritual

It is often suggested that the ritualization of social relationships on a societal level is a feature of the simple "mechanical solidarity" type of society, and therefore the study of ritual is widely held to be the domain of the social anthropologist. V. Turner (1969b: 10), for example, holds that "with advances in technology, increasing division of labour and the extension of 'organic' solidarity the social range and cultural scope of ritualization tend to contract . . . The total system or 'global society' seems to have surpassed thresholds of size and complexity beyond the capacity of ritualization to bond . . ." This assessment is implicitly based on the belief that ritual is always spontaneously generated by those who make up the total social unit and that "ritualization cannot be externally imposed on human aggregates" (*ibid.*). The description of the system of socialist rituals in the Soviet Union, a large modern industrial society, has proved both these generalizations to be wrong. Ritualization on a large scale has been possible for two reasons. First, due to social planning and conscious cultural management, there is a much greater standardization in Soviet society and culture than in capitalist industrial societies. Secondly, ritualization has not spontaneously evolved but, even if not imposed, has certainly been instigated and directed from above. To make large-scale ritualization of Soviet society possible a complex organizational framework has been gradually evolved. A description of this framework and an analysis of the orientations underlying it are given in this chapter.

THE FORMAL STRUCTURE

The introduction of the new ritual has by no means been a heavily organized and centrally directed affair from the very beginning. On the contrary, up to 1964 this new movement existed only in some parts of the Soviet Union, it was mostly initiated by local organizations and the new rites differed in form and content, though not in essence, between geographical areas. Also the organization of activity was being carried out by different social and political bodies in the various areas. As far as any organization existed on a republican level it was often exercised through the atheist Knowledge Society (*Nauka i religiya* 1973, 4: 32). Significantly, this organizing body was later considered as being socially too narrow, representing, as it does, only the atheist aspect of Marxist–Leninist ideology.

The first initiative for the development of new socialist rituals was taken in the Baltic republics of Latvia and Estonia and in Leningrad city at the end of the fifties. After 1963, several other regional capitals of the RSFSR and some areas of the Ukraine followed suit. It came from the Young Communist League, the Knowledge Society, and, to a lesser degree, from the Communist Party. Although they were concerned with developing a whole range of rites, in those early years only a secular wedding rite and, a little later, a secular rite to mark the birth of a child were introduced. Permanent organizational support was given by the local political authority, the soviet or council. Some republican and regional conferences on ritual were already conducted between 1962–4 (Rudnev 1967: 9).

The big turning-point came in 1964, after the subject of developing and introducing new rituals had been considered in the resolutions of the Central Committee of the Party. This followed the November 1963 session on atheist education during which the Central Committee's ideological commission had singled out the introduction of the new secular rituals as one important way to reduce religious involvement. Although relatively little space had been devoted to ritual within the wider problem of atheist education (only one paragraph out of four-and-a-half pages of resolutions, according to *Partiinaya Zhizn'* 2, 1964: 25), this declaration of moral support by the most influential political body in the Soviet Union had immediate effects. These resolutions were given further impact by a decree of the Council of Ministers about "the elaboration and introduction into life of the new civic ritual" (Rudnev 1979: 177) and by an All-Union conference on the subject of ritual under the leadership of the Central Committee's department of propaganda and agitation, which worked out the basic methodological and organizational principles for the introduction into Soviet life of the new holidays and rituals. They stipulated the following:

(a) an organic connection of the new holidays and rituals with the whole system and way of life (*obraz zhizni*) of the Soviet people at the present stage of communist construction

(b) the expression in every new custom of a definite progressive idea and of the principles of communist morality in combination with the specificities and forms of every custom

(c) a synthesis of the logical and the emotional in every holiday and ritual. The utilization of varied means of aesthetic and emotional influence

(d) an atheist direction, counterposing new to old religious rituals

(e) the principle of internationalism of the new rituals and holidays. Maximum utilization of everything progressive in national or popular traditions. Struggle against survivals of bourgeois nationalism

(f) universality and systematic character of the new holidays and rituals, continuous and ubiquitous introduction of them into the daily life of the Soviet people.

In many republics activity towards developing the new ritual was either started for the first time or was given a big new impulse. "The call of the Party to strengthen the education of the workers on the glorious revolutionary, military–patriotic and labour traditions of the older generations of the Soviet people called forth a well-known acti-vization of work on the part of the cultural–educational institutions and public organizations in our republic" (Gerandokov 1970: 22). In the RSFSR the Council of Ministers adopted a resolution "About the Introduction into the Life of the Soviet People of New Civic Rituals" within a month of the Party Central Committee's recommendations (Aliev 1968: 5). After 1964, systematic organization of the new rituals began to evolve all over the Soviet Union. According to El'chenko (1976a: 60), the head of the Central Committee's department for agita-tion and propaganda in the Ukraine and a member of the republican commission:

the formation of the new ritual began to transform itself from a campaign, implemented in the main by the forces of various public bodies (*obshchestven-nost'*) and cultural institutions into a planned direction of ideological and economic activity by Party and state organs, capable of centralizing and uniting the efforts of organizations most varied in profile.

In many republics councils or commissions were formed to co-ordinate the work on the new rituals for the whole republic and to assist local bodies in their practical work. They were being formed under the auspices of different political bodies in the various republics: under the Council of Ministers (executive governmental organ), the Central Committee's department for propaganda and agitation (Party), the

Supreme Soviet (parliamentary body), the Ministry of Culture or under a mixed commission with members from the first three of the above-mentioned bodies. Besides having members from some or all of the three chief political bodies, representatives of a great variety of social, political and cultural organizations also serve on these commissions, such as the Communist Youth League, the Trades Union Council, Institutes of Culture and Creative Collectives, for example, Houses of Popular Creativity, as well as individual artists and scholars. Often these commissions are divided into sub-committees or working parties, each one with responsibility for a particular group of rituals and liaising both with people and organizations at grass-roots level and with the central commission. The main task of these commissions is to co-ordinate and guide local work. In order to do this effectively, they do research, publicize local experience, work out recommendations and systematic instructions for specific rituals and give practical help to those working at the local level (Ranne 1972: 186). The republican council or commission may work out the complete scenario of a new ritual in all its details. It commissions scientific research work on the subject and organizes regular seminars and conferences at various levels. At these, participants relate their local experience, discuss with each other specific problems and sometimes observe and evaluate a new ritual in operation (Aliev 1968: 5; *Nauka i religiya* 1973, 4: 39; Lobacheva 1975: 19).

These republican organizing commissions are supplemented by parallel local commissions at the level of the region, district, town, village or even individual collective farms or enterprises. There is no uniform pattern of organization or hierarchy of authority over all the Soviet Union. In some geographical areas commissions may exist at all these levels, in others there may be only a scattered organization. Some of these commissions work consistently and effectively. Others operate more haphazardly and take an opportunistic approach to the matter to satisfy the Party line (Aliev 1968: 254). Many of their members have no real commitment to the task or, at the lower levels, are ill-qualified to organize such work (*Kommunist Estonii* 1968, 7: 30–1).

Local commissions are most frequently formed under the auspices of a Party committee but can also be gathered under Councils of Elders (in Muslim areas), the Executive Committee of local soviets, atheist or other public organizations. If the local Party organization is not the main organizer it is always involved in some capacity, and the chairman of such a commission is usually a Party man (see Ranne 1972: 184;

Zots and Poluk 1978: 93). Ritual, according to El'chenko (1976a: 57), is regarded by many Party people as "an ideological weapon" and the work concerned with it as "one of the most important sides of ideological work" (*ibid.*: 61). Like the republican commissions, the local ones co-opt members from all areas of life who might contribute something to the creation and effective performance of a new ritual. The large number of people involved in these commissions is indicated by the figure for Penza region (RSFSR) where 2400 enthusiasts work in 340 public commissions (Fursin 1977: 5n). Practical help, particularly as far as the main *rites de passage* are concerned, is given by the local soviet.

The scope of activity of these commissions varies from area to area. Some of the most advanced ones, like those in Leningrad or Syryanovsk (Kazakh SSR), work out their own scenarios for the various rituals. Others take over the scenarios devised by the republican commission and merely adjust them to local conditions, while yet a third group may mechanically implement recommendations made by the central commission. In addition, local commissions may engage in propagandizing the new rituals through the various means of mass communication and, most importantly, supervise and monitor the actual performance of the new rituals. For this purpose they may have a permanent seminar, where they can discuss practical and theoretical problems which have arisen out of the day-to-day work, and devise ways to improve the impact of specific rites. The long-term establishment and acceptance of the new ritual will depend, in the last resort, on the work of these local commissions.

In recent years the Communist Party at the all-Union level has made no further policy decisions or announcements on the subject of the new rituals and holidays. When the subject came up at the twenty-third Party Congress in 1966 there occurred a careful avoidance of the word "ritual" (*obryad*), and the pronouncements have been on a strengthening of the "three holy Soviet traditions" instead (*Resolyutsiya XXIII sëzda KPSS* 1966: 24). The resolutions of the twenty-fifth Congress in 1976 contain no reference to the subject at all. The Komsomol, in contrast, at its eighteenth Congress made a fresh commitment to support existing initiatives and to introduce further new rituals, particularly youth rituals (*Nashi prazdniki* 1977: 94).

It remains completely unknown by what process it is decided that a certain stage in the development of an individual, a group or of the whole society needs ritual formulation. We know, however, what happens once such a decision has been made. How then is a particular rite devised and implemented? The process of its creation and implementation reminds one of both the scripting and producing of a play and of the introduction of a new piece of political legislation. A number of members of the republican or the local commission (usually workers in the cultural–educational field) get together and, pooling their various skills, work out the script, the scenario and the symbolism of the ritual, as well as details about the music and poetry and the name and date in the calendar of the new holiday or ritual. The results of this work are then submitted for examination to the whole commission or council. If the latter approves the prototype it then makes practical recommendations on how the new ritual can be introduced into daily life. It also prepares cadres and the material–technical base for the new ritual or holiday. As is the case with a new play, several rehearsals are made. The rite is performed in one particular collective and is judged both by those who "produced" it and by those who performed it. If necessary, it is altered on the basis of these criticisms. Only then does the republican commission take steps to introduce the new ritual on a republic-wide scale. (This account is based on Khasanova 1976: 70–4.)

It needs to be pointed out here that the "dramatists" involved do not work in a cultural vacuum inventing the script and the symbols, nor do they produce such individualistic work as a dramatist for the theatre might. They are firmly rooted in the three "holy" Soviet traditions and widely utilize pre-existing elements of ritual, symbolism and art. Very often the "new" ritual is not very new at all. It may be a revival or an adaptation of an old pre-Soviet ritual or may merely join together into an agreeable whole various elements which, up to then, had existed in isolation from each other.

Like a new play, the new holiday or ritual is popularized by an extensive "advertising" campaign. Massive editions of placards and photographic albums about the new ritual as well as brochures stating its scenario bring it to people's notice. The first performances are given coverage in the press and on television, and discussions of the new ritual within various political organizations are encouraged (*ibid.*). In the Muslim areas intermediary bodies, such as Elders' or Women's soviets (a Soviet version of a Women's Institute), are utilized to influence those who cannot be reached by the media or by political organizations (Berestovskaya 1968: 42; Gerandokov 1970: 38). Even when a ritual has been established for a while it is still carefully monitored, and further changes and/or additions may be made by regular seminars devoted to the improvement of rituals (Rogozina 1973: 71; Genkin 1975: 131ff).

A different set of organizational problems surround the actual performance of the rituals. Here we need to consider what human, material and cultural resources are employed to stage rituals and ceremonies. Besides variations between different geographical and socio-demographic areas, patterns of organization differ between rituals performed all the year round (e.g. the life-cycle rituals) and between those staged only at annual or bi-annual intervals. Concerning the life-cycle rites, masters of ceremony or Ritual Elders (in the Ukraine) may perform their duties full- or part-time, depending on the demand, for pay. No special term to describe the person conducting the rituals has evolved in the Russian areas, where he is usually referred to by the neutral word *Zaveduyushchii*, translated as the leader, head, person-in-charge. In rural areas and for the less well-established funeral rite the officiating person usually carries out his duties on a part-time basis. People recruited for this work are often headmasters, teachers or Party workers (*Kommunist Estonii* 1968, 7: 31, 33).

Some masters of ceremony now take a short training course, developing their oratorial skills and receiving some information about the essence of the rituals and the psychology of the participants in the ritual. In a few areas the subject of the new holidays and rituals has already been introduced into the curriculum of teacher training and other cultural–educational institutions, and a course of study designed particularly for masters of ceremony has been worked out in some republics (*Nauka i religiya* 1973, 4: 33; El'chenko 1976: 67). In other areas, People's Universities (a kind of Evening Institute) or periodic seminars on the subject of ritual perform this role (Kampars and Zakovich 1967: 235). Many writers in the field feel the latter kind of training to be inadequate and argue for a general institutionalization of training in institutions, educating workers in the field of culture and education (*Kommunist Estonii* 1968, 7: 31; Aliev 1968: 225; El'chenko 1976a: 69). They complain that many masters of ceremony are inadequately prepared for this work, which requires a high level of political maturity, delicacy in interpersonal relations and a feeling for the artistic side of the ritual. One author justifies the demand for more training by pointing to that received by a priest (*Kommunist Estonii* 1968, 7: 31).

Just as state churches have done for centuries, some workers in the field also want to institutionalize the teaching of ritual competence for participants by including ritual songs in the curriculum of schools

(Kampars and Zakovich 1967: 237; Shneidere 1969: 37). Although there is, at present, no systematic teaching of ritual competence in schools that is comparable to religious instruction in many Western countries, there is, nevertheless, a good deal of fragmentized teaching, preparing the children both emotionally and cognitively for the important Soviet rites and holidays. Thus most of the basic ritual songs (see appendix A) are already taught at school, and children's school readers contain a generous amount of material on specific mass political holidays, on Soviet symbols and on the values expressed in most rituals. A content analysis of a third-year reader of the early seventies (O'Dell 1978: 76) established the following: of 175 lessons which had to be dedicated to the various topics in the reader, teachers had to spend:

six on Octobrists and Pioneers
nine on Our Native Army
ten on Lenin
seven on the anniversary of the October Revolution
eight on Soviets build a new life
six on International Workers' Friendship
eight on International Women's Day
nine on Our Native Land (i.e. on patriotic themes).

Although May Day did not figure as a subject in the third-year reader it was prominent in readers for both the first and the second year (*ibid.*). Some authors also recommend sociological and social–psychological research to get a better understanding of the ritual requirements of various social and national groups (Kampars and Zakovich 1967: 235).

Besides human resources, material support for the organization of ritual is of crucial importance. What resources are needed and who provides them? The staging of life-cycle rites involves considerable expenditure for permanent ritual halls, payment of masters of ceremony, musicians, orators, as well as for various ritual attributes, such as printed invitations, certificates, badges, flowers and candles. From the very beginning, participants in the rites have had to pay only nominal sums or have had the rites performed completely free of charge (*Torzhestvennaya . . .* 1974: 11). The organizations legally responsible for the registration of births, weddings and deaths do not have any financial means of their own to stage the life-cycle rites and depend completely on other bodies for finance. This has not always been forthcoming. The expenses have usually been carried by the local soviet but sometimes, particularly for funerals, contributions have been made by collective farms, enterprises, trades unions or similar bodies (Ranne 1972: 184; Teplyakov 1972: 93). But there has been a continuous shortage of funds, and in some areas the organizations responsible for the staging of rites are poverty-stricken and cannot provide adequate facilities (*Izvestiya* 22 September 1973: 5). It has been suggested that the State should finance such an important part of ideological work (e.g. Mytskyula 1968: 56). Some republican governments have responded to such demands. In the RSFSR, for example, the Soviet of Ministers has released funds for providing purpose-built accommodation (Zuev *et al.* 1974: 57), as well as financing efforts to devise the scenario for a funeral rite by sponsoring creative workers in various fields (Kampars and Zakovich 1967: 234). Not only did the Council of Ministers provide funds but they also instructed town planners to make provision for ritual halls in any plans for future building developments. Similar support has been provided by the Ukrainian republican government (*Nauka i religiya* 1974, 4: 33).

Whereas during the early years, the life-cycle rites were staged on a shoestring budget using makeshift accommodation and weakly utilizing artistic means, today many, but by no means all, urban areas have come a long way from this. In most big towns there now exist special buildings or halls in which the rites can be staged effectively. Most are Wedding Palaces, Palaces of Happiness or Palaces of Solemn Events (in the Ukraine), designed either just for the performance of the wedding rite or for both wedding and birth rites. Some towns, for example Leningrad, have a separate palace for the latter. A well-provided republic, like the Ukraine, is said to have 311 ritual "salons" and 32 "festive halls" (Zots 1976: 24). Funeral pavilions, either purpose-built or converted from a cemetery chapel, are, as yet, found relatively infrequently. It is interesting that the funeral pavilion in Leningrad has been provided as part of a newly built crematorium, a relatively recent phenomenon in the Soviet Union. On some cemeteries there has been set aside a special area called "Mourning Square" (*traurnaya ploshchad'*).

The organization of the various rituals of initiation, which require fewer resources, follows different patterns. These rituals are organized and financed primarily by the social or political organization into which ritual participants are being initiated. Assistance is usually given by the local Party, Komsomol or trades union organization. Thus the ritual of initiation into the working class, for example, is organized jointly by the Party, Komsomol and trades union organization of the enterprise where the initiands work. Some large enterprises, which are

53

particularly active in staging rituals and ceremonies, have their own permanent organizing committee whose work is approved by the enterprise's Party and trades union committees. (See, for example, Grishchenko and Kakonin (1974: 10) on the Magnitogorsk metallurgical combine.) If there is no clear organizational responsibility, as with the school-leaving ritual or the Baltic "Summer Days of Youth", the Komsomol, the political organization of the young, steps in. None of the initiation rituals require purpose-built accommodation but are most effectively staged in any surrounding with symbolic qualities that relate to the particular "holy tradition" into which the young people are being initiated.

With holidays of the calendric cycle, yet another pattern of organization prevails. Where such a holiday serves a distinct community, such as a collective farm or enterprise, the organization and finance is carried by that community. Where a holiday is designed to attract a more dispersed population, organization is usually carried out by the Party with the help of various co-opted organizations and individuals.

To sum up this section, the creation and introduction into everyday life of a system of socialist holidays and rituals has evolved gradually from various local political initiatives. Initially it developed fairly haphazardly without a lot of central co-ordination. Although from around 1964 onwards organization has become co-ordinated at the level of the republic, local initiative has remained a strong force in the development of the new rituals. The moral and practical support received from 1964 onwards from the highest Party circles has naturally been important in maintaining the impetus of the local initiative and in stimulating new activity. Among the local organizations introducing and promoting the new rituals, the Communist Party and its youth movement, the Komsomol, have consistently assumed the leadership and have involved themselves most actively in the work. They have, however, not monopolized it and have drawn in a wide spectrum of other organizations and talented or influential individuals. While they appear to have had considerable success in involving the latter group of persons, institutions and individuals in the fields of culture and of the creative arts have been more difficult to mobilize. The lack of interest in the "ritual question" by workers in the field of culture has been stressed by several writers along the lines of the following comment printed in *Izvestiya* (22 September 1973: 5): "In several towns I talked to dozens of registry office employees, and all of them talked

54

about the complete or nearly complete brushing-aside (*ustranenie*) of the 'ritual question' by republican and regional institutions of culture.''

SOME CONFLICTING ORIENTATIONS IN THE ORGANIZATION OF RITUAL

Voluntarism versus constraint

The political and cultural elites, to use an analogy, provide the theatre, the script of the play, the director and producer, but the actors have to come from among the ordinary Soviet people. It is necessary to examine how the Soviet people become involved in performing the new rituals and to what degree their involvement can be described as either voluntary or constrained. There is no easy answer to these questions. While most Soviet ritual specialists would hasten to assure us that participation is entirely voluntary, a careful examination of the practice in different areas and with regard to the various rituals reveals that the answer is more complex and that a more differentiated approach needs to be employed.

Looking at the mass political holidays, it is common knowledge that participation in its central ritual, the procession–demonstration, is organized from above. Each work collective selected for participation in the demonstration during a particular year mobilizes as many of its employees as will make up a contingent. Usually enough volunteers can be found but occasionally some pressure may be necessary.

Turning to the rituals of initiation into social and political collectives, one needs to define the word "constraint" more widely. Although participation may be formally voluntary the membership of a small, clearly defined group, such as, for example, the new young workers of an enterprise, puts social pressure to participate on each individual. Resentment of such pressure, however, cannot be too widespread, or else the ritual could not be staged convincingly.

Yet a different situation prevails as far as familial life-cycle rituals are concerned. Here participation is again formally voluntary. Although pressure by the small collective to participate can be discounted, the moral pressure of the large collective – militant atheist public opinion – which proscribes participation in the traditional religious *rites de passage* must be considered a constraining influence. In addition, there are various more direct pressures exerted on individuals which put a question mark over the voluntary nature of participation. I am referring to such practices as sending personal invitations to those eligible for a particular ritual (Berestovskaya 1968: 23; Baturin 1976: 114); officials visiting parents straight after the birth of a baby, sometimes even in hospital (Lisavtsev 1966: 105); asserting influence through superiors at work or Elders in Muslim communities on people who are either still unsure or have decided to have a religious rite performed. Thus the chairman of the town commission for rituals in Sevastopol (RSFSR) reports how a young couple was persuaded to change from a religious to a socialist wedding rite after members of the commission and a superior of the bridegroom at his place of employment had worked on them for a whole week (Veselev 1973: 66ff). Sometimes a combination of all three methods is employed and, as one author notes with pride, "these common efforts bring positive results" (Berestovskaya 1968: 23). Such practices, it must be pointed out, have been reported mainly in studies of the sixties. They seem to have been adopted in areas where a rite was relatively new and ritual specialists were still anxious about its acceptance. In areas where the life-cycle rituals are well established and performed with some sophistication such practices would be decried. Persuasion, however, through propaganda popularizing the new rites, is exerted in all areas.

Concerning holidays of the calendric cycle, which try to attract a more general and more diffuse part of the population, there is no way to pressurize people to participate in their central rituals, and participation is entirely voluntary. Unfortunately there are, in the literature, no data to show whether participation in the genuine sense, rather than just spectatorship, is forthcoming or not.

This short review of the ways in which people become involved in the performance of socialist rituals has brought out that participation, although constrained in several ways, has a large measure of voluntariness in it. It would be naive to accept without reservations the Soviet claims that participation is completely voluntary. But it would also be wrong to maintain that, because there is an *organized* system of rituals, rituals are imposed from above on the Soviet people. Such practices as reported above can mobilize the uninformed, the undecided and the inert, but they cannot make the hostile participate. If participation in a religious rite is precluded because of informal pressure against it, individuals are not driven to participate in a socialist rite as the alternative. Changes in the life cycle need not be marked by any public ritual but may be celebrated privately after having been recorded in a registry office. Furthermore, surveys have shown (e.g. Zhirnova 1971: 73) that the performance of the socialist wedding rite is for the large majority of young people a genuine choice rather than something that cannot be avoided.

In any case, it is impossible, in the long run, to impose ritual on unwilling people without destroying the ritual in the process. As has been pointed out earlier, the efficacy of ritual as a social regulator depends on a fusion of social or moral injunctions with positive emotions engendered in the individual participant. If people were constrained to participate these emotions would not develop. A ritual failing to elicit a positive emotional response would either perish, or it might be continued as an empty form. We know from the literature that, for various reasons, the first has frequently been the case. As to the second possibility, one can hardly believe that the new Soviet ritual has been maintained for around fifteen years without having had any efficacy whatsoever. My claim that participation in the ritual is to a large extent voluntary does not imply that there is always an immediate response to the new ritual. On the contrary, acceptance is a gradual process, and a good deal of persuasion is necessary to convince people that the new ritual offers appropriate channels for expressing basic emotions.

Spontaneity versus direction

Western writers making a theoretical analysis of ritual, as well as critics of the new Soviet ritual both inside and outside the Soviet Union, maintain that the notion of organization is irreconcilable with ritual and that ritual will not develop unless it evolves completely spontaneously as a popular creation. Some even go so far as to claim that there can be no such thing as a *new* ritual but that ritual, by definition, is steeped in tradition (Struve 1969: 760; M. Wilson 1971: 129). An article by Petukhov in *Novy Mir* (1969, 6: 274), which created a stir in the Soviet Union, described the new rituals as paper flowers, created by those who cannot wait until living flowers will grow. This and similar arguments are vigorously repudiated by Soviet ritual specialists who, it seems to me, put forward more valid counter-arguments (see Filatov 1967: 22; Fursin 1972: 166; Ugrinovich 1975: 161ff). Such critics, they say, forget that a large and well-established part of the ritual of our Western civilization, namely Christian religious ritual, originated as the result of a similarly controlled and consciously organized effort on the part of the ecclesiastical elite. Even rituals seemingly free of the direction from an ideologically conscious and organized social group, such as popular or folk ritual, has not evolved completely spontaneously. It has initially required some organizing body or individuals, who have perceived the requirement of a specific social group, to become staged effectively. The distance in time from the creation of a ritual has obscured the fact that ritual specialists have been involved. Also, the groups for which the folk rituals were created generally resembled more the "community" type, so that the social distance between theorists and practitioners of ritual was not such a marked one.

The belief that organized ritual cannot succeed is also based on the idea that "organized" necessarily means "invented". As I shall show below, although the two sometimes go together in practice, they are not inevitably associated. Whether or not a ritual becomes successfully established does, therefore, not depend on the absence of organization but on the exact nature of that organization. It is a question of whether or not a balance is kept between direction and spontaneity in this organization, or, in other words, whether direction remains mere guidance or becomes regimentation.

Soviet ritual specialists, in theory, are agreed that a balance between direction and spontaneity has to be preserved, but differ on the weight which is to be given to each. Trotsky, writing in 1923 about the possibility of creating a new system of rituals, was quite adamant that the spontaneous creativity of the masses had to be given the greatest weight and that the creative intelligentsia should only give guidance. The Party is not even mentioned by him:

It is only by the creativity of the general masses of the population assisted by the creative imagination and artistic initiative, that we can, in the course of years and decades, come out on the road of spiritualized, ennobled forms of life. Without regulating this creative process we must, nevertheless, help it in every way. (Trotsky 1973: 47)

Ritual specialists writing at the present time have changed the balance more in favour of direction and give both sides equal weight.

Rituals in our time arose as a product of artistic and everyday life creativity of the popular masses, on the one hand, and by planned goal-directed work of the institutions of Party and soviet and of Soviet public organizations, on the other. (Kryvelev 1977: 36)

In their practical work, however, ritual specialists do not observe such a perfect balance. Planned, goal-directed work is paramount. It is, at most, guided by popular need and is responsive to spontaneous popular creativity.

What form then does popular participation in the creation of the new ritual take? First, there is consideration and utilization of *past* popular creativity as found in established pre-Soviet rituals and culture in general. This has taken the form of quite extensive co-optation into the system of new holidays and rituals of old complete rituals and of selected ritual actions or symbols. These have usually been adapted to conform to present ideological requirements, and very often the mere forms have been adopted (for details of this syncretism, see chapter 12). This co-optation of the old rituals or elements thereof, it should be noted, is as much motivated by a need to channel and thus control their impact as by a readiness to invite popular participation. But whatever the motivation behind this incorporation of established symbolism, the fact remains that the new rituals are not invented. They are not a product of the imagination of ritual specialists but have had to take into consideration what has been created by popular "spontaneity" through the decades and centuries. Even this process of syncretism, though, does not evolve spontaneously but occurs as "rational synthesis", preceded by conscious selection from the past.

Secondly, popular participation of a passive kind is involved in the consideration, by ritual specialists, of popular need of either individuals or groups. Such need is sometimes inferred from the degree of acceptance or non-acceptance of a new ritual and, at other times, is consciously articulated in demands expressed by participants, particularly during the pilot stage of a new ritual. How far such needs are actually taken into consideration and are allowed to shape the new rituals is rarely made explicit by ritual specialists and remains very vague. A few examples of responding to group needs (of an ethnic or national kind) are the incorporation into the new ritual of some specific local ritual actions or symbols, for example the inclusion into the life-cycle rites in the Ukraine of the local embroidered rug (*ruzhnik*). Inclusions of this kind are widespread and are actively encouraged by ritual specialists. These very minor adjustments to ritual form enable them not only to satisfy group demands but also to avoid uniformity by adding local colour. Consideration of individual needs is also given by concessions to individual taste in the choice of music and to requests for greater privacy in most life-cycle rituals. The latter will be discussed in detail below. In both cases, it should be noted, consideration of participants' needs involves only slight adjustments, affecting the form rather than the content of the rituals.

Thirdly, and most importantly, mass participation is involved when spontaneous popular creation of a whole ritual or of a ritual sequence is acknowledged by, and receives organizational support from, ritual specialists. To enable such spontaneous participation to occur in the first place, scope must be given for spontaneous creativity to unfold. The historical study of the ritual of the mass political holidays in chapter 10 has shown that in the first decade of Soviet power this scope existed and was utilized. Then, social diversity was still great and organization was relatively loose and not completely in the hands of specialist organizations. At the present time, organization is central-ized and is exclusively the task of bodies which predetermine every detail, not only of the mass political holidays but of ritual and cere-mony in general. In this context very little scope for spontaneous creativity remains. Indeed, very few examples are reported in the literature on the subject. One notable exception to this rule has been the seemingly spontaneous creation, by Leningrad school-leavers, of the school-leaving ritual "Scarlet Sails". Leningrad ritual specialists certainly adopted, and gave organizational support to, this new ritual. But in the process they killed all spontaneity and, by adding to its content and form, completely changed its spirit from a romantic affair just for school-leavers to a political mass demonstration (for a detailed description of this process, see Laskina 1976).

To conclude, the main expression of popular participation in the new ritual is the incorporation into it of pre-existing elements that are considered to be part of a widely accepted popular culture. In this respect socialist ritual is new only in the sense that it brings together traditional elements in a new combination. Although some conces-sions to present popular demand have been made these have only been minor and have mainly affected the form of the new ritual. The greatest concessions to individual need, it will be shown below, have been made in the life-cycle rituals where they have affected the under-lying orientation. Direction, more often than not appearing as regim-entation, is paramount and determines the general nature of the new ritual. Some of the more enlightened ritual specialists deplore exces-sive regimentation, express a desire to base themselves on mass creativity and are aware of serious deficiencies in this respect (e.g. Brudnyi 1968: 1973; *Nauka i religiya* 1973, 4: 41; El'chenko 1976a: 62). But the organization of the new ritual militates against the realization of these desires. Even ritual specialists of this kind, however, would dampen spontaneous popular creativity which expressed orientations irreconcilable with the ideology of Soviet Marxism–Leninism on which the new system of rituals is based.

The collective versus the individual

Ritual, I said earlier, relates the individual to the collective. Ritual provides ready-made channels which allow the individual to express his feelings while at the same time funnelling them into a socially accepted direction. This transformation of individual into social consciousness is accomplished, as V. Turner (1967) points out, by a fusion of the emotional (the individual) and the ideological (the social) through the power of ritual symbols. To be effective, that is to accomplish its task of tying the individual to the collective, ritual must therefore keep a balance between focussing on the individual and on the collective. It is now in order to examine to what extent this balance has been maintained during the various stages in the development of the socialist ritual and how it is preserved in the various kinds of the new ritual.

The Soviet theoretical work on ritual, although familiar with the internal structure of ritual and the mechanisms which make ritual effective in general, does not fully consider their implications when making recommendations for devising and implementing the new rituals. The very fact that most ritual specialists carry out this work in their capacity as members of the Party or local government apparatus and associated political organizations, as workers in the field of ideology (agitation and propaganda), makes them focus on the ideological side of the new ritual, on the requirements of the social or political collective, rather than on those of the individual. The new ritual is being considered primarily as a tool for political socialization, and the satisfaction of individual needs is seen by most writers in the field as a subsidiary function, rather than one of equal importance. This approach is exemplified by the most recent work on the new ritual, *Nashi prazdniki* (1977), which, being a collective effort by a large number of authors, can be considered as being representative of the approach of most ritual specialists at the present time and is thought to be authoritative by Soviet workers in the field (it was pointed out as such to me on several occasions). The ten pages of the book devoted to a theoretical discussion of the new Soviet ritual in general dwells

61

chiefly on its function of being "an important means to educate the masses" (*ibid.*: 1) and hardly considers the needs of the individuals participating in it. This rather one-sided approach, however, is not taken by all theorists of the new ritual. A few of them, for example Brudnyi (1968), take a socialist humanist approach to the introduction of socialist ritual and are as much concerned with how the new ritual benefits the individual participants as they are with its rewards for the political collective.

As might be expected, there is also a difference in attitude to the new rituals between ritual specialists (i.e. the theorists of the movement) and between those engaged in the practical work who are constantly in touch with the clients, as it were. When talking to people engaged in the day-to-day running of the palaces in Moscow and Leningrad where life-cycle rites are performed, the directors and masters of ceremony, I found a different set of priorities. Preoccupation with the primary function of the new ritual (as stipulated by ritual specialists), political socialization, was not very great, but concern for the emotional satisfaction of the ritual participants was at the forefront of their minds.

In addition to these rather general differences concerning the balance between focussing on the individual and on the collective, there are more specific variations in attitude and practice. These depend, first, on what stage in the development of Soviet socialist ritual we are studying and, secondly, with which sub-section in the general system of rituals we are concerned. Looking at the development of socialist life-cycle ritual historically, one is immediately struck by the fundamental difference in orientation to the life-cycle rites in the twenties on the one hand, and the sixties and seventies on the other, as well as by a less striking change in attitude between the sixties and the seventies. In the twenties, when the *Oktyabriny* (a registration of a new-born child) and "Red Weddings" were introduced as the first secular alternatives to the corresponding Christian religious *rites de passage*, there was no attempt to keep a balance between satisfying individual needs and achieving the ends of the collective. As the account of one such occasion, given below, demonstrates, the needs of individuals for emotional expression were not only ignored, but individual sensibilities were often violated. Far from being the centre of the rite, the individual was a mere tool for achieving the ends of the collective. The important turning-point in a family's life became a mere pretext for a lesson in political demonstration:

In the front corner of the club a detachment of Pioneers with the scarlet banner sing to the quiet beating of a drum: "We are the young guard of workers and peasants . . ." The chairman declares: "Comrades–Pioneers, I suggest you turn to the mother and invite her (to come) over here." The audience applauds and shouts "Hurrah!" When all have entered the club the young mother declares: "The child belongs to me only physically. For its spiritual education I hand it over to society." Applause. The chairman takes the child in his arms, and the Pioneers unwind over him the cloth of their banner. "We, the Pioneers, swear to help the new member to proceed through all three schools: that of the Pioneers, the Komsomol and of the RCP and to become an upright citizen. With honour we take the newly born girl into our detachment." The chairman reads out an official diploma given to the new-born by the comrades from his place of residence: "On the day of the seventh anniversary of October the administration and the workers of the house solemnly take into the membership of their collective the new-born and name her Maya, in honour of the international proletarian holiday of the 1st of May." Music, shouts of "Hurrah!" Applause. The orderly of the house's medical cell (*sanyacheika*) reads out and hands to the mother a second diploma about the assumption of patronship over the child. The new citizen is given a portrait of Rosa Luxemburg, and the mother (receives) a diploma and a book about motherhood. (*Izvestiya* 1924, quoted by Veresaev 1926: 23–4)

As might be expected, such an approach to the creation of ritual was doomed to fail. This lesson was learnt by ritual specialists who sought to introduce socialist life-cycle rituals from the late fifties onwards. They became much more concerned to maintain a balance, though in the early years of that period the requirements of the collective still frequently overshadowed those of the individual. Then it was not an occasion just for the family and close friends, but representatives from various social and political collectives impinging on the life of the individual asserted their presence with long, repetitive speeches. Also the verbal content of ritual formulae emphasized the status of citizen of Soviet society with its attendant obligations rather more than the status of a member of a family. From the late sixties onwards, when the wedding rite and the rite of Solemn Registration of the New-born Child were well established in most areas of the USSR, the demands of the collective became less dominant and were expressed more discreetly. Although there are still differences in this respect between geographical areas, one can say that, generally speaking, in the life-cycle rites care is taken to maintain a balance between focussing on the individual and the collective. Furthermore, some ritual specialists express concern about those of their colleagues who have not yet come round to this way of thinking. Deprecatory comments on the socialist life-cycle rituals by Western writers, such as Unger (1974: 196), emphasizing the public, collective-orientated nature of the life-cycle rituals, are therefore adopting a rather one-sided and somewhat outdated interpretation of this particular group of rites.

The same attempt to maintain a balance is being made in relation to the ritual of the revived holidays of the calendric cycle, celebrated by the various national groups. Unlike the life-cycle rites, however, where the individual and the collective are relatively well integrated and form an harmonious whole, in the holidays of the calendric cycle the normative injunctions of the socialist political collective are often clumsily inserted or tagged on.

Turning to the rituals of initiation into a social or political collective and to the ritual of the mass political holidays, one finds that the demands of the collective completely obliterate the individuality of participants. Incorporation into a specific collective in the first case, and reaffirmation of loyalty to the overarching general collectives – state and Party – in the second case, dominate these rituals. Although some concessions are made to the individual, such as calling every member of the group by name in initiation rites, the individual remains a mere constituent part of the group rather than an individual personality. Abandonment of individuality and submersion in the collective is carried farthest in the mass political holidays. This insistence on articulating the norms of the collective at the expense of the individuality of group members may account for the unimaginative uniformity often encountered in this group of rituals and goes some way towards explaining the much slower rate of their acceptance.

Part II

vvvvvvvvvvvvvvvvvvvvvvvvvvvvvvvvvvvvvvvvvvvvvvvvvvvvvvvvvvvvvvvvvvvvvvvvvvvvvvvvv

The nature of Soviet socialist rituals

The six chapters of part II are all devoted to the empirical study of the various rituals performed in Soviet society at the present time. They describe the ritual scenarios of the major rites performed, and descriptions are given of regional variations where they exist. These chapters also give short accounts of the development of the various rites and indicate how particular rites relate to the general system of rituals and to the ideology embodied in them. Following Ortner's approach (1975: 135), the descriptive accounts are supplemented by some remarks about the problematic realities of Soviet society to which particular rites are addressing themselves (their "model of" aspect) and about the reorientations towards these realities which ritual specialists are trying to effect (their "model for" aspect).

The extremely wide range of rituals in the Soviet system has been sub-divided for presentation according to the following criteria, which are not always mutually exclusive. Chapter 5 deals with rites focussing primarily on the individual as a member of a family, while chapter 6 is concerned with his incorporation into (or, in one case, separation from) social and/or political collectives, excepting only those based on common labour. The latter have been included in chapter 7 which is devoted to the large and diverse group of labour holidays and rites. Chapter 8 is about the holidays and rituals which relate the individual or the group to seasonal changes and to a number of diverse and often unrelated clusters of values from the political ideology that are tagged on to them. Those holidays which concentrate strongly on the labour requirement accompanying a change in season have been included in chapter 7. Chapters 9 and 10 describe rituals relating the individual or specific groups to the whole society. While chapter 9 deals with the mass political holidays and rites which focus on the military–patriotic aspects of Soviet ideology, chapter 10 is concerned with the two main mass political holidays of the revolutionary tradition. This chapter differs from the others in this section in that it gives a detailed historical account of these two holidays from 1918 up to the present time, relating both changes and continuities in their ritual content and form to the changing and constant broad concerns and general problems of Soviet society during its sixty-odd years of existence.

5

Familial life-cycle ritual

First of all it is necessary to focus on the problematic social realities which have contributed to the creation of the life-cycle rites and on the new value orientations the rites are intended to transmit. The attitude of Soviet political elites towards the family as a primary social group consists of two conflicting orientations towards it. On the one hand, a socialist developed industrial society with pretensions to world economic and political leadership, and opposed by a strong bloc of capitalist societies, depends on a strong and stable family. The latter is needed to supply the State with recruits for its industrial and military armies and to assist the State in the inculcation of the discipline necessary for the operation of a modern economy and army. But the Soviet family, like that in other modern industrial societies, is becoming increasingly unstable and incapable of performing certain of its roles as defined by the State. As Lapidus (1978: 286) points out, "Rising divorce rates, signs that marriage itself is declining in attractiveness, increasingly serious problems of juvenile delinquency, widespread alcoholism, and many additional signs of general family instability has made the Soviet family . . . the focus of anxious scrutiny." At the same time the existence of the family as a relatively independent agency of socialization is correctly feared as an alternative source of norms and values and is thus regarded as a serious obstacle to the process of establishing total ideological domination. Consequently measures had to be adopted to further the objective of strengthening the family while, at the same time, limiting its capacity to socialize its members in ways deviating from that sanctioned by the official ideology.

Ritual has been regarded as one means which can achieve both these objectives. Both the very creation of familial life-cycle rites in general and their more specific features of emphasizing Soviet socialist norms of conduct in the family and definitions of sex roles are seen by ritual specialists as supporting and strengthening the family. At the same

67

time the new familial *rites de passage* are regarded as being vehicles for the transmission of values, correcting the family's deviant value orientations and its harmful tendency to put the welfare of its members above that of the larger collective. Thus the rites oppose an atheist to a traditional religious world view. They also underline the notion that individuals are supported by the State and have to reciprocate with a conscientious performance of social duties. They emphasize the fact that families have not only obligations to each of their members but to the whole society and to the State. The rites make it clear that family affairs are as much a concern of the State as they are of the individual family members and that family socialization must inculcate the norms and values of the official ideology.

THE BIRTH RITE

A ritual to mark the birth of a child first emerged in the early twenties under the name *Oktyabriny*. Both in name (derived from the Russian word for October, referring to the Revolution) and in content and form it resembled more a political demonstration than an individual life-cycle ritual (for a detailed description see Ugrinovich 1975: 114). It failed to gain acceptance beyond a small band of political enthusiasts and proved to be a short-lived experiment. A new attempt to ritually formulate the birth of a child was not made until 1963 in most republics. Although it is now accepted by a large minority of new parents it is by no means generally established. In many areas its organizers are struggling for wider acceptance, and the ritual is still at the formative stage. While the ritual is well established in some of the western republics, excepting only Catholic Lithuania, and in Leningrad and moderately well established in other areas of European Russia it has as yet found little acceptance in the traditionally Islamic areas of Central Asia (Lobacheva 1972: 7).

The lack of firm and general acceptance is manifested in the large degree of diversity in this ritual between geographical areas, even in its very name. Although the content is basically the same in all of them, there are differences in emphasis on the constituent elements, expressed in different ritual forms. At one end of the scale are those birth rituals enacted in some of the large towns of the western parts of the Soviet Union, where the ritual is well thought out, is firmly established and has a secure material base. Here great emphasis is laid on the emotional requirements of the individuals involved, and the social and political collective does not intrude too much. At the other end of the scale is a procedure of marking the birth of a child which completely disregards the emotional requirements of its parents. In many rural areas, where both the buildings and the personnel that are necessary to stage an impressive ritual are lacking, a birth may be marked, in the words of a Soviet commentator, in the following way: "The parents receive a certificate about the birth of their child, and that is all. There is no more solemnity and emotionality in this than in receiving a permit for buying concentrated fodder or in paying agricultural taxes" (*Kommunist Estonii* 1968: 29). In between these two poles fall birth rituals where organizational conditions are adequate but where the forms of the ritual are still too reminiscent of political meetings and must reduce the emotional impact on the participant individuals considerably.

Just as diverse as the forms of this ritual is its name in different areas. The official designations of this ritual as "Solemn Registration of the New-Born Child" or "Ritual of Name-Giving" have proved too cumbersome to gain general acceptance. In many areas the old religious term *krestiny* (Christening) has been so tenaciously adhered to that even ritual specialists have succumbed and adopted it officially (e.g. Kampars and Zakovich 1967: 16, 17; Mytskyula 1968). In many areas, after a lot of heated discussion, the institution of godparents has now been introduced into the ritual. These are variously called Honorary Parents, Appointed Parents (*Nazvannye roditeli*) or Godparents (*Krestnye roditeli*). They perform similar functions as those demanded of godparents in the ritual of baptism, except that they are made responsible for the child's upbringing to society, rather than to the Church.

The following description of a birth ritual is of that enacted in Leningrad which has served as a model for many other towns. Some of the variations from this pattern will be pointed out after that.

The first Solemn Registration of the New-Born Child in Leningrad was performed in 1963, after a systematic preparation for this event by the town's Party and Komsomol committees. In 1965 the town received a handsome building that was converted for the performance of this ritual; the building is called *Malyutka* (baby palace). This palace provides a curious combination of services, making provision for both ritual and purely instrumental, even scientifically orientated action with reference to the new-born child, and thus indicates the secular orientation of Soviet ritual. Besides providing space for a ritual and a banquet hall the palace also contains a baby shop and, more

69

importantly, a mother-and-baby room with a doctor and a nurse in attendance. This dual orientation is also reflected in the literature the parents receive in some areas. Besides a "beautifully finished" birth certificate and a letter of congratulations from the local soviet, parents also receive a leaflet offering guidance on aspects of baby care and child education. Also available is a booklet with names that are thought to be desirable. The Leningrad booklet is arranged like a calendar, each day containing the name of a person "who is the pride of the Soviet Union" (Rudnev 1966: 173). In addition there is a section with forgotten Russian names and one with new Soviet names. Parents apply for the Solemn Registration of their child not later than five days after the mother's return from hospital, and then parents and administrators together determine the day. The palace undertakes to send out invitations to the organizations were mother and father work or study.

On the day, parents and guests arrive at the palace, where the mother and child go into a waiting-room apart from the other guests. At an agreed time all enter the ritual hall to the tune of the song "Fly away doves". In recent years the repertoire of songs has changed slightly and now includes a hymn specially composed for that occasion. Today's parents also have the option, for a small charge, to have the musical items rendered by a professional choir, whose members are festively attired in long white lace dresses and dark suits. Special seats are prepared for parents, godparents and grandparents. It is thought particularly important to involve the latter, who are often the carriers of religious influence, in the new ritual. When the music stops the master of ceremony announces that Leningrad Urban Soviet of Workers' Deputees registers the new citizen of the USSR in accordance with the law on marriage and the family of the RSFSR. "Today", he continues, "is registered the son (daughter) born to X and Y (name of parents). In accordance with the wishes of the parents he (she) is given the name X. In honour of the new citizen the Soviet anthem will be sung" (quoted by Ugrinovich 1975: 126). Then a deputy from the soviet congratulates the parents and gives them the birth certificate, a letter of congratulation from the executive committee of the Soviet and a memorial medal. The latter has on one side the Lenin memorial against the background of a Leningrad scene, and on the other side is a five-cornered star in the rays of the sun and the name and date of birth of the child. The letter of congratulation also contains admonitions to educate the child as a good citizen. A few words are addressed to both

70

the parents and the grandparents. A closing speech contains the following words:

Dear Parents! Today is for you a great and significant event – a new member of the family has been born. This is a joy not only for you but for our whole society. Children are our happiness, our joy, our future . . . I wish you to raise and educate your children (to become) healthy, joyful, bold and not fearing difficulties. From childhood implant in them love of work and of our great Motherland. (Quoted by Rudnev 1974: 95)

After relatives and colleagues have congratulated the parents and handed them presents, the ritual comes to a conclusion with the song "Let there always be sunshine". (As this song seems to be a part of most birth rituals its words are set out in appendix A.)

A Solemn Registration of Birth in Latvia is similar in content and form to the Leningrad ritual but is less severe as well as making an appeal to the emotions through a wider use of symbolism and ritual attributes. (The following description is based on *Torzhestvennaya registratsiya . . . 1974.*)

The procession of the parents with their child, godparents and guests are led into the ritual hall by two young children from a local kindergarten. These are in national dress and carry on a special tray the birth certificate and two small unlit candles. They all pass through a cordon of more young children in national dress holding garlands of flowers. The ceremony is opened by a specially commissioned reciter with the following words (my translation):

> Life becomes brighter and more beautiful
> Much quicker is its wonderful course,
> Suddenly here in our Soviet family
> A small person is born.
> Today we are celebrating in honour of him to whom
> belongs the future, and we are saying to him
> "Hail, new citizen of our great Soviet state". (*ibid.*: 6–7)

Then the parents are asked to take the small, unlit candles (pink or blue, according to the child's sex) from the children's tray and to light them from two large burning candles on the ritual table. Throughout the ceremony, recitation of verse and music are interposed. At its conclusion, the father is handed the birth certificate and, often, a book of stories, while the mother is presented with flowers and a letter of congratulation from the local soviet. These are usually given by a deputy from the soviet who says a few words about love for the native

71

place, about passing it on to the child, about his hope that the child's love for the birthplace will turn into love of the Motherland.

A birth ritual conducted in the Krasnodar region of the RSFSR emphasizes a future social role of the child by including in the ritual a group of Young Pioneers. They salute the new citizen and hand the parents a Young Pioneer scarf. In this ritual the attempt is made to impress their social duty on the parents more indelibly by making them promise in writing to bring up their child as "a glorious son (daughter) of the great Motherland" (Lisavtsev 1966: 105–6).

Although the ritual performances described so far contain several pointed references to the fact that the new-born child is as much a new citizen of Soviet society as he/she is a new member of a family, the individual parents and their child remain the centre of the ritual.

Another well-developed and firmly established birth ritual is the Ukrainian version. In its interpretation of the significance of birth, it shifts the balance further away from the family and puts more emphasis on the individual's inclusion into the larger political unit. The family remains, however, the focus of the ritual. The following detailed account of such a rite is given in *Nashi prazdniki* (1977: 134ff). The parents and their guests, led by the ritual elder (*starosta*, the traditional word for a village elder or headman and also for a church elder), enter the ritual hall to the tune of the following song, rendered by a choir or a trio of bandore players:

> A radiant light has spread –
> A man was born in the world.
> Mother and Father we are meeting
> We propose their health.
> We meet them. (My translation)

Then the ritual elder's assistant solemnly announces:

There will be performed the ritual of name-giving and registration in the book of records of civic acts of the new-born son (daughter) of —— (mother's name) and —— (father's name). The ritual will be conducted by the ritual elder, the deputy of the soviet —— (name).

The ritual elder enters the hall and, stopping by the ritual table, addresses those present:

I am glad to greet you, dear guests, in this bright hall! Your son (daughter) and grandson (granddaughter), esteemed parents, grandmothers and grandfathers, was born at a fine time when the centuries-old dreams of progressive humanity about a just social system and a happy life for toilers has been made a

72

reality by the selfless creative labour of the Soviet people, led by the Communist Party. It falls to our new generation to complete the cause begun by the great Lenin, the name of which is communism.

Then another song, called "Anthem (*Velichal'naya*) to the New-Born", is rendered. This song, which seems to have been created for the occasion, echoes the words of the ritual elder. Then the elder asks the parents:

Esteemed   (name of mother) and   (name of father)! How did you decide to name your son (daughter)?
Father: In the family council we decided to call him (her) —— Let him (her) grow up and obtain good fame for his name – by work, diligence and painstaking study.
Elder: Esteemed —— (name of mother) and —— (name of father)! I ask you to come to the table and authenticate with your signatures the document about the birth of your son (daughter) —— (name of child) as a citizen of our great Motherland – the Union of Soviet Socialist Republics.

The parents thank him and sign the document. A song called "Anthem to the Parents" is rendered. Another short speech by the ritual elder declares the completion of the registration of the child. He hands the parents the certificate and a memorial medal in the shape of a star. He continues:

Dear parents! In the name of the Soviet state, on the instructions of the —— Soviet of People's Representatives I sincerely congratulate you on the birth of your son (daughter). Remember about your holy duty before our socialist society – to raise your son (daughter) as a worthy fighter for the full triumph of communism. Inculcate in him love of work and of his great Soviet Motherland. Let him be honest, just, good and respectful so that Mother–Motherland will be proud of your son (daughter). On its part, socialist society guarantees and offers your son (daughter) its citizenship with full rights, all opportunities, all material and spiritual values for his all-round harmonious development and the exercising of his inclinations, capabilities and talents. The way in which these opportunities will be utilized depends a lot on you. Set him an example of respectability in every big and small matter. Let him also be a dependable support in your old age. Family happiness and prosperity to you, dear friends!

The song "With what does the Motherland begin?" (for the text see appendix A) is played. The ritual elder turns to the grandparents:

Highly esteemed grandfathers and grandmothers! In your lifetime you did a lot of work, brought people much good, raised good people who now have become parents themselves, and you have received grandchildren. Allow me to sincerely congratulate you on the birth of your grandson (daughter) —— (name of child). Let him grow up to be a joy for you, give him your generous

73

and loving kindness and strengthen your family links, cement the continuity of generations!

After this guests and relatives congratulate the parents. This basic scenario receives minor adjustments and additions in the various parts of the Ukraine in an attempt to add local colour.

A rather remarkable version of the birth rite has in recent years been performed in a Penza maternity hospital. According to a description in the newspaper *Nedelya* (1978, 48), the ritual begins with the sounding of a fanfare. Then "in the right corner of the spherical screen a red spot begins to blaze, a complete imitation of the rising sun. And it is dispersing beams, longer and wider. Then everything suddenly flares up in red, yellow, green, as if a rainbow were flowing over the surface. In this culminating moment, to the sound of the finale of Tchaikovsky's First Concerto, Tamara (a medical nurse) comes out with the child in her arms." The screen continues to iridesce in all colours, and the parents are addressed with the words: "Under the peaceful, brilliant sun of the great Soviet Homeland for happiness and glorious deeds" a child has been born (*ibid.*).

In some areas of the Soviet Union the individual approach is often lost through a lack of resources or political overzealousness on the part of the organizers. Thus in many areas a birth ritual is arranged for a number of families together, and any public building may be used to stage it (see Berestovskaya 1968: 35; Gerandokov 1970: 36). There may be a large number of congratulatory speeches, with public representatives from a wide spectrum of social life, stressing their contribution to the happy state of affairs into which the child has been born. These speakers may include a representative from the local soviet, from the collective farm or industrial enterprise where the parents work, from the Party and from the local school (see Khachirov *et al.* 1973: 43ff).

The registration ritual is often followed by a tree-planting ritual in an Avenue of the New-Born or a Park of Happiness. The birth of a girl is marked with the planting of a fruit or lime tree and that of a boy with the planting of a chestnut or maple tree, each tree bearing a small plaque with the child's name and date of birth.

THE WEDDING RITE

The wedding rite was the first of all the life-cycle rituals to be instituted and is the most widely established and accepted. After short-lived

74

experiments with it during the early post-revolutionary period, and again during the early fifties, it became more permanently instituted from about 1960 onwards. At the present time it is being celebrated in all the Soviet republics in both urban and rural areas, although the provisions for its celebration differ widely, particularly between town and country. Wedding rites are performed either in purpose-built or converted wedding palaces, also called Palaces of Happiness, and, in the Ukraine, Palaces of Solemn Events, or in palaces of culture, clubs, buildings of local soviets or registry offices. According to one source, in 1970 there were 600 wedding palaces situated in republican and regional capitals (Rudnev 1974: 82). At present the demand to have one's marriage celebrated in one of the palaces exceeds the supply (*Izvestiya*, 22 September 1973: 5). For example, in Moscow only one-third of all weddings could be celebrated in a wedding palace during the middle sixties (*Torzhestvenno . . . 1966*: 6). In general, only when it is the first marriage for at least one of the partners can it be ritually celebrated in a wedding palace (*ibid.*). Public buildings in which the wedding rite is conducted are usually decorated with emblems such as a flowering branch of an apple tree, two entwined rings or, most popular, a male and a female hand stretched out toward the sun.

These wedding rites are attempts to provide an occasion where individual concerns and feelings can be expressed but at the same time can be related to the wider societal context. They stress the interest of society in the individual and individual obligations to society as well as expressing Soviet moral norms on family life. The secular focus of the rite is detailed in the ritual attributes, and in the speeches, which put the happiness of the young couple firmly into their own hands.

A fairly typical ceremony would proceed like this:
The bride and groom and their guests arrive at the palace in decorated limousines. In the palace they can buy flowers and presents, and a photographer is on hand. While the bride and her attendants are led to one waiting-room and the guests to another, the groom attends to the legal formalities of the wedding in another part of the building. At an arranged time a procession, with the couple at its head, is led into the ritual hall to the sound of solemn music, usually traditional classical music such as Mendelssohn's Wedding March, the Wedding March from *Aida* (Filatov 1967: 40), Tchaikovsky's First Concerto or the Polonaise Glazunov (Rogozina 1973:6). The ritual hall in one of the Moscow palaces I visited is a handsome and light room furnished with only a large solid table, facilities for the orchestra, some flower

75

arrangements and a bust of Lenin. Those I visited in Leningrad are very similar. The ceremony is conducted by an employee of the local soviet, and a deputy of the soviet may also attend. The master (or mistress) of ceremony is dressed in festive dark clothes with a red sash over his (her) shoulder. The bride and groom are dressed in the same way as English couples who have a church wedding. The master of ceremony stands behind the table, the couple stand in front of the table at some paces distance and the guests sit or stand in the rear of the room.

The ceremony is opened with a speech by the master of ceremony. After many alterations, the following speech is now being delivered in Leningrad's wedding palaces and in many others in the country where Leningrad's pioneering work has been copied. (The following is based on Rogozina *ibid.*: 7ff.)

Respected —— and —— (name of bride and groom)! We have been entrusted by Leningrad Soviet of Workers' Deputies to register your marriage. Before the act of solemn marriage allow me to remind you that the Soviet family is a union of people warmly loving each other, having decided to go through life together. It is the most important cell of our state. Soviet law protects the family and facilitates its strengthening.
Having made the family union you do not only take on new civic rights but also new great civic obligations. Nobody is forced to enter marriage but, having entered it, you will be obliged to submit to its laws, its high moral demands. The basic moral principle of the Soviet family is the consciousness of responsibility for the life and happiness of a near one. In connection with this I must ask you: Is your decision to enter marriage mutual, free and sincere?
Are you prepared to create a harmonious, strong family, to care for each other and to provide a fitting education for your future children?
I ask the groom to reply.
I ask the bride to reply.

After an affirmative answer by the bride and groom the official says:

In the presence of the deputy of Leningrad Urban Soviet —— and of witnesses —— and —— in accordance with both your wishes, your marriage will be registered today on the —— (date). I ask the bride and groom to sign their names in the book of records (*aktovoi zapis*).

A speech in another area of the USSR emphasizes both the humanistic emphasis of Marxist–Leninist ideology and the role of the family in the state with phrases like:

Remember, you are masters of your familial happiness . . . Let your family be a good exemplary Soviet family . . . A strong, good family is the might of our Motherland. (Veselev 1973: 70, 72)

While the couple and the witnesses sign the record traditional classical music is being played quietly. When the music stops the master of ceremony again turns to the couple:

As a sign of faithfulness and mutual love I ask you to put on each other's hands the rings!

The deputy of the soviet then hands the couple the certificate of marriage, and the master of ceremony speaks the following concluding words:

In accordance with the Law on Marriage and the Family of the RSFSR your marriage is registered. I pronounce you husband and wife.

After some more music, congratulations to the couple are extended by all present, according to a predetermined order. The official then declares the ceremony closed, and all leave the hall to the tune of a wedding march or a waltz. In the adjoining banquet hall the bride and groom drink champagne from a common glass, then all the guests drink to their happiness. After this, they all leave to continue the celebrations in another place.

A more overtly political variation of this wedding ritual is being performed in the Ukraine (see *Nashi prazdniki* 1977: 140ff). There the reception room of the Palace of Solemn Events holds a vessel for torches which are solemnly lit from an eternal flame at each opening of the palace. The ritual hall itself is decorated with the political symbols of both the USSR and the Ukraine – flags, emblems and a bust of Lenin, as well as with an object of traditional popular culture – an embroidered wedding runner (*ruzhnik*) placed on the ritual table.

The wedding procession is met in the reception room by the assistant to the master of ceremony or ritual elder with the following words:

Esteemed —— (name of bride) and —— (name of bridegroom). Please, come up to the eternal flame. This flame is a symbol of our memory of those who gave their life for the freedom and independence of our Soviet Motherland, for the communist ideals, for a clear sky above us, for our happiness and the happiness of our children. May such a flame eternally burn in your hearts!

The assistant then gives the bridegroom a torch. The bridegroom lights it from the eternal flame. The bridegroom and the bride with the lit torch take their place at the head of the wedding procession. The doors of the ritual hall open and as soon as groom and bride have stepped across the threshold the choir greets them with the song,

"Bridegroom, take your young [bride]". (Words of the song are not supplied.) The assistant to the ritual elder solemnly announces:

Into marriage are entering the citizens of the Union of Soviet Socialist Republics —— (name of bride) and —— (name of groom). The solemn act of marriage will be conducted by the head of the department of records of civic acts, the deputy of the urban soviet —— (name).

Fanfares call "Listen all!". The deputy enters and stands behind the table. He or she addresses the couple and their guests:

We are glad to greet dear guests in this hall! You —— (name of bride) and —— (name of groom) gave each other your hands at a fine time. Under the peaceful sky of our beloved Motherland, the Soviet people, led by the party of Lenin, goes along the bright road towards communism. You, the daughter and son of your heroic people, its hope and future, today enter into marriage union and create a new family, the primary cell of our society. The Soviet government strengthens and sanctifies a healthy, strong family, founded on the mutual respect of the spouses.
Executing the high duty of a representative of the Soviet state I ask the young people to answer: Are you entering marriage with mutual agreement? Is your intention to create a new family sincere?
I ask the bride to answer.

The bride answers.

I ask the groom to answer.

The groom answers.

I ask you to authenticate your marriage union.

The bride and groom go up to the table and sign the marriage certificate. After them the witnesses sign. The master of ceremony then says:

In the name of the law of the Ukrainian Soviet Socialist Republic the mutual display of the will to a joint marital life of —— (name of bride) and —— (name of groom) is confirmed. From now on you are man and wife, founders of a new family, and the perpetuators of your family to the benefit of our socialist state, the immortality of the Soviet people and of your personal happiness.

The choir sings an anthem. The assistant brings the rings. The master of ceremony turns to the newly married couple:

Put on these rings as a symbol of marital faithfulness and of the indestructability of marriage ties.

The bride and the groom put the rings on each other's fingers. The master of ceremony hands the young couple their marriage certificate. He says:

Dear friends! Take the marriage certificate as a memorable document of your family, recognized by the Soviet state. I cordially congratulate you on the birth of your family, I wish you good fortune and a life full of great well-being and good friends. Live amicably! Be generous in work and love! From this minute everything becomes common to you: work, dreams, joy and sorrow. Drink to happiness from your wedding cups and congratulate each other as spouses!

The young couple are brought cups of champagne. They drink from the cups and congratulate each other. Turning to the young couple, the ritual elder continues:

Dear —— (name of bride) and —— (name of groom)! The people most dear to you – your parents – have come to congratulate you. Always be a firm support to your fathers and mothers. Thanks are due to your parents who gave you life and raised you. Today they give you their blessings for an independent family life. Honour them for their love and care for you.

The young people bow to their parents. Music is played. The master of ceremony turns to the young couple:

Dear young people! Take with you this torch with the holy fire. Let it be your family relic. And through all your life carry the flame of love and devotion to our Motherland, the fire of the heroes' hearts, defending its freedom and independence, increase the glory of our great Soviet Motherland!

In conclusion, the master of ceremony turns to the parents and friends of the young couple:

Esteemed parents and guests! Congratulate the newly-weds, wish them happiness and well-being. Good luck to all of you!

In other republics, particularly outside the bigger towns, the wedding rite may be performed in a more modest manner. It may take place in a building not designed for the purpose, and several couples may have to share a ceremony. The latter fact is deplored by those who report it, and it is probably only a transitional phenomenon.

Besides this public wedding rite (*brakosochetanie*) there is the more private family and community based wedding ritual (*svadba*). While the family oriented ritual has been widely retained in simplified form without interruptions, the community related ritual had gradually died out in the Russian areas since the Revolution. In recent decades, however, many of its elements have been revived in the countryside. This traditional popular wedding ritual both precedes and follows the central public rite. It is very colourful and rich, and a description of it falls beyond the scope of this study. (For descriptions of popular ritual in both Russian and non-Russian communities, see Dunn 1971.)

Although this part of the wedding festivities is more immune from direction by ritual specialists, attempts have been made to influence public opinion against those elements incongruent with Soviet morality, such as sequences presenting the woman in a subordinate role. At least one author (El'chenko 1976a: 40) argues for a further extension of control over this traditional popular ritual. In Leningrad, where the traditional ritual had become extinct, a new ritual scenario for the wedding festivities was devised in 1976 (by the staff of the Museum of Ethnography). Not only was a special "ritual complex" provided to stage it in, but also professional producers and artists to assist with its performance (Rudnev 1979: 139ff).

In some of the Central Asian and Caucasian republics with a predominantly Muslim population religious ritual has been so closely intertwined with the whole elaborate complex of the traditional popular wedding ritual that it has proved difficult to integrate the new socialist ritual into it. Change in these areas therefore had to proceed much more slowly and gradually, and one may find weddings being celebrated that express various stages of change. The great complexity of this process of change and the problems it presents for specialists of the new Soviet ritual are well brought out in the study by Lobacheva (1975), a Soviet ethnologist. Three basic types of wedding festivities are described. First, there is the old-style, traditional wedding which faithfully preserves the Islamic popular ritual as well as some of the religious ritual, and eschews all modern Soviet ritual. Secondly, there is the transitional wedding with most of the traditional popular rituals preserved, but ritual forms have been shortened and adapted to modern living. While Soviet specialist ritual is not integrated into this complex of modernized traditional ritual, couples celebrating their wedding in this form will frequently take part in it as a separate ritual a few days before the traditional wedding. In both these types of wedding the upholding of the traditional elements serves not only to express an identification with the general Islamic tradtition, but regional variations also express identification with particular local traditions and national groupings within the broader Islamic cultural world. Third, there is the modern Soviet wedding which has shed all traditional Islamic features and consists of the socialist wedding rite followed by festivities that are distinctive in their paucity of ritual. These cannot be distinguished from wedding feasts in other urban Soviet areas except that, being in part political show cases, they are of a very public nature rather than a family affair. This is expressed both in the choice of guests and of locale. Both Lobacheva (*ibid.*) and Aliev (1968: 207) note with regret that the new "Komsomol" weddings, as they are popularly called, have lost an important dimension by repudiating all traditional ritual and by relegating the family to a background position. Of these three types, the transitional type is by far the most frequent, while the Soviet type appears to be relatively rare. A survey conducted in Uzbekistan by Lobacheva and Tul'tseva (1977: 34) brought out that a large majority of people (80 per cent) were in favour of a fully or partly traditional wedding without the Soviet wedding ritual.

Another republic in which the new wedding ritual has been unable to replace the traditional religious rite to any significant extent is Catholic Lithuania. There, according to the Catholic Committee for the Defense of the Rights of Believers (*Radio Liberty Research Bulletin* 265/78),

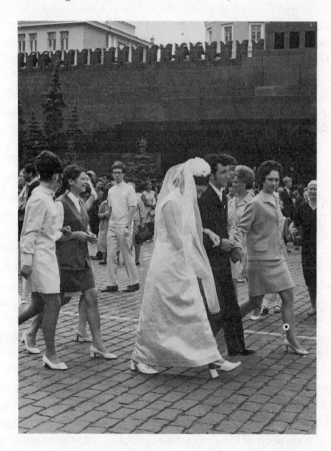

Bridal couple after their visit to the Lenin mausoleum in Red Square

50 per cent and 90 per cent of couples in urban and rural areas respectively still have a church wedding.

In both urban and rural areas in many parts of the Soviet Union, two other, more spontaneous, ritual acts have become associated with the wedding rite in recent years. Many couples now drive from the wedding palace straight to the local Lenin memorial or to the Eternal Flame in memory of fallen soldiers to place some flowers and stand (for a minute) in silence. A different rite is the planting by the young couple of a young family tree in Parks of Family Happiness (Filatov 1967: 40).

In recent years, a revival of the institution of engagement has also been advocated. In some areas silver and golden weddings are being celebrated with a public ceremony. All these measures are motivated by a growing concern about the high divorce rate and are believed to increase the stability of the nuclear family (Gerandokov 1970: 32). In Leningrad, young couples are also given public practical support after the wedding by the provision of a Club for Newly Married Couples, where they can develop social contact with other couples and, more importantly, with specialists who give help and advice on the many problem areas that the couple may confront. A course of lectures by highly qualified speakers and individual consultations of the marriage-guidance type are also provided (Rogozina 1973: 15ff).

THE FUNERAL RITE

Although a secular funeral rite has been performed for public figures from the time of the Revolution, efforts to establish it for ordinary Soviet citizens have begun relatively late, that is from the middle sixties to the early seventies onwards. Up to then ritual specialists had shied away from its institution because they realized the great philosophical and organizational problems involved in creating and conducting a secular funeral rite. Even at the present time the funeral rite still presents problems. It is significant that a recent authoritative work on socialist rituals and holidays by a number of experts in the field, *Nashi prazdniki* (1977), completely omits the subject of the funeral rite. Other authors freely admit that conducting a socialist funeral rite is considered to be a very difficult task. Efforts are being made in some areas to overcome the latter problem by setting up short training courses for organizers of funerals. These give attention to such problems as the content of the grave-side speeches and the manner of their deliverance. Speakers are urged to personalize each funeral as much as possible, to link the endeavour of the deceased to that of the living and to find mournful, moving words while avoiding sentimentality and false pathos. There is a wariness to the possibility that standardized state orators, "Ciceros of the Cemetery", may be created (Gerodnik 1970: 79ff).

The crucial significance attributed to successfully coping with a secular funeral rite is expressed in this statement by a ritual specialist: "The struggle between the old and the new does take place not only on the barricades, not only in the economic and political field but also in the resting-places of the dead" (*ibid.*: 6). In those areas where ritual specialists have given serious thought to the existential problems brought by death and have formulated their answers in emotionally elevating form, there have resulted viable secular alternatives to a religious funeral rite. My estimation of the long-term success of this rite is based partly on its inherent merit and partly on an evaluation of the acceptability of the religious alternative. The secular rite is commendable in attempting to give secular answers to such questions as: What is the meaning of life? How can a person "live on" after death? A secular funeral, according to Kampars (1969: 24), should result in "a serious meditation about the meaning of life, about the great responsibility of the living to life, to him who has gone and to those who have remained behind, to one's own conscience". The whole ritual is meant to express the idea "that man lives on earth only once, that there is no other life beside the earthly one, and that the value of everybody's life is, therefore, determined by his concrete earthly affairs. The life of every honest man is a valuable contribution to society" (*ibid.*). The socialist funeral rite is meant to pay respect to the deceased and to offer emotional release to the living. Unlike the traditional religious rite it attempts to lighten feelings of grief and pain and to turn men's thoughts firmly back to life and the living. The acceptance of the socialist funeral will be aided by the fact, shown by sociological research, that religious answers to existential questions are becoming unacceptable even to a growing number of "believers". Here I refer to the great decline of the belief in the immortality of the soul, in eternal bliss and a meeting of all in a life beyond the grave. Various Soviet surveys have shown that around 50 per cent of self-identified Orthodox no longer believe in a life beyond the grave (Basilov 1967: 159, 160; Yablokov 1969: 140; Alekseev 1970: 235). These people attend funerals not to pray for the soul of the departed but to express and share their grief.

In areas where the rite is well established it is celebrated in the following way: the ceremony proceeds under the overall direction of a state-employed (part-time), specially trained official. Like the religious rite, it consists of two parts, one enacted either in the home of the deceased or in the funeral pavilion or House of Civic Funerals on the cemetery and one at the grave-side. In the pavilion the coffin stands on a raised platform and is flanked by a guard of honour formed by four friends who wear red armbands with black edging. A photograph and any medals of the deceased are displayed on a cushion as a visible manifestation of services rendered to society. An orchestra is in attendance, playing traditional classical mourning music. Friends and relatives each say a few words about the merits of the deceased, putting particular emphasis on services rendered to society. A short speech by the official on the same theme may conclude with words such as:

Life continues, and everything that the deceased has managed to achieve will continue. His causes are alive in ours, his beginnings we shall complete, everything is left to men. (Brudnyi 1968: 154)

or

The Citizen of the Russian Soviet Federative Socialist Republic   (full name) has concluded his life's journey. The Motherland takes leave of her son (daughter). May a good memory of him (her) eternally be preserved in our hearts. (Quoted by Rudnev 1979: 181)

After such a speech all those wishing to say farewell to the deceased go around the coffin, closest relatives last. The coffin is then covered and carried towards the grave by the four escorts, preceded by wreaths and medals. The rest of the mourners follow in solemn procession. At the grave-side candles are lit, and, by pre-arrangement, a person who was close to the deceased says the last words. A minute's silence follows. After the coffin has been lowered down into the grave all the nearest relatives and friends of the deceased throw earth onto it. When efforts by ritual specialists to exclude this religious symbolic action from the socialist funeral rite were defeated by popular habit, it was attempted to eliminate the religious meaning of the action by introducing it with the following secular interpretation:

And now, comrades, in accordance with popular custom, let us throw onto the grave three clumps of earth – of that earth which feeds us and delights us with the colours of life and gives everyone of us eternal rest. (Quoted by Gerodnik 1970: 90)

This action may be followed by the recitation of a verse, perhaps Rozhdestvenskii's "Requiem". (For the text, see appendix A.) A communal mourning song concludes the ceremony. This short summary shows that the secular rite, although not as rich in symbolism and as full of sensuous impact as the religious rite, has a dignity of its own and offers its particular answers to some perennial human dilemmas.

The change-over to a socialist funeral rite has begun to profoundly affect the social significance and general appearance of cemeteries. Whereas in the capitalist West inequality and social distance between different socio-economic and religious or ethnic groups in their life-time is perpetuated after death, in Soviet society the greater equality between the living is also extended to the dead. Religious and ethnic divisions perpetuated in the West have been eliminated by the Soviet system, and economic considerations, paramount in the West, do not dictate the choice of a burial plot in Soviet society, where it is obtained free of charge. However, outstanding merit in political life or other fields secures privilege in life and death in Soviet society. As regards the appearance of cemeteries, attempts have been made to minimize their association with church and religion, although a few concessions to religious believers have been made in this respect. In some areas of the Baltic republics and of the RSFSR pavilions of mourning have been purpose-built, or the interiors of cemetery chapels have been stripped of religious attributes. Graves are now being marked with marble stones instead of the traditional wooden crosses. Epitaphs have an optimistic tenor and often contain a literal or symbolic reference to the earthly achievements of the deceased. There have been efforts to clean up and beautify cemeteries. Public opinion has been mobilized against neglect, hooliganism and petty crime on graveyards and for helping with their upkeep. "Neglect of cemeteries", says Gerodnik (*ibid.*: 28), "evokes a tendency towards *social slovenliness*, creates cynics and nihilists." In the Baltic republics of Latvia and Estonia they have gone further and have used landscaping and monumental art to turn cemeteries into Parks of Rest for both the dead and the living. (The preceding account is based mainly on the work of Gerodnik *ibid.*: 17ff and Rudnev 1974: 122ff.)

Also expressed in this socialist funeral rite is a new healthy attitude to death which is now lacking in Western societies. Soviet ritual specialists do not approach death and mourning with stealth or with withdrawal from those affected by it, but try to make the family's loss and resulting burden of responsibility those of the community. An

effort is made to actively involve friends and colleagues in the preparation and performance of the funeral rite. If the deceased was in
employment at the time of his death a representative of the working
collective often delivers the main speech. Once buried, the dead are
not forgotten but are remembered during annual remembrance ceremonies (see below). Continuing love and respect for them is expressed
through Books of Remembrance, memorial plaques and sculptures.
The living are linked to the dead by efforts to change cemeteries from
gloom-laden, neglected places to "Parks of Rest" or "Parks of Good
Memories".

In conclusion, it must be pointed out that the above description
applies as yet only to a few parts of the USSR, while in many places the
secular funeral is not yet considered with the necessary seriousness.
Letters to the Soviet press complain about "heart-breaking conditions"
in many cemeteries and describe undignified funeral rites. In some
areas the old order continues unbroken, particularly in the predominantly Muslim Central Asian republics (Lobacheva 1972: 7). But the
examples of the socialist birth and wedding rites have shown that
experience about their successful performance in some areas is soon
utilized in other, less advanced areas, although one should expect the
socialist funeral rite to be accepted at a slower rate than the other
life-cycle rites.

REMEMBRANCE DAY

Remembrance ritual for the heroes of the Revolution and the Civil War
is as old as the Russian Marxist revolutionary movement, and remembrance ritual for the fallen heroes of the Great Patriotic War has a
central importance in Soviet public life (for details see chapter 9). But
Remembrance Days for ordinary Soviet citizens were only instituted
after the introduction of a socialist funeral rite had begun. The predominantly political tenor of ceremonies for dead heroes made them
unsuitable as prototypes for a general Remembrance Day, and new
forms and content had to be devised. The new Remembrance Days are
in part occasions to express personal familial sentiments and in part
political ceremonies, evoking "holy" revolutionary, military and
labour traditions by celebrating the memory of those associated with
these traditions. The new *general* Remembrance Day ceremonies frequently subsume a ceremony particularly for Soviet heroes.

Such Remembrance Days were first celebrated in 1958–9 in Estonia and Latvia. Although this ceremony has since spread to other parts of the Soviet Union it is well established and widely accepted only in the two Baltic republics and in the Ukraine (*Nashi prazdniki* 1977: 145). Initially Remembrance Days were conceived of as an anti-religious measure and were usually arranged on the same day as, and in competition with, the traditional religious equivalent. In areas where such ceremonies are well established they have proved to be more popular than their (church) religious counter-parts (Gerodnik 1970: 113; Ranne 1972: 195). The fact that the public sector can bring into play more material and cultural resources than individual churches to make these mass ceremonies memorable has given the socialist ceremony a great advantage over the religious equivalent. Over the years Remembrance Days have turned into mass ceremonies, requiring major efforts of organization. Cemeteries are tidied up, radio equipment is installed, orchestras, choirs and orators are booked and special transport is laid on. The scenario of a Remembrance Day varies from area to area, but the elements common to all are the laying of special wreaths, speeches, spiritual (*dukhovny*) and symphonic music, choir and communal singing, declamations and recitations of poetry. Some of the latter had to be created for the occasion, and the work of Estonian artists – giving rise to a new genre of art – receives a special mention in the literature on the subject. Extracts from declamations and verse rendered on such occasions show a deliberately secular orientation as well as having an appeal to patriotic sentiments. Thus the first Remembrance Day in the Kazakh town of Syryanovsk was opened with the following speech:

Today we are gathered here to remember people dear to our hearts departed from us. And these are not just our relatives and close friends. These are also our fellow citizens, those people who built our town, forged its glory. Let the Day of Remembrance become a good tradition. It is no accident that this is a spring day: the joy and happiness of the present life have been achieved by the work of our fathers and the dependable hands of our mothers. Let this day become a day of our general respect towards the affairs of those who have left us, a day of solemn promise to continue the good work of our fathers and mothers.

Similar thoughts are expressed in the following extract from a speech given at an Estonian memorial service:

Our fathers and grandfathers, buried here, worked and fought in the name of a better life. They bequeathed to us the wish to make it even brighter. Before us, the living, stand great tasks. We are faced with working and learning, with fighting for our own happiness, and for the happiness of our children and grandchildren, for the happiness of our friends in the whole world – in this lies the essence of life of Soviet people!

These sentiments are also echoed in poetic form in the second part of the following song, while the middle part is unusual in acknowledging sadness and grief.

Song of Parting
Eternally rotates the wheel of time
Swiftly run out the days of our life
Suddenly comes the time of parting –
Our companion–comrade leaves us
Our hearts are filled with sadness
And our soul is heavy (*tyazhelo na dushe*).
But the road of life leads further still
The cares and joys of life call us
All the best, friends.
All the best, friends (*Tak v dobryi put'*).
(Quoted by Gerodnik 1976: 67 – my translation)

After the collective public solemn remembrance families go to the graves of their own deceased members for a private remembrance. Up to now Remembrance Day has become established only in some areas as an occasion where private and public sentiments about the dead can be expressed and successfully combined to stage an impressive mass ceremony. Its wider acceptance might be eased by the fact that it is less intensely personal and existentially problematic than the funeral and by the special character of the main religious equivalent. Russian Orthodox Remembrance Days, such as *Radonitsa*, are not highly spiritual occasions solely devoted to mourning. Traditionally, *Radonitsa* has been a day of both mourning and rejoicing, of feasting with the dead forefathers as invisible participants. Such temporal orientation may ease the change-over to a completely this-worldly secular Remembrance Day.

6

vvvvvvvvvvvvvvvvvvvvvvvvvvvvvvvvvvvvvvvvvvvvvvvvvvvvvvvvvvvvvvvvvvvvvvvvvvvvvvvvvvv

Rituals of initiation into social or political collectives

The sudden and great proliferation of rituals of initiation for the young in Soviet society has to be seen in the following social context. The successful socialization of the young with the social and political values of a society guarantees the continuation of a social order and is thus seen as a vital task by the political elites of any type of society. In Soviet society it is considered particularly important in view of the fact that political elites aspire to total ideological domination and depend on a more comprehensive and controlled socialization process. Whereas earlier generations acquired the desired value orientations as much through the experience of fundamental social changes and critical events as through direct ideological education, the present young generation is only subject to the latter influence. Its members are said to frequently insulate themselves against this method of socialization and consequently show a weakly developed political commitment and a disproportionately large interest in material comfort (see the discussion of this aspect in chapter 2).

In this situation the rituals of initiation have become an alternative means of political socialization, believed to be more effective than conventional ones. These rites link the endeavour of the individual to that of the collective, and in the process transform the loyalty to, and pride in, the small and often intimate collective into loyalty to the larger collective, Soviet society. In the words of one ritual specialist (Rudnev 1974: 119) these rites are meant to inculcate "respect for social order, the laws of the state and of society, for its sacred objects, its honour, memories and symbols". Besides trying to generate such a general political commitment each specific rite also attempts to relate children or youths to selected value complexes of the general ideology in order to restructure attitudes towards mere specific problematic social relations. These will be highlighted in the discussion

89

of particular initiation rites or other rituals revolving around collectives for the young.

There exist in the Soviet Union large political youth organizations, schools of political activism, for three different age groups – the Oktyabryata (for the 7–11 age group), the Young Pioneers (for the 9–14 age group) and the Leninist Communist Youth League or *Komsomol* (for the 14–26 age group). Membership of the Young Pioneers, although voluntary, is almost universal, while membership of the Komsomol and the Oktyabryata is more selective. These youth organizations have existed almost from the beginning of the Soviet state and have always had some kind of formal procedure to admit new members. In recent years, however, entry has acquired a much more elaborate ritual formulation. Initiation rituals take place all through the year, but preferred times are the eves of a national political holiday in a place connected with Lenin or the "heroic" revolutionary or military past. In Leningrad, for example, new members are initiated at the Finland Station or in the Smolny Institute (Rudnev 1966: 159), in the Lenin museum, on the cruiser *Aurora* or at the war memorial at Piskarevska cemetery; in Moscow, on Lenin's birthday, in front of the mausoleum or, otherwise, in the Lenin museum; in Volgograd by the Monument to Fallen Soldiers, a place of national pilgrimage; and in Sevastopol by the monument commemorating its defence in 1941–2, or by the "Twice Glorified Malakhov Burial Mound" (Fursin 1973: 564).

Initiation into each youth organization may either take place separately for each youth organization, or it may be part of a grand, combined occasion where three generations of builders of communism meet. The latter takes the following form: the initiands meet at an appointed place and march with flowers and flags to the place of initiation where they are met with applause by a group of Old Communists and/or other "heroes" of the Revolution and the Second World War (Gerandokov 1970: 26). The opening words are spoken by a leading member of the local Komsomol organization. They are about the honour and holy obligations of membership, and they refer to heroes from the ranks of the Komsomol. The second speech is delivered by a Communist veteran who talks about the October Revolution and asks the neophytes to "preserve the purity of the glorious

labour and fighting traditions of their fathers and mothers" (Rudnev
1966: 160). Veterans then give membership cards to the new Young
Communists. After that one of the neophytes, in the name of all the
others, gives a solemn oath of loyalty "to guard the purity of the
Komsomol banner, to continue work begun by the Komsomol at the
dawn of Soviet power, to be foremost in labour and study, and to
preserve and augment the glorious traditions of our fathers and
mothers". The oath of allegiance does not appear to be standardized
for the whole country. In the Karbadino-Balkar ASSR, for example, a
much longer version is given by the initiands which is notable for its
explicit hero-worship:

I —— (name) – a member of the All-Union Leninist Communist League of
Youth – swear in front of my comrades, in front of communists: to dedicate all
my life, a long or a short one, to the people! I swear to remember those whose
banner was given into our hands by our fathers and forefathers. I swear to be
similar to Nikolai Ostrovsky and Zoya Kosmodemskaya and to the heroes –
Young Guardists, to the Heroes of the Soviet Union X and Y, to all those who
were fighters and not cowards!
To burn and not to smoulder!
To seek and to vanquish!
To find and not to surrender! (Gerandokov 1970: 27ff)

In Leningrad the ritual was concluded by the solemn instruction of the
new recruits in their duties by the Komsomal secretary. In the Karbadino-
Balkar ASSR a communal singing of The International brought the
ritual to its conclusion. Then the Komsomols marched off to lay
wreaths at the memorials to fighters of the Revolution and the Second
World War. A similar ritual then follows for the Pioneers, with the new
Komsomols handing over their old Pioneer scarves to the initiands.

I observed initiation rituals solely for Young Pioneers in both Moscow and Leningrad, both taking place in their Lenin museum. In
Leningrad the children assembled in the cloakroom, where they lined
up and received their new scarves and badges. Carrying the scarves
over their outstretched right arms and flowers in their left hands they
walked in formation up to the ritual hall. There, directed by their
leader, they lined up in single file and, after a few words from the
leader, collectively gave the Pioneer oath:

I —— (name of child called out by each child himself), a young Pioneer of the
Soviet Union, in front of my comrades solemnly promise to warmly love my
Soviet motherland, to live, learn and struggle as bequeathed to us by the great
Lenin and as the Communist Party teaches.

After this various children in turn recited words of a similar content. Then some older Pioneers put the scarf and badge on each child. An old Bolshevik, or similar hero or just the Pioneer leader, addressed the children with a command like the following:

Young Leninists! For the struggle for the cause of the Communist Party be prepared.

The children answered in unison:

Always prepared!

(In Leningrad several phrases of similar content were pronounced.) After this the banner carriers (two older Pioneers) lifted up the Pioneer banner and ceremoniously marched it past all the children out of the ritual hall. Bugle fanfares and drum beating concluded this formal part of the ritual.

In all the rituals that I observed it was notable that these young children took the occasion very seriously and performed their quite substantial parts in it with great competence and dignity. Parents' interest in the ritual was expressed in the fact that several parents were always present to watch, and that nearly all the children wore freshly laundered white shirts and white socks and, despite the almost prohibitive prices, carried fresh flowers.

After the formal part of the ritual, the Pioneer leader took the children on a tour of the museum and gave them an illustrated talk on Lenin's life and deeds. At the various busts of Lenin children would often quite spontaneously put down their flowers. In Moscow, on the eve of Lenin's birthday, instead of a tour of the museum, the children are taken into the mausoleum.

Besides these rituals of initiation, the Communist youth organizations have many other elaborate rituals. Particularly important is the annual celebration of their organizations' birthday. For the Pioneers this celebration takes the form of an All-Union parade on which the children "report to their Motherland about their glorious causes". The rituals performed are not so much directed towards a celebration of the internal life and history of their organization but are designed to relate the organization and its individual young members to society, particularly to those events and objects in which its value system has become crystallized. This parade is best described in the words of those closely involved in the staging of this ritual (*Nashi prazdniki* 1977: 95–6):

The Pioneer parade . . . The insistent sound of the horns. The beating of the drums. In front of the detachment is the scarlet banner. It is solemnly carried by a banner carrier and his assistants – the "best of the best" Pioneers of the detachment. The Pioneer rows are as if touched by a gust of wind: hands are raised together above the head – a salute of the banner. Solemnly measuring their steps, the banner carriers go past the formation of children in their red kerchiefs. The children accompany with their eyes the banner of their detachment. Now it has gone round the whole formation and has come to a standstill on the right flank. Every ten minutes the guard of honour at the banner is changed . . .

In solemn silence the Pioneer detachments go to the memorial. At the head of each detachment a boy and a girl carry wreaths. The banner carriers with their assistants go in front. At the memorial they bend their knee, and the scarlet cloth is dipped. The voice of a reader renders the words of "The Requiem" and "Eternal Glory to the Heroes". The representatives of the detachments lay wreaths. A salute to the heroes. May their memory be eternal! And deep gratefulness for everything – for happiness, for life. And again hands are raised in the air in salute, in a Pioneer salute to the fallen heroes.

While initiation into the Young Pioneers and, to a lesser degree, into the Komsomol is a frequent occurrence in Soviet life I encountered no

Young Pioneer parade in Red Square

93

evidence that the Party itself ritualizes the acceptance of new members. Initiation into the Party has been mentioned only once in the extensive literature on ritual. It was said to be a development only recently introduced in some districts of Leningrad (Rudnev 1974: 33). While such an initiation rite seems to be a significant omission (see p. 32), ritual surrounding important changes in the Party has been more frequent in recent times. For example, when the Party was purged of all its inactive members in 1973 and new membership cards were issued, attempts were made to raise the quantitatively reduced Party to a higher level of significance in front of the whole society by ritualizing the issue of new Party cards to its most prominent members. Party card no. 1 was issued to Lenin and card no. 2 to Brezhnev in a solemn ceremony.

EDUCATIONAL ''RITES DE PASSAGE''

School entry

There are several rituals marking the passage of the child and young adult through the educational system. While the initiation of young people into technical–vocational schools and secondary special schools (i.e. schools for future industrial workers) and into institutes of higher education (excluding universities) are very recent, poorly elaborated and only partially accepted rituals, the initiation of the young child into his first school is based on a long Russian tradition and is universally performed. These rituals on the first of September used to involve only the children or youths and their schools or institutes. In recent years efforts have been made to involve the whole Soviet public. The first of September is now called "Day of Knowledge", and a variety of events take place which try to inculcate the importance of education and ideological instruction in a wider audience.

Rituals transforming a child from an infant into a school child are celebrated in two variations. In Estonia, Spring Days for Children in June are arranged for all children due to go to school in the following September. Although some aspects of these celebrations prepare the children and their parents for the coming transition, they have more the character of a giant party than of a *rite de passage* (for details see Ranne 1972: 190). In other parts of the Soviet Union, celebrations on the first day of school, called "The First Bell", are strongly ritualized. They proceed in the following way: early in the morning teachers and

94

First Bell ritual at the beginning of a new school year

new pupils are congratulated on the radio, and school songs are transmitted. Parents receive congratulatory cards from friends and comrades at work with best wishes for the child in his new stage of life. The first walk to school leads through streets decorated with jolly characters – for children – and slogans – for parents (Nagirnyak *et al.* 1970: 65). An hour before the first lesson of a new school year begins, old and new school children assemble outside the school in festive attire and holding flowers. At a signal, they line up in two ranks, older children on the right, younger children on the left. Each class is flanked by its teacher and Pioneer leader. In front of them stand the head-master, other teachers and parents. At another signal bugles are sounded, and the banners of the school's Pioneer and Komsomol detachments are solemnly carried out. The headmaster congratulates the new pupils and their parents on beginning school and then issues the command: "All pupils to be led into the school!" To the tune of a march, they enter the assembly hall and line up along the walls. A bust

The First Day at school

of Lenin on a platform is flanked by a guard of honour. Children place flowers by the bust. After the bugle signal "Listen all!" and another speech, older children are ordered to give the new pupils their first reading book. Then the First Bell is rung. This is done collectively by the three best pupils of the preceding year. Another command is issued: "Older pupils are to lead pupils of the first year to their class rooms!" Then the first lesson begins (based on Rudnev 1974: 120).

School-leaving rituals

Seventeen is the official school-leaving age for all children in the Soviet Union, and most Soviet youths, particularly in urban areas, now conform to this norm. The last day at school at the end of June is a very special day for these young people. In many areas it is concluded by the ritual of "Ringing the Last Bell", an act reserved for the best pupil of the year. In some areas a school-leaving ritual after school hours has developed in a seemingly spontaneous and relatively unstructured way. Over the years, however, organization and direction from interested collectives have turned these celebrations into more formal and controlled events.

In Moscow there exists a tradition that, during the evening hours of the last school day, youths from all over the town converge on Red Square dressed in festive clothes. Holding hands, they sing their favourite songs, dance, enact allegorical scenes and put on masks. They all fall into complete silence when the steps of the changing guard of honour at Lenin's mausoleum can be heard (Brudnyi 1968: 125). In Leningrad a similar ritual takes place. Here this day falls during the famous "White Nights". A romantic poem about the White Nights, in which suddenly the scarlet sails of a boat (*brigantina*) can be seen through the white haze, has given both name and emblem to this ritual – Scarlet Sails. In the early years the ritual was similar to that performed in Moscow. The young people came to the banks of the Neva straight from an official school-leaving ceremony in the local club. The ritual consisted of light-hearted spontaneously evolving gaieties during evening hours, followed by a complete silence upon the opening of a Neva bridge that brought the outline of the pre-revolutionary battleship *Aurora* into sight. On this evening, says Rudnev (1974: 121), "the young people are like all-powerful masters of their own town". In 1971 the preceding official ceremony was adapted to this development by taking it out of the clubs into the central Kirov Park of Culture and Rest.

After some years, at the request of some young participants in the Komsomol paper *Smena* for refreshments, decorations and organized entertainment, the Komsomol organization moved in and the whole occasion took on a structure and extended over the whole day (see Laskina 1976: 108ff). Inevitably the standard social and political didactic speeches and mass displays were introduced and created a heavily organized mass event. Its only distinction from other mass events now lies in its original emphasis on nautical themes and images (*ibid.*). It does not become clear from the description how this development has been received by the young people and whether the "directed" and the "spontaneous" parts of the school-leaving celebrations have become integrated.

This Leningrad ritual has been copied in some other areas. While the northern Russian town Pskov provides similar natural preconditions for its performance, the ritual in Tashkent, named "Tashkent Dawns" (Lobacheva 1975: 103), is a more mechanical imitation.

Initiation as students

An initiation ritual for new students has not yet been generally established (*Nashi prazdniki* 1977: 109). It appears to be a recent development
that takes place mainly in institutes of higher education of a technical
college type, but also in a few universities.

One initiation ritual described in the literature (Rogozina 1973: 60ff)
is for students of a Polytechnical Institute and takes place on the first of
September in the Institute's stadium. The stadium is decorated with
placards, flags and transparencies and is equipped with radio speakers. The guests – other students, parents, Pioneers from schools under
the Institute's patronage — are on the stands. The members of the
presidium of the ritual sit on a special rostrum erected by the main
stand. At the centre of the stadium, on its own rostrum, towers a
symbolic "Cup of Knowledge".

At 9.30 a.m. the initiands draw up according to faculties on the side
field of the stadium. At the head of the whole column are two young
men and two young women carrying a large version of the Institute's
emblem. At the head of each faculty column the same number of
youths carry the emblem and motto of the former. There is also a
separate column of banner carriers, who are the Institute's best students and activists of the student scientific society. They are dressed in
the uniform of student building detachments.

At 10.0 a.m. the gradually intensifying roll of a drum is heard which
then breaks off sharply. The fanfares demand "Listen all!", a march is
struck up and the initiands enter the main field of the stadium. They
arrange themselves on the running-track opposite the main stand. The
members of the presidium and the guests of honour on the main
rostrum rise to their feet. In front of the rostrum sixteen initiands line
up, eight to say the oath for all the initiands and eight bearing torches.
Then the secretary of the Institute's Komsomol committee commands:
"Attention! Carry out the banners!", and the banner carriers enter the
main stadium to the beating of drums. While they file past the stands,
an announcer tells the history of every banner and speaks about the
students who have been awarded the honour to be banner carriers.
When the banner carriers have lined up next to the initiands, the
Komsomol secretary reports to the chairman of the presidium – the
principal – that the participants of the parade are lined up. The principal greets them and says some words of congratulation. Again the
signal sounds, "Listen all!" The eight representative initiands climb up

to the rostrum and read the text of the oath over the microphone. One of them says:

Entering the ranks of Soviet students I swear to carry out Lenin's legacy, to study persistently in order to become a highly educated, creatively thinking specialist!

The other seven confirm this with:

I swear.
To be a worthy citizen of our great Motherland, to participate actively in public life, to work untiringly for the affirmation of the high principles of communist society.
I swear.
To hold holy and to augment the revolutionary, military and labour traditions of the Leningrad Polytechnic Institute!
I swear.
To justify the high trust of the Motherland, opening for me the wide road towards knowledge!
I swear. I swear. I swear.

All sing the Soviet anthem. After another fanfare signal, "Listen all!" the command is given to light the "Cup of Knowledge". The eight torch bearers set the cup alight and stand around it with burning torches. After a short speech, the oldest scholar of the Institute gives those initiands who read the oath a symbolic key to the Institute. Other speeches follow. Another fanfare precedes the command to the initiands to form their columns for a solemn parade. To the tune of a march, they leave the stadium. At 12.0 p.m. the new students gather in the lecture hall, and their studying begins.

In another institute of technical education the initiands marched with banners and torches to a place where heroes of the Revolution were buried. "Here by the Brotherly Graves the first-year students bowed in loyalty to the behests of the fathers, in loyalty to the cause to which they dedicated their life" (*Nashi prazdniki* 1977: 109).

In general, these rites combine old, pre-revolutionary and even international elements of ritual with those of socialist origin. I was amazed to read that the old European student song in Latin, "Gaudeamus Igitur", was a part of many of the rites (Rudnev 1979: 161).

THE PASSPORT RITUAL

Since 1976 all Soviet citizens reaching the age of sixteen have been receiving a Soviet internal passport or identity card. Up to that date,

99

only inhabitants residing in towns, urban areas, State farms and a few other selected areas received this document. It is a record of the holder's residence, employment and marital status and assists the authorities in keeping a check on the internal movement of citizens. It had been a feature of Tsarist society, where it served the purpose of tying the peasant to the *mir*, the village commune. It was reintroduced in 1933 as a means to increase control over labour movement, when the big influx of unskilled labour from the countryside into urban indust-rial areas jeopardized industrial labour discipline. As it was withheld from collective farmers they became as tied to the land as their serf ancestors had been. Although it is thus, in the words of Soviet legal authorities, "a most important means of protecting public order and State security" and mainly serves to restrict freedom of movement, it is promoted by ritual specialists as a document which, on its reception, turns young people into full and equal citizens. In fact, however, most important rights and obligations are not incurred until the ages of eighteen or nineteen. I am referring to the rights to vote or to get married (in the RSFSR) and to the obligation to do national service, and official school-leaving age is not until the age of seventeen. Equating the reception of the internal passport with the initiation into citizen-ship becomes also a dubious practice when one considers that such a passport will only be universally available to collective farmers by the late 1980s. People of special merit receive their passport before the general population of a given collective farm, together with the sixteen-year-old youths.

Until the early sixties, this passport was just collected from the local militia without any ceremony. Now it is, in the words of Rudnev (1974: 33), "a governmental–civic act of initiation into the citizenship of the USSR" and is usually celebrated on the eve of the Day of the Constitution. Initiands receive an invitation by post to attend the ritual. It does not appear to have been adopted in all republics. In Estonia and Latvia, for example, a Day of Maturity is celebrated at the age of eighteen. One author rather vaguely states that it is being celebrated everywhere, but has not yet become a true ritual (Brudnyi 1968: 121).

This ritual is particularly well established in Leningrad where, according to Rogozina (1973: 42), "it has entered the life of all Lenin-grad inhabitants by now" and is performed every month in all districts (Rudnev 1979: 40). The ritual was first staged in 1963 in the Museum of the Revolution. Now a Passport ritual is being arranged separately for each town district, with variations in form but not in essence between districts. Organizations involved in its staging are police departments, departments for culture of the Town Council Executive, the heads of palaces of culture and of clubs, and the Komsomol (*ibid.*). One such performance in a palace of culture in 1972 is described as follows (based on Rogozina 1973: 45ff): the palace of culture is festively decorated with the Soviet emblem, with posters and transparencies bearing words from the classics of Marxism–Leninism, by present political leaders and by Russian and Soviet poets "about the meaning of life and the calling of man and of a citizen". Guests of honour are a deputy of the district soviet, a representative each from the district committee of the Party, the Komsomol and the passport department of the police. Guests asked to participate in the ritual are a veteran of the Second World War, a hero of the Revolution and a young shock worker who is a Komsomol activist. The opening speech addresses the young people with the following words:

Dear friends! From the very day of your birth you have enjoyed the care and love of your Mother-Motherland (*Mat'-Rodina*), the rights written into the Soviet constitution – the right to study and to rest, the right to a happy, peaceful childhood. The present day is significant for the fact that, having received your passport, you become a citizen of the Soviet Union with full and equal rights. And this means that each one of you not only receives great rights, but also that serious obligations are laid on him, holy and honourable obligations to the first socialist State in the world. Your duty is to execute these obligations with honour.

Dear young people! Today is a festive day not only for you who receive their first passport but also for your relatives and friends. For this holiday are gathered the young as well as those who already for many years carry with honour the title of citizen of the Country of Soviets, who by their work and their exploits all through their lives more than once justified this high calling. To greet you and wish you well on your way into the big life several generations of Soviet people have come. Thanks to them, your elder comrades, you could happily grow up and study. You will receive your first passport from their hands. Remember this day! Towards those who give you your passport you may always turn for help, for advice when choosing your way of life.

After this opening speech the master of ceremony introduces the three heroes of the Revolution, the War and of Labour with tales about their respective heroic deeds. Each in turn says a few words about the heroic past and about present tasks in their particular field of activity and then proceeds to give a group of young people their passports. The national anthem is played, and all stand up. One of the initiands replies on behalf of all of them to the preceding speeches and promises to fulfil the obligations that are placed on them. After a break, the more informal part of the evening offers a concert and dancing.

In other areas the following variants of this ritual are notable. The decorations of the ritual hall may follow a theme such as "Your hero, the Young Communist!" or "I am a citizen of the Soviet Union!" (*ibid.*: 42), or it may be decorated with the portraits of young heroes who have performed great deeds at the age of the young initiands (*Kak provesti* . . . 1966). Persons of ritual importance may be an elderly Bolshevik, a former sailor of a famous battleship, a participant in the storming of the Winter Palace during the Revolution (Rudnev 1966: 173), a person who knew Lenin personally or a Party member since 1917 (Rogozina 1973: 44). Sometimes these heroes wear red sashes decorated with the State emblem and all their medals. The ceremonial may include such ritual acts as the solemn bearing of the State emblem, listening to Lenin's speech "What is Soviet power?" or making a solemn oath of loyalty to the Soviet Motherland by the initiands, with their passports in their hands (*Kak provesti* . . . 1966: 6). The solemn rendering of political songs or verse may form an important part of the ceremonial. The description of a Passport ritual in Petrozavodsk/RSFSR, for example, mentions five each of carefully selected verses and songs. Of these, Mayakovsky's "Poem about a Soviet Passport", either in full, or the last few lines, seems to be a focal part of the ritual in many areas:

Chitaite,	Read,
Zaviduite,	Envy me,
Ya – grazhdanin	I am a citizen
Sovetskogo Soyuza.	Of the Soviet Union.

Also popular are the songs "My Wide Native Country" (*Shirokaya strana moya rodnaya'*) by Dunaevskii, "The Song of Troubled Youth" (*Pesna trevozhnoi molodosti*) by Pakhmutova and Yakerson's "The Relay Race of Generations".

COMING-OF-AGE RITUALS

In the RSFSR, I said above, young people are ritually initiated into only one narrow part of adult life at the age of sixteen, namely into that aspect of citizenship relating to the holding of an internal passport. In the Baltic republics of Estonia and Latvia, in contrast, coming-of-age rites at the age of eighteen mark a more general and complete transition into adult life. They take place at the more appropriate time of life when young people find themselves confronted with many new rights and obligations. These rites were initially created as anti-religious measures to weaken the impact of the Lutheran confirmation rite. Later they developed into rituals with a distinctive character of their own and a wider purpose. While the religious confirmation rite signals only the religious maturity of a young person, the socialist coming-of-age rite marks the recognition of a general social and political maturity and the entry into adulthood on both an individual and a social level. The socialist rite is thus more akin to initiation rites of youths in "primitive" society, differing only in its disregard of sexual maturity.

The coming-of-age rites of the two Baltic republics have been copied in other Soviet republics. In these an equivalent religious rite is not known. A much shorter version of the rite tends to be performed, and it is less well established. In some of these republics they have not taken root at all and have now been abandoned (*Nashi prazdniki* 1977: 105). The first ritual of this kind in the Baltic republics was performed in 1957 on a small and modest scale. Over the years it has gradually grown in scale and in popularity among young people. During the early years there was a lot of opposition to the new ritual from parents and, to a lesser extent, from the managers of enterprises where initiands worked. At the present time, according to *Nauka i religiya* (1977, 7: 45), it is welcomed by young and old alike, and in Estonia industrial enterprises even contribute financially to the complex of activities called "Summer Days of Youth". The popularity of this rite is also underlined by Baturin (1976: 114), who calls it "a firmly established mass ritual".

The Day of Maturity proper, on the first Sunday in July, is preceded by many weeks or even months of preparation of the initiands, which culminate in the events of the final week. While in most republics these preparations take place during the initiands' spare time over a long stretch of time, in Estonia they are concentrated into as many as six Summer Days of Youth that are spent during work or school time in a camp set up for the purpose. Urban working youths may get only a few days' release, but rural youths may spend the whole week there (Ranne 1972: 191). These Summer Days have been introduced and are organized by the Komsomol organization, with some support from the Party. Every young boy and girl rising eighteen receives a personal invitation to participate, as well as a specially created badge and a kerchief to be worn during the Summer Days. The latter is inscribed

103

with the name of the town or rural district and with the words "Summer Days of Youth" (Baturin 1976: 114).

The preparatory programme usually starts with a ball at which the young people get a chance to get to know each other and the planned programme of events. These are of both a social and an educational nature. The young people are instructed in such diverse topics as their civic rights and obligations, their history, militant atheism, beauty care, household management and economics. In recent years they have also received a "careers advisory" type of education. Special evenings are arranged to meet the inevitable heroes representing the "holy Soviet traditions" as well as contemporary political figures, famous sportsmen, composers, authors and artists. During sports and amateur dramatic events, art competitions and quiz games the young people have an opportunity to interact (Brudnyi 1968: 123; Ranne 1972: 192).

Those who spend the Summer Days of Youth in the camp have a similar programme of activities as well as some that are peculiarly suited to camp life in a beautiful and remote location. There are more intimate meetings around the camp fire with heroes of the Revolution and the Second World War and torchlight processions to war memorials. Also notable are the attempts to dramatically recreate historical, conspiratorial meetings of communist partisans in the woods, often with the participation of a surviving partisan. This is said to be particularly popular with the young (Baturin 1967: 251).

Both the urban programme of events and the rural Summer Days culminate in the final celebrations of the Day of Maturity, held on a mass scale in a town or district centre that is decorated with flowers and banners. The day starts with a festive procession of the young people around the town to the sound of music. The young girls wear white dresses (styled differently from confirmation dresses) and the young men dark suits, and both hold either candles (Ugrinovich 1975: 132) or flowers (Ranne 1972: 192). The ceremony is opened by the singing of both the Soviet and the republic's anthem. Then the secretary of the Komsomol district committee makes a speech, congratulating the young people on their coming-of-age, wishing them happiness and expressing his hope for a worthy passage into adult life. His speech is followed by short addresses from all those who have guided and educated the young people up to this stage – parents, teachers, representatives from places of work. Then the young people receive an album of photographs and a congratulatory letter from the Central

Committee of the Estonian Komsomol, which contains an address by Lenin to Komsomols in the early post-revolutionary period that urges them to build communism. They also receive flowers and presents from parents, friends and work mates. The ceremony is concluded by a speech from one of the young people thanking the Party, the government, the Komsomol, the schools, the enterprises and farms as well as their parents for the care given to them so far, and promising that they will justify the honour and confidence bestowed on them. The day ends with a big concert by the best orchestras in the republic. A tradition has developed to lay wreaths at the monuments to Lenin and to fallen heroes (Ranne 1972: 192, 193; Baturin 1976: 114).

Although these coming-of-age rituals are generally considered to be well established and almost universally accepted, some criticisms of short-comings are made. These have partly resulted from the very success of the ritual. Numbers are becoming too big, particularly in the camps, to develop genuine collectives. The immense task of preparing and organizing these events has been met with a waning enthusiasm on the part of the Komsomol. There are said to be too many speeches, lectures and declarations and not enough ritual acts (Mytskyula 1968: 54).

INDUCTION INTO THE ARMED FORCES

It is a big break in the life of a young man to leave familiar places and loved people for a number of years and to set out for a new, completely different environment. The tradition to ritually mark such an important event as induction into the armed forces dates back to pre-revolutionary times. Then it was a private ritual involving family and local community, in which feelings of anxiety about a harsh and uncertain future were mingled with excitement at the opening of new horizons. This event was usually accompanied by excessive drinking. At the present time conscription is still widely regarded as an occasion "to spend the last penny on merry-making" (Grishchenko and Kakonin 1974: 59). Although ritual specialists assert that at the present time enlistment into the armed forces is a joyful occasion and that "the people love their armed forces, care about them, live with them one life" (Nagirnyak *et al.* 1970: 203), it is widely known that enlistment is as much as ever considered to be an unavoidable evil, or worse, something to get out of if one can. The immense popularity of higher education, according to Smith (1976: 393), is partly due to the wish to become exempt from conscription. Problems do not stop once the young people have entered military service. There is a growing body of literature expressing official concern and worry about the disregard for traditional authority and the disenchantment with military life in general displayed by the enlisted (see sources quoted in Wolfe 1968). According to Wolfe (1968: 133), "from a social and political viewpoint the new generation (of conscripts) is creating problems of morale and assimilation into military life on a scale hitherto seldom encountered in the Soviet Union".

It is against this background that we must view the development, from the early sixties onwards, of a public ritual of "Induction into the Armed Forces". This dwells on the incorporation into a new honourable collective rather than on parting, and attempts to arouse feelings of joy and pride about this incorporation. Moral and practical support from, and responsibility to, the young man's working collective instead of to his family are underlined. Collectives are expected to give their young men social and political training before enlistment, to keep in contact with them during service and to receive them back with honour on their return. This is facilitated by the practice to keep their places in enterprises open for them.

The ritual is usually organized and conducted jointly by a military organization, by representatives from the recruits' place of work and by local Komsomol and/or Party organizations. The ritual varies considerably in form between different areas and between working collectives within an area and, according to Soviet commentators, "has not yet found its face". The ritual may be organized on the basis of individual enterprises or collective farms or on the basis of residence.

If the former, it is held in the enterprise or farm itself or in its palace of culture or club. It may be held for individual brigades in the workshop's Red Corner. It is introduced with a speech by a works' or farm representative emphasizing the reciprocal ties and obligations between the collective and its conscripted members. The following are extracts from such speeches:

Always remember that you are a representative of a famous collective, preserve and remember the revolutionary, military and labour traditions of your enterprise, keep a constant contact with us, your success shall gladden us. We shall wait for you! (Rudnev 1974: 53)

or:

Leading you to military service we, the workers, office workers and engineering–technical staff, your fathers and mothers, brothers and sisters, your older

106

comrades and near ones, at this solemn hour congratulate you on your entry into the glorious Armed Forces of the Soviet Union . . . (Rogozina 1973: 54)

Such an appeal is particularly effective if an enterprise has a glorious tradition to guard and a strong collective identity. After such a speech on behalf of the working collective, the recruits give a solemn oath in front of the factory or farm banner to fulfil their obligations honourably. On some collective farms the whole village comes to see the young men off (Zav'yalov 1973: 11). The enlistment cards are usually given out by a number of men representing the different "heroic traditions" of the Soviet Union, particularly the military one. Other speakers may be the mother of a conscripted youth who lost both husband and brothers in the last war, but urges everyone to defend Soviet borders, even if it leads to new sacrifices, or it may be a soldier who has recently completed his service and talks about the rewards of it. The prospective soldiers may also be given small parting presents to remind them of their work mates. This ritual at the actual place of work may be followed by an evening film show in the palace of culture. Here, films are shown which bring to life heroic events from both the revolutionary and the military past (Grishchenko and Kakonin 1974: 61).

If the ritual is performed for recruits residing in a certain geographical area it is done on a larger and also more impersonal scale in the local stadium, near a notable war memorial or on the field of a famous battle. The following description is of such a ceremony in a town in the Karbadino-Balkar ASSR (based on Gerandokov 1970: 24ff).

Decorated cars, carrying the recruits, converge on the stadium from surrounding regions. On arrival the recruits form themselves into a column in front of the stand where their friends and relations are sitting. The ceremony is opened by the regional Party secretary. Then the regional military commissar takes the platform. He informs everybody of the peaceful intentions of the Soviet Union and explains the need for a strengthening of Soviet defence capacity by reference to the aggressiveness of the imperialists. Then he addresses the new recruits with the following words:

Now your turn has come to carry out your filial duty. The people trusts you to preserve its freedom, its happiness. We deeply believe that you will not disgrace the honour of the glorious working people of Karbadino-Balkariya.

After the new recruits have been congratulated by everyone present, one of them swears, in the name of all, to hold sacred the order given by parents and older comrades. Some enlistment rituals conclude with the presentation to each young man of a little red sack holding a clump of earth to take with him as a reminder of his native land (Nagirnyak *et al.* 1970: 205; Zav'yalov 1973: 11).

In some areas the ritual is given more emotional impact by the greater utilization of military attributes and by ritualizing the new military role of the called-up youths. There, regimental banners are carried ceremoniously into the stadium by soldiers to the sound of fanfares. The called-up youths parade to the tune of a military march and clapping by the audience to the main tribune where they line up under a banner (Rudnev 1966: 161ff). In Sevastopol the called-up men are given the banner of ships which have excelled in battle, the banner standing for the relay baton passed from the elder to the younger generation (*Nashi prazdniki* 1977: 119). In other areas the ceremony is opened by a spectacular procession of open vehicles displaying "allegorical pages of a chronicle of heroism of the Soviet people", that is depicting famous war scenes and heroes. Then the first command is given to the youths by the regimental military commander calling them into the ranks of the army. On their first ceremonial march the recruits pass portraits of war heroes from the local area and salute them (Brudnyi 1968: 137ff). Another variant of the ritual is an organized conducted tour for all the enlisted of each local place that has a connection with a war hero, with a short talk at each location given by a local person.

Parallel to these organized public ritual performances, which emphasize the incorporation into a glorious new collective, some spontaneous private rituals have developed which dwell on the aspect of parting and on the accompanying uncertainties. In some regions of the Ukraine friends and relations pin to the young men's clothes commemorative ribbons or small handkerchiefs. On the point of departure each young man detaches one and throws it out of the vehicle to a mother or girl friend to pick up. This is meant to ensure their safe return home. In other areas the girl friend may plant a tree, give some of its leaves to the young man on his departure and promise to tend it in his absence (*ibid.*: 140). In some places it is becoming a tradition for enlisted men to pay a visit to a famous war memorial to give a private oath of allegiance (*ibid.*; Fursin 1973: 56).

7

vvvvvvvvvvvvvvvvvvvvvvvvvvvvvvvvvvvvvvvvvvvvvvvvvvvvvvvvvvvvvvvvvvvvvvvvvvvvvvvvvvvvvvvvvvvvv

Labour ritual

The central place of labour, particularly of the industrial working class, in the ideology of Marxism–Leninism and the indispensable role it has played and must go on to play in the actual development of Soviet society has been recognized by ritual specialists. It is expressed in an exceptionally large number of labour holidays and rituals, relating both to industrial and, to a lesser degree, to agricultural work. These have to be seen in the following problematic social context. Although the official ideology proclaims the working class to be the leading force in Soviet society, in practice it is relatively powerless both in the political and in the work situation, as well as being underprivileged in terms of material rewards and social honour in comparison to the intelligentsia. A twofold consequence of this state of affairs has been a disproportionately strong preference among young people for professional occupations and, resulting from this, a shortage of quali-fied manual labour, and a tendency by those already in manual occupations to produce shoddy or even faulty goods. Given the fact that political elites are still highly dependent on a loyal and disci-plined working class for both ideological and economic development reasons, the trends described above constitute a serious problem for them.

The labour rituals described in this chapter are seen as one step towards easing this problem. These rituals are designed not only to direct society's attention to the importance of manual labour and upgrade its status in the public opinion; they are intended also to relate both workers and collective farmers to the values of their society and to turn working collectives into cohesive communities, in which a wide spectrum of members' social relations comes under the direction and the control of the group. On a more prosaic level they are meant to increase labour discipline and the quantity and quality of labour output.

RITUAL IN INDUSTRY

Most labour rituals are staged by a combined effort of Party and/or Komsomol and trades union organizations. These occasions are given a festive and weighty appearance by bringing out the enterprise banners and by forming a guard of honour of the collective's best workers. Other characteristic activities on such days may be an exhibition centred on the factory and its work or a competition testing workers' knowledge of their trade or of their factory's history (Rudnev 1966: 162).

Besides being ritually distinguished, individuals or collectives may also be rewarded materially. Both ritual honour and material reward are carefully graded to present stimuli for yet higher labour achievement. In theory, the moral stimuli applied in ritual take precedence over material ones (Momylev 1975: 39–43).

Although labour ritual has existed from the very beginning of the Soviet period it was first introduced systematically and on a large scale only in the early sixties. While a few rites are now performed in most large enterprises, others have remained as local traditions. One of the most widely performed rituals is that of initiating young workers into the working class.

INITIATION INTO THE WORKING CLASS

This ritual was first started in the early sixties in Leningrad, and it is now so widely established that it is described by one writer as a "mass holiday" (Genkin 1975: 23, 64). The following description is of a ritual enacted for new workers of the famous Leningrad Kirov (formerly Putilov) works (based on Brudnyi 1968: 127ff). The ritual starts with some veterans of labour lighting a giant torch from the blazing flame of the factory's open furnace. Before bringing it to the ceremony proper in the factory's palace of culture, they carry it around the whole town during the evening hours as a symbol of Leningrad's remarkable labour and revolutionary traditions. The factory palace of culture is festively decorated with slogans on the walls, such as "Hail to the New Generation of Workers", "Be Worthy of the Traditions of the Fathers", "Labour Lays the Way to the Stars" etc. On a raised platform, against the background of the Red Flag, sit the factory's veteran workers and leading people from the town's Party, Komsomol and trades union organizations. In the audience are parents and friends. After an initial fanfare by bugle players, the chandeliers "blaze up", the doors open and the new workers enter to the tune of a solemn march and the clapping of hands. After the young workers have sat down various heroes of labour and the Revolution relate their experiences on a cinema screen. Then the drums start up and the guard of honour brings the torch into the hall. A representative of the initiands goes up to the torch and gives the labour oath:

We swear to follow always and in every way the traditions of the Petrograd proletarians.
We swear.
We swear to carry forward with honour the baton of our fathers.
We swear.

After this oath the ceremony continues with further speeches, congratulations, music and film.

Other towns and factories stage a similar ritual but have their own distinctive symbolic actions. Another factory with a distinguished revolutionary history, the Kiev Arsenal works, gives local colour to this ritual by presenting a dramatic juxtaposition of working life in the factory in 1863 (a historic year for the factory) and in the 1960s (Kampars and Zakovich 1967: 72). The giant metal-working combine in Magnitogorsk/Urals, with its heroic labour record, has at the centre of its ritual the showing of a film which is a complete record of the history of the combine and the town which grew up around it. It shows the arduous and heroic work of the founders during the early thirties, the important milestones between that glorious past and the present and concludes with shots of the present initiands in their various work situations. In the accompanying commentary the words "Russian miracle" and "legendary achievement" frequently crop up (Grishchenko and Kakonin 1974: 44). This last initiation ritual stresses more than others the idea of "passage" from one status to another. The former teachers from the Technical School or the initial training course formally declare to the young people's future mentors at work that the young men and women can be considered ready for a new stage in their lives (*ibid.*: 48).

Other local variants of the ritual have initiands give their promise of political loyalty and good labour performance while kneeling in front of the enterprise's Red Banner and kissing its "scarlet cloth". Certain measures, like inscribing their names into books of initiation or receiving commemorative certificates or Laws of Workers' Honour (which lay down acceptable work performance), are designed to give permanence to these promises (Gerandokov 1970: 9; Lobacheva 1975: 108). In some factories the call for a good work performance is given structural support by putting each initiand under the patronship (*shefstvo*) of an experienced worker. The ritual has its own repertoire of traditional Soviet songs, such as "We are the Smiths", "March of the Enthusiasts", "The Young Guard", "March of the Communist Brigades", "The Working Class is Marching" (*Idet Rabochii Klass*), "Meetings with Glory" (Nagirnyak *et al.* 1970: 191). Mayakovsky's famous verse is sometimes recited as the opening sequence of the ritual (Belousov 1973: 14–15):

Ya schastliv,	I am happy
Chto ya – etoi sily chastitsa	that I am part of this force
Chto obshchie	that even the tears in the eyes
dashe slezy iz glaz.	are common ones.
Silnee i chishche nelzya	It is impossible to commune in a stronger
prichastit'sya	and purer way
Velikomu chuvstvu –	with the great feeling –
po imeni klass.	of class. (my translation)

The rite has given birth also to some new poetry, such as the verse quoted by Gerandokov (1970: 9):

Rabochie ruki po pravu	Workers' hands we rightfully
My chtim, kak oporu strany,	consider the support of our country,
Net pesny, dostoinoi ikh	There is no song adequate
slavy,	to [express] their glory,
I net na svete tseny.	and in the world [there is] no price.
	(my translation)

This initiation ritual is designed to mark an important transition in the life of a young person, to link him to a new collective and to provide him with new goals and ideals. It is also meant to make foremen and engineering–technical staff aware of their responsibilities for the new workers (Lisavtsev 1966: 71). At the same time the ritual seeks to realize important concerns of State and Party: to replenish the ranks of the working class, "to mobilize workers for the utilization of inner productive reserves and to involve them in the movement for a communist relation to work" (Kuchiev 1974: 64). The necessity to replenish the ranks of the working class has become a particularly pressing objective at the present time, when the "pyramid of desire" of youths for higher education rather than for manual work is becoming incompatible with the "pyramid of supplies" available in the economy (Kulagin 1974: 17). The prolonged pressure on youths in the past to set their sights higher than "becoming a simple worker" (*ibid*.: 18) has been so effective that it has now become imperative to change the balance in the other direction. Rituals of labour are one of the various efforts made at the present time to upgrade the status of manual work in public opinion and in the individual evaluation of the young. All these goals are pursued by appealing to the "glorious traditions" of the past and by emphasizing continuity of endeavour. Both are invoked through the considered choice of time, place and participants of the ritual as well as of appropriate symbols.

Other labour rituals are less evenly diffused or are specifically local traditions. Some ritually mark out a labour collective, a specific occupation or industry, while others bring individual workers of merit to the notice of the collective. A working collective is honoured when a factory, workshop or brigade celebrates an anniversary or a noteworthy occasion. Particular trades are honoured by holidays dedicated to individual occupations, for example Day of the Miner. Individuals are singled out by such diverse rituals as First Labour Rating, First Wage, Acceptance into a Brigade of Communist Labour, presentation of a labour decoration, a labour anniversary, a retirement ritual, Election of Veterans or an Honouring of a Worker's Dynasty. In addition, general labour holidays are intended to involve the whole working population of a given area. There is no space to describe all these holidays and rituals, but significant features of some from each group will be highlighted below. (For descriptions of labour rituals and holidays in different areas of the Soviet Union see Rudnev 1966: 162ff; Berestovskaya 1968: 4; Gerandokov 1970: 5ff; Kuchiev 1974: 61ff; Lobacheva 1975: 108f; *Nashi prazdniki* 1977: 41ff.)

An example of a ritual distinguishing a particular enterprise is the Founder's Day of the Leningrad Kirov works. Its central activity is a labour report by four generations of the enterprise's workers and by groups connected to the factory by patronship. Such reports consist of making "labour presents". These may amount to so many tons of scrap metal collected by the schoolboys coming under the works' patronship; of tractors built by members of the enterprise's Komsomol group in their spare time; of over-fulfilled plans by workers; and of so many lectures given by veterans of labour. These reports are made at the various "holy" places in Leningrad, mentioned above (the description is based on Rudnev 1974: 60). Collectives within a factory, such as a brigade of special merit, may be honoured by having bestowed on

113

them the title "Brigade of Communist Labour", by giving its members special badges and certificates of achievement or by an oratorial or dramatic recreation of the brigade's history (Gerandokov 1970: 6; Rudnev 1974: 58).

A way to honour a more diffuse collective are holidays of individual occupations or branches of industry. Although holidays of a few occupations were already created in the 1930s and 1940s, a systematic calendar of occupational holidays was instituted only during the 1960s. It is not clear on what basis these occupations have been selected and how widely these holidays are actually celebrated. One team of authors (Nagirnyak *et al.* 1970: 10–11) give the impression that there is a well-established fixed annual calendar of holidays dedicated to eighteen different occupations or branches of industry which cover almost the whole spectrum of manual occupations and which are being observed all over the Soviet Union (for details see the ritual calendar in appendix B). In practice, there appears to be quite a big variation between republics and even within them. The ritual calendar of one medium-sized town, for example, contained only five such holidays of occupations (Genkin 1975: 61). Other authors too (e.g. Kampars and Zakovich 1967: 169; Aliev 1968: 169; Ugrinovich 1975: 150) have stressed that most of these holidays are not very securely established and generally are not well regarded. On all the lists seen by me, the great majority of holidays are for manual workers. The few professions mentioned are lower professions and have few university educated members. One author suggests paying more attention to the holidays of trades whose members are culturally backward and socially at a low stage of development, such as construction workers and agricultural workers (Lisavtsev 1966: 76).

These labour holidays are said to have the following basic components: a labour report (i.e. a report on labour achievement) at a festive meeting; honouring of innovators and victors of labour competitions; honouring a worker's dynasty in the given occupational field (Nagirnyak *et al.* 1970: 15ff). Organized lectures and discussions, evenings of labour glory, the declaration of competition results for "the best of the profession" as well as mass spectacles and sports events are additional components of these holidays in some areas (*Nashi prazdniki* 1977: 42). The holidays are preceded by several weeks of labour competition.

The low popularity of the labour holidays is probably due to the fact that they do not serve, and are not sustained by, a genuine collective, but are merely decreed from above for a given category of people.

Consequently they have no authenticity and are regarded as dull and uniform (Ugrinovich 1975: 150).

More successful are the holidays of labour devoted to a town's dominant industry, where the majority of the population is in some way involved. An interesting example here is the rituals and other festivities conducted by the Lenin metallurgical combine in the Ural town of Magnitogorsk. This town owes its existence to the combine and has become a symbol of the Soviet Union's industrial achievement and technical supremacy (Grishchenko and Kakonin 1974: 7–8). Having such a "glorious" history of labour achievement the combine is well placed to engage in periodic ritual celebrations. One such was the celebration in the early seventies of the "The Pouring of the 200-millionth Ton of Steel". The central ritual action was, as the name indicates, the pouring of the actual 200-millionth ton of steel.

Among the rituals developed around individuals or families of workers, the "First Wage" and the "Honouring of Workers' Dynasties" are noteworthy, albeit for different reasons. The ceremonial handing over of a young worker's first wage is interesting not for its symbolism but for the expressed intention it serves. It is meant to eliminate the entrenched tradition of making a new worker buy drinks for all his mates, thus launching him on the road to heavy drinking. The argument behind this action is that if the mood is heightened by ritual action alcohol as a stimulant of mood will become superfluous (Rudnev 1966: 162).

The ritual of creating "Workers' Dynasties", in contrast, is notable for its vivid symbolism. The word "dynasty" tries to signify that the worker in Soviet society occupies as elevated and honoured a position as was held by the high nobility in Tsarist Russia. A Worker's Dynasty is established when three or more generations of one family (these may include from three to thirty persons) have either worked conscientiously in one factory, or when a family has produced several generations of people who have distinguished themselves in some way in the political or military field or in their labour. They need not necessarily all be manual workers (Sukhov 1976: 61). These Workers' Dynasties are now widely established and ritually distinguish a very large number of workers. One large machine-building factory in the Urals, for example, in 1974 had 1700 dynasties comprising 8000 members (Momylev 1975: 38). In 1974 the first all-Union rally of Workers' or Labouring Dynasties was held, and in many regions of the Ukraine such rallies now occur regularly (Zots and Poluk 1978: 89).

An extended family is turned into a Worker's Dynasty during fac-
tory-based celebrations. During such celebrations the family's history
is told with illustration and documentation. Individual members of the
family talk about their life and about how they distinguished themselves in one of the fields mentioned above. Sometimes family members even act out their family history, recreating the most dramatic
episodes. At the end of the evening they inscribe their names into Rolls
of Honour of Workers' Dynasties and receive some sort of certificate or
badge to indicate their new honour. A "dynastic" evening may also
include an exhibition of some of the products made by various members of the dynasty and of "family valuables", such as medals, orders,
testimonials and prizes. Such a construction of family history often
brings to life the history of the whole local community at the same
time, and is therefore interesting and important both to the honoured
family and to the audience (for descriptions see Nagirnyak *et al.* 1970:
20; Sukhov 1976: 61; Zots 1976: 21).

Other rituals deeply ingrained into the texture of Soviet industrial
life are those that come under the heading of Socialist Labour Competitions. These have also a strong instrumental component, and their
ritual aspect is not always recognized by Soviet writers. They have
their origins in the socialist *Subbotniks* and, more directly, in the
Stakhanovite Movement of the 1930s. The *Subbotniks*, dating from
1919, established the principle of giving one's labour over and above
what is required by the terms of one's employment, that is working
on a Saturday (*Subbota*) for the good of the State (for further details see
p. 212). The Stakhanovite Movement developed in 1935 as a means to
increase labour discipline to an industrial working force over-weighted
with unskilled, under-educated, recently urbanized workers. It introduced an element of competition into this type of labour. Such competitions, with some variation, have been held ever since and have
extended their scope all the time. The renewed emphasis on socialist
competition in recent years, according to McAuley (1977: 24), has to
be seen in the context of the leadership's frustration with the failure of
more sophisticated methods of revitalizing the economy, such as economic reform. These competitions are a permanent feature not only of
all industrial enterprises but of all areas of Soviet public life. In recent
decades the emphasis of competition has been not only on increasing
the quantity of output but also on improving its quality, as well as on
the level of technical and political competence of the workers. Even
more ambitiously, some socialist labour competition is intended to

induce participants to change their whole way of life and to conduct their social relationships both inside and outside the industrial enterprise according to the moral postulates of the communist Moral Code.

The most recent variant is the Movement for Communist Labour, under which brigades and individuals in industrial enterprises compete for the respective titles of Brigade and Shock Worker (*Udarnik*) of Communist Labour. Those who compete have to follow the command of the Movement "to study, to work and to live in a communist way". The Movement for Communist Labour aims at nothing less than creating the new Soviet man. The internal organization of the Brigades of Communist Labour shows a recognition of the fact that the restructuring of a moral outlook depends on the presence of a moral community to set goals and to stimulate and support individual efforts by positive and negative sanctions. Efforts are being made to turn brigades into genuine communities whose members take a lively interest in all aspects of each other's lives. Each brigade keeps a diary in which, for every member, are noted such important events in his life as the completion of a course of further training, a marriage, a birth or death in the family or enlistment into the army. The collective demonstrates to the individual member its interest in those events in various ways. The brigade holds meetings to discuss how its members work, study, participate in public life and order their family relations. In short, the whole life of each member is laid bare before the collective. Contacts with members are kept up even when they have left the factory (Aliev 1968: 164).

This Movement for Communist Labour has become a well-established part of Soviet life. In 1968, over thirty million working people participated in it. Even wider participation is achieved in the less ambitious Socialist Labour Competitions. These take place annually and do not involve the forging of permanent moral communities. They involve not only individuals or brigades, but competitors may also be such large units as enterprises, towns, districts, regions and even republics within the Union.

In the Magnitogorsk Lenin metallurgical combine, for example, such competitions are firmly established annual events, although they have not yet developed "final ritual forms" (Grishchenko and Kakonin 1974: 49ff). A competition for the best young worker starts three months before the final judging and is introduced with much publicity. During those three months competitors are watched closely on all aspects of their work and social performance. To be considered socially and

117

politically sound the worker must be active in both these aspects of life and must be trying to better his qualifications. The victors (there is one in every branch of work) receive a diploma and a souvenir present (e.g. an engraved watch). Their work-places are decorated with pennants and their portraits are displayed on stands of honour (*stendy Pochety*) in the combine's palace of culture. Repeated winners get the highest labour rating, are taken on visits to other factories to spread their experience, and they are known by name all over the combine and, through newspapers, in the town. The "champions" may go on to town-wide or district-based competitions.

Such competitions are not only designed to raise the labour effort and discipline of participants; they are also occasions to create "heroes of labour" who, by their example, spur on the less ambitious or less committed to greater efforts. One Soviet author expresses the wish to see the best Soviet foundryman or turner becoming as famous and celebrated as the best Soviet hockey or chess player (Kulagin 1974: 62), while another puts heroes of labour on the same level as military heroes (Momylev 1975: 33). One attempt to accord workers the same honour as traditionally honoured social groups or individuals is given by the custom of creating "Rooms of Labour Glory" in Galleries of Honour, where pictures of the workers who drove the first Soviet bulldozer, tractor, etc. are exhibited (Nagirnyak *et al.* 1970: 20).

The more modest Communist Subbotnik dates back to 1919 when workers on the Moscow–Kazan railway line decided to give their labour voluntarily on their rest day to help improve the disrupted economy and to show their support for the Communist Party. A report of that first Subbotnik by a participant (*Pravda* May 1919, quoted by Lenin 1976: 164) brings out well both the instrumental and the ritual aspect of Subbotniks. Having described the disciplined labour and high productivity of this voluntary work team the reporter finishes with the following words:

When the work was finished those present witnessed an unprecedented scene: a hundred communists, weary, but with the light of joy in their eyes, greeted their success with the solemn strains of The International. And it seemed as if the triumphant strains of the triumphant anthem . . . would spread through the whole of working-class Russia and shake up the weary and the slack.

The Subbotnik did, indeed, quickly spread, and it became a mass "holiday" during the next year. The labour given on that and following occasions was not as well organized and productive, and was sometimes even a little anarchic, and the ritual aspect came to predominate over the instrumental.

The Subbotnik has been retained up to the present time, and instrumental and ritual aspects are again of equal importance. It is now celebrated annually on the Saturday nearest to Lenin's birthday (22 April), and involves both white-collar and manual workers. This date is particularly fitting, as it commemorates both Lenin's support for the Subbotnik and enables people to express their attachment to Lenin in a concrete and active way by making him "labour presents". The Subbotnik has developed a long way from its inception in 1919. While in that first year fifteen workers gave their labour to repair three steam engines, in 1975 around 140 million people created production worth a billion roubles (Fursin 1977: 27). As one Soviet ritual specialist puts it: "Ever brighter burns the fire of work enthusiasm lit in 1919" (Rudnev 1979: 33). Before groups of workers start on their labour task for the day, they have a solemn meeting at their enterprise, office or university lecture hall to remind participants of the purpose of their labour. Manual workers continue to work in their ordinary jobs, often with saved raw materials to enhance the "gift" status of production. Many white-collar workers, students, school-children and pensioners perform manual tasks devoted to the cleaning-up and beautification of public spaces. When I observed the activities on the occasion of Lenin's birthday in 1978 in Leningrad, I noted small groups of people everywhere, cheerfully cleaning and tidying up verges and parks to the accompaniment of revolutionary music from loudspeakers. Enquiries about people's attitudes to this extra working day established that most people did it gladly and used the occasion to execute a pressing task which could not be accomplished during normal working hours. Another reason for its popularity may also be the fact that it involves a role reversal for all those usually engaged in "mental labour". It thus offers a rare occasion to discard for a day a system of social stratification arising from the level of education, which is no less rigid than that of capitalist society, and to enact the cherished old communist myth that all labour is equal and that there are no social differences between physical and mental labourers.

RITUAL IN AGRICULTURE

Holidays and rituals of labour were introduced much later on collective farms than in urban–industrial areas. They do not appear to be as widely established as those in industrial enterprises, and in many cases their ritual is either weakly developed or exists in a very crude form. The greater geographical and social isolation of collective farms has meant that successful new ritual forms are not quickly dispersed between them or from town to country. Also the greater shortage of active and well-qualified political and cultural cadres hinders the speedy introduction of socialist ritual. The much higher level of religiosity in the countryside may also act as a braking factor. Consequently, more collective farms than industrial enterprises do "their own thing" which, although more original, remains dependent on the limited local cultural resources.

Soviet authors writing about agricultural labour ritual are particularly concerned, for two reasons, that it be increased and improved. One author sees such ritual as a means to raise the status of agricultural work which, according to him, is very unpopular and attracts only those people who have failed in everything else (Lisavtsev 1966: 72). Others see the introduction of agricultural labour ritual as a means to oust Christian and Islamic religious holidays, which are still strongly entrenched in the countryside. Most frequently under attack are the various local Saints' Days, which are said to be connected with widespread drunkenness and absenteeism at a crucial time in the agricultural year. It is suggested that Saints' Days are most easily replaced by a secular holiday, because they are now only tenuously connected with religious sentiments (Rudnev 1966: 165; Filatov 1967: 81ff; Kampars and Zakovich 1967: 216; Kuchiev 1974: 64). Thus, as has been frequently the case in Soviet history, despite a recognition of a particularly urgent need for correct political socialization of the rural population, the organizational capabilities of political bodies have not proved equal to the task.

The most widespread agricultural holidays and rituals of labour are the Initiation as Cultivators (*zemledel'tsy*) or Grain Collectors (*khlebobory*) and a Harvest Festival, as well as such variations on a basic theme as "Holiday of the First Furrow" or "Holiday of the First Sheaf". In addition, there are some of the traditional holidays of national groups, combining popular and labour ritual, which have been revived in recent years. Most of these holidays are in two parts, with traditional rural amusements following the ritual first part.

INITIATION AS GRAIN COLLECTORS

This ritual is now quite widely performed, but takes different forms in the various geographical areas. In some areas it is separate, in others it is celebrated as part of a general labour holiday or as part of a more comprehensive *rite de passage*, marking changes in the productive life of three generations. On this latter occasion veterans are led into retirement, "foremost workers" are honoured and new agricultural workers are initiated into their work collective and into their chosen specialized field of work. The following description of an initiation ritual, performed separately, is an account of the practice in some areas of the Northern Ossetian ASSR (see Gerandokov 1970: 9ff). Many of its constituent elements are also present in the ritual as celebrated in other areas.

The young initiands arrive at the rural club in cars decorated with slogans appropriate to the occasion. Together with their relatives and with farm veterans of labour they enter the club. A poem is read out to set the mood:

> I know a lot of glorious occupations,
> Miner, smith, geologist and pilot,
> Creator of verse and skilled metal-worker
> It would be impossible to count them in
> a whole year.
> And they are honoured in my native area,
> But I love my own trade –
> The trade of a simple grain collector. (My translation)

The veterans, led by the most honoured one as banner carrier, go to the stage, and the young men and girls line up in front of it. The secretary of the local Komsomol organization hands each young man a set of tools and each young girl the white overall of a milkmaid, and both receive a book on the latest findings of agricultural science. Veterans pin to the chests of the young people the badge of the corn collector, featuring the hammer and sickle framed by ears of corn and flowers in the rays of a rising sun. After that there is a speech by the headmaster of the local school who tells how the boys and girls grew up, studied and acquired habits of work. Then, to the sound of drums, Young Pioneers enter and greet the farm youths. Their leader carries a beautiful small chest, filled with farm earth, and hands it to the master of ceremony. The initiands go up to him. The first takes a clump of earth in his hand, and the others, putting their hands on his, join him in making the following promises:

Entering the ranks of the grain collectors of my Motherland I solemnly
promise:
To love the soil, to be faithful to it and to care for it like a proprietor would
(*po-khozyaiskii*);
To respect work – the source of abundance and happiness;
To master my trade to perfection;
To constantly introduce into production everything new and advanced;
To constantly study and pass on my experience to my comrades at work;
To hold dear the honour of my collective;
To live and work in a communist way;
To consider holy the revolutionary and labour traditions of the older
generation;
To be devoted to the native Communist Party;
To give all strength and energy to the building of communism;
We promise that we will firmly continue along the road of our fathers and carry
with honour through life the high calling of a Soviet grain collector. (My
translation)

After the reading of a poem the young people sign their names to the
accompaniment of soft music. Then they are addressed by a veteran
with a speech which stresses their indebtedness to the older generation and reminds them again of the obligations already expressed in
their solemn promises. Congratulations and admonitions from other
members of the collective farm follow. Then the farm's banner is
brought to them, and each of the initiands in turn kneels down and
"presses his lips to the scarlet cloth". After one of the youths has made
a speech in reply, they all leave the stage to the tune of a march. The
occasion is concluded with a concert for everyone.

HARVEST DAY

Harvest Day is not only an ancient Russian holiday but has also been
encouraged from early Soviet times as a secular holiday. According to
Harper (1929: 227ff), from 1923 onwards it was revived and given a
new interpretation by the Komsomol organization. During this time of
alliance between town and country, young urban workers were sent to
the villages to impress on the peasants the secular and scientific nature
of agricultural work, as well as to conduct general political agitation.
The slogan of the holiday was: "In union with the town the village goes
along the path blazed by Ilych" (*Nashi prazdniki* 1977: 60). Apart from a
procession with banners and slogans and an exhibition of the products
of labour it had few ritual or even festive elements in it. In 1929 a special
resolution of the Party's Central Committee widened the focus of this

holiday to become the "Day of Collectivization and Harvest". It took on "the character of a wide political campaign, the basic content of which was the mobilization of the broad labouring masses of town and country for the cause of the socialist reconstruction of the Soviet village" (*Massovye prazdniki* . . . 1961: 257). By 1930 it had become a general holiday. We know that a Harvest Day of this type did not become a permanent calendric holiday, but none of the sources give us an idea for how long the early version remained in general existence.

Harvest Day as a holiday combining traditional pre-revolutionary and new socialist ritual directly connected with the harvest was revived as a publicly organized holiday only from the early sixties onwards. At the beginning, only individual collective farms observed it, but gradually it has become established more widely. The intention behind its reintroduction has been the replacement of some or all of the religious holidays, in both Orthodox and Islamic areas. Usually it has replaced the Orthodox local Saint's Day. Collective farm assemblies, after much educational and propaganda work, have been persuaded to adopt Harvest Day as a public holiday in place of a religious holiday. Formal announcements of such practices have appeared in the local papers informing potential urban visitors of the change (Vestnikov 1964: 60ff; Rudnev 1966: 165; Gerandokov 1970: 21; Kuchiev 1974: 64).

This new holiday has not yet found a unified ritual form, but consists of an odd assortment of ritual acts and mere entertainment. In most areas there is little evidence that Harvest Day is a holiday with a long tradition, and both old and new ritual is weakly utilized. Most Harvest Days have the following elements: a festive procession with agricultural products; a meeting or report on work results; an honouring of heroes of labour; a dramatized presentation or concert on the theme of Harvest Day; and a Harvest supper and/or some form of organized amusement.

In Slavic areas the festivities usually start with the solemn presentation on an embroidered cloth of a huge traditionally decorated loaf of bread baked with flour from the new harvest. It is sometimes inscribed with a figure denoting the amount of grain delivered by the farm to the State (Filatov 1967: 88). Sometimes there is a parade for showing off farm tools or horses. One author notes with disapproval that these are the traditional tools rather than modern, powerful machinery (Brudnyi 1968: 110). The dramatic element may be a personification of Harvest accompanied by Golden Autumn, thanking all those present for their good work and giving out premiums for outstanding work. On the bigger farms it may be a massed gymnastic display in which music, colour and movement combine to convey the various stages of growing and harvesting the corn, picturing not only the labour but also the rural merriment after completing the labour (Abramyan 1966: 14).

In some of the traditional corn-growing areas of the USSR, for example in the Ukraine, Harvest Day draws on old traditions, the ritual of which has been carefully adapted to the changed political ideology. Here the Day is also still referred to by its traditional name *Dozhinki* or *Obzhinki* (from the verb *dozhinat'* – to finish reaping). In pre-revolutionary times the central ritual action consisted in placing a picturesque, plaited wreath of corn on the head of the estate's landlord and wishing him and his family well; or the wreath was presented to the village's prettiest girl who was then led in procession from house to house with traditional songs. In both cases the honoured person (or her parents) had to provide a harvest supper for the rest of the village. Now the wreath is presented to a person of authority in the collective farm and is meant to symbolize the "labour victory and glory" of the collective farmers. Whereas the landlord considered it beneath him to take part in the feast he provided for his workers, there is said to be no such division between management and the workers of the collective farm. Changes are also reflected in the appearance of the wreath. In some areas the corn ears are no longer plaited into a circular shape but into a five-cornered star, or the wreath may be decorated with the emblems of Soviet power. Some of the traditional harvest songs have been retained while others, the religious or feudal sentiments of which are no longer in keeping with the present political ethos, have been replaced with new socialist songs. (This account is based on Kampars and Zakovich 1967: 51ff.)

SABANTUI

Another holiday of labour, based on ancient traditions, is Sabantui. It is celebrated by the Kazan Tatars after spring sowing. Sabantui, unlike most other traditional holidays, continued to flourish all through the post-revolutionary period, although some changes have been introduced. Whereas traditionally it was held at the end of April to *meet spring sowing*, it now occupies a more convenient date in early summer (on the nearest Sunday to 24 June) during a lull of work between sowing and harvesting and marks the *end* of sowing.

Traditionally, the ritual start of sowing by the village's most respected inhabitant was followed by traditional Tatar games and competitions, in which strength and dexterity could be tested and shown off. The winners received hand-made prizes, prepared by the village's young women all through the winter. The most important competition was the battle of the sashes (*bor''ba kushakakh*), and its winner, the *batyr*, became a sort of folk hero. The games and competitions were followed by jollities for the young people which afforded a kind of annual "marriage market". Although Sabantui was a Tatar folk festival it was never ethnically exclusive, and all other nationalities in the area were welcomed to participate. This characteristic, together with its genuine "folk" nature, probably accounts for the fact that it was allowed to continue without much interruption up to the present time. Most of the traditional elements have been retained. The traditional games have maintained their popularity and the main game – the Battle of the Sashes – is still the undisputed centre of the holiday. Presents given to the victors of the competitions in the smaller communities still include the traditional embroidered shirts and cloths that are made by the hands of the community's young women. Their collection on the eve of the holiday by young men on horseback is as much as ever an important and spectacular part of the holiday (Urazmanova 1977: 99).

But some contemporary details have been added, such as an honouring of shock workers, a political parade at the start of the holiday and the inclusion in the programme of competitive games and such modern sports as light athletics, football and volley-ball (Magdeev 1976). Prizes for the victors now also include consumer goods, like radios, washing-machines and watches (Urazmanova 1977: 99). The fact that the new socialist ritual elements have not become an integral part of the holiday, but are regarded as alien intrusions liable to distort the nature of the holiday, is indicated by Urazmanova's comment: "All this [the congratulatory speeches, the honouring of shock workers etc.] is fine if it does not lose a sense of proportion. Occasionally unfortunately, the congratulations and giving out of [labour] awards . . . delay the holiday and weary those gathered" (*ibid*.: 100).

The biggest change in Sabantui has not been in the details of its content, but lies in the spirit of the holiday. Traditionally, it was a holiday based in the small, face-to-face community, and was staged by that community for its members. The competition of the traditional games was one between individuals, and victors were rewarded only with prizes made by individual women. The holiday has retained this spirit in some of the smaller rural communities, where the village elder

125

still plays a very active part (*ibid.*). But it has lost it in many others, particularly where it has been made an urban holiday. In the larger communities it is often staged in the impersonal surroundings of a park of culture or a stadium, and it is organized by all sorts of social and political collectives, including enterprises. Although the central competition, the Battle of the Sashes, is still held between individuals, they no longer fight for their own glory but as representatives of the various collectives (*Massovye prazdniki* . . . 1961: 268).

In other Muslim and Russian areas similar though less distinctive holidays of the agricultural cycle, such as the Holiday of the First Furrow or the Holiday of the First Sheaf, have been revived during the last two decades. These are very ancient holidays of pagan origin. Their essence was an attempt to influence the course of natural agricultural development by the application of magic. At the beginning of the twentieth century they combined a magico-religious orientation with a focus on the popular national culture of a particular Muslim group of the Caucasian and Central Asian areas of Imperial Russia and of the Soviet Union. At some time in the early Soviet period they became discredited with the political authorities and gradually fell into oblivion.

From the early sixties onwards these agricultural holidays have been revived. Stripped of their religious and magical elements, they have become labour holidays which combine the standard Soviet labour rituals with a ritualized performance of the agricultural labour act central to the holidays (e.g. ploughing the first furrow). They have retained elements of the traditional popular culture of dress, food, games and amusements to give the holiday distinctiveness and local colour.

HOLIDAY OF THE FIRST SHEAF

Although agricultural work is now very mechanized and sheaves are normally no longer part of the rural scene, a holiday of this name has been revived in many Muslim areas. On this day a sheaf is assembled and, decorated with garlands and flags, is ceremoniously paraded past a line of all the farm's brigades. It is then placed on a stage by a farm veteran who wishes all the farm inhabitants a happy holiday. A young machine operator takes the stage to thank the veteran and to call on all the brigades to enter into competition on the following day when the harvest starts in earnest. After this, various informal entertainments take place (*ibid.*: 252ff). In other areas a more modest celebration immediately precedes the field work. Before the machine operators go into the field there is a parade followed by a Festive Session (*Nashi prazdniki* 1977: 63–4).

The following holiday scenario is another variation of this basic theme. The essence of this holiday, celebrated at the beginning of the harvest in some Muslim areas, is expressed in its central ritual. It takes the form of an examination of readiness for the beginning of harvest work and is conducted out in the fields. On arrival in the field, the villagers are greeted by march music, played by a local group. After a short speech, the chairman of the collective farm gives work tasks to every brigade, and the machine operators submit their plans about the gathering of the harvest. Socialist pledges are made, and a date for the completion of the harvest is determined. Then the brigades line up at the starting-point. After the oldest farmer has thrown the first ear of corn to the best operator of a combine harvester, the starting tape is cut. The farm "enters the battle for the gathering of bread without fail" (based on Kuchiev 1974: 64).

HOLIDAY OF HAMMER AND SICKLE

This entirely Soviet holiday of labour was designed to express the unity of interest between workers and collective farmers, between town and country. It is an occasion on which "representatives of the collective farm peasantry symbolically give account of their economic activity to their patrons, representatives of the urban working class" (*Nashi prazdniki* 1977: 57). Although this holiday is relatively new, it is based on an old Leninist ideological principle – the alliance of workers and peasants – and on a well-established related principle of organiza-tion – the idea of patronship. The Alliance of Workers and Peasants was established at the beginning of Soviet power and is said to have been decisive to the Bolshevik victory in the Civil War. This notion of alliance has remained current up to the present time, although varying ideological emphasis has been given to it during different periods of Soviet history. While it has always been referred to as the "friendly" alliance it has been at best a rather-one sided friendship, putting the interest of the urban working class first. At worst, during the years of War Communism and later, during collectivization of agriculture, it has been a bitter struggle for supremacy by the working class on behalf of the Party and a fight for liberation from this disadvantageous partnership by the peasantry. The alliance has never been one between equal partners but has always been based on the idea of patronship of one social class over another. Patronship is assumed by the group which is considered to be both ideologically and culturally at a higher level of development and which, on the strength of this, gives friendly assistance to the group at a lower level. It is against this background of an always uneasy union, vacillating between co-operation and exploitation, that the Holiday of Hammer and Sickle has to be viewed.

This holiday has become an annual or bi-annual event in many parts of the Soviet Union, celebrated at the convenient time of September when all the field work is finished. Each holiday meeting involves the workers of one or several urban factories and the members of a collective farm in a near-by rural area, who are connected to each other by the ties of patronship. In the Ukrainian capital of Kiev and the surrounding countryside the holiday has been celebrated in the following way. The festivities start on the collective farm, where the whole farm collective gathers in the morning for a solemn review of the completed harvest and an honouring of the best workers. An older collective farmer reminds his fellow farmers of the great help rendered to the farm by the Kiev workers during difficult times, and he calls on the collective to hold holy, and to strengthen, this friendship. A young farmer, in reply to this speech, promises on behalf of the collective to do so. The Party secretary invites everyone to participate in this holiday, and the farm collective, in specially decorated vehicles, sets out for the place of celebration in the nearby town.

They stop their vehicles a little distance away from the place of celebration and march the rest of the way on foot. There, in a large square near a big park, columns of urban workers have lined up in a semi-circle to receive their rural guests. On approaching the semi-circle the collective farmers are met by girls with bread and salt. This is followed by various speeches of welcome by the industrial enterprise's "best people": shock workers, victors of socialist competition, veterans of labour. The farmers then present a huge sheaf of wheat to their hosts. After that a representative of the farmers gives a report of the farm's labour achievements during the past year. He finishes by calling on the young workers to co-operate with the farmers by perfecting the mechanization and automation of the more labour-consuming processes of agricultural work. The farmers' report is followed by a similar one from the industrial workers talking about successes in the fulfilment of the plan and about the main events in their working collective. Then a young girl farmer and a young worker together read out the text of an oath about loyalty to the great cause of Lenin, loyalty to the Motherland, the people, and to friendship. The hymns of the Soviet Union and of the Ukraine are sung. After an exchange of flowers and souvenirs all the participants of the festivities march with music and singing to the nearby park. Here the festivities continue in a more informal manner, although entertainment is still focussed on the theme of the holiday. Before the rural guests depart they issue an invitation to the workers to come and participate in the celebrations of their forthcoming Harvest Day (the account is based on *Nashi prazdniki* 1977: 57–8). In many areas, where this holiday is celebrated, there has become established a concluding ritual of planting a "tree of friendship" along specially designated "Avenues of Friendship" (Nagirnyak *et al.* 1970: 40ff).

This meeting of workers and collective farmers on the Holiday of Hammer and Sickle is often followed by other formal and informal meetings. The groups exchange not only hospitality and gifts but, having become acquainted with the nature of each other's work, also exchange physical assistance, share work experience and equipment, as well as social and cultural provisions (Lobacheva 1975: 127). It does, however, appear to be a somewhat one-sided exchange with the urban groups having a lot to offer, and the rural groups needing most of the help.

vv

Holidays of the calendric cycle and their ritual

Besides the labour holidays of the agricultural cycle described in chapter 7, there is another group of annually recurring holidays which are distinguished both by a religious element of a Christian, Islamic or pagan kind and by a rich tradition of folk ritual and custom. These mark the seasonal changes and are taken in both rural and urban areas. Whereas once these holidays were celebrated by the whole population of a given religious/national area of what is now the Soviet Union, and were organized by the community itself, at the present time they no longer occupy such a central part in the annual cycle of the more urbanized and less community oriented Soviet population. Also their organization is no longer carried by the participants themselves.

Those holidays, in which the religious motive is still central, like the Orthodox Easter or Whitsun, are, of course, not a part of the system of officially promoted holidays. On the contrary, their celebration is frowned upon by the political authorities, and efforts have been made to weaken their impact by counterposing them to new socialist holidays. Efforts to oust the major Christian holidays were first made in the early twenties when the Young Communists (*Komsomol*) celebrated a rival "Komsomol Christmas" or "Komsomol Easter" with colourful and boisterous carnival-type parades, aimed at blaspheming God and trying to ridicule religious institutions and functionaries. These celebrations were considered offensive by many Communists as well as by believers, and orders to stop them were received from the Party (Brudnyi 1968: 71ff). There was no replacement for many years, and the main religious holidays have continued to enjoy widespread popularity. In most areas of the Soviet Union a large minority or even a majority of the population still celebrate them in various ways (for details, see Lane 1978: 63).

From the sixties onwards, the continued popularity of these Chris-

130

tian holidays, particularly in the countryside, has prompted new efforts to weaken their influence. These include the introduction, in some areas, of new socialist holidays to replace the religious ones. A Holiday of Spring has been introduced to compete against the Russian Orthodox Easter (often the Orthodox Easter coincides with May Day). New holidays of summer, such as a Holiday of Song in some parts of the Ukraine (Kampars and Zakovich 1967: 210) or a Holiday of the Birch in many Russian areas, are intended to replace the Christian Whitsun. There are differences of opinion between ritual specialists as to what tactics to adopt in relation to these new holidays. Some advocate putting the new "secular" holiday on exactly the same date as the religious one. Others fear that such a choice might inadvertently strengthen the religious holiday. They either urge extensive educational work to accompany the introduction of an alternative holiday to prevent misunderstandings (Sukhanov 1976: 8), or they prefer to celebrate the new socialist holiday on a separate date in the same season (Kampars and Zakovich 1967: 217ff). Yet another tactic in weakening the Christian holidays has been to detach the associated folk ritual and custom and to attach them to a newly created Soviet holiday. An example of this practice in Estonia is the transfer of the custom of colouring eggs at Eastertime to a new spring holiday called "Day of Birds" (Mytskyula 1968: 52). Another example is the transposition of the popular ritual of Christmas to the New Year holiday, which will be described in detail below.

Other holidays, although of religious origin, are now celebrated only as traditional folk holidays and are officially encouraged or even sponsored. Notable in this group are the all-Soviet New Year celebrations, the Russian "Seeing-off of Winter", formerly the Orthodox *Maslenitsa* or Shrovetide, the Islamic *Novruz* and *Lola* (a tulip festival), and such summer solstices as the Latvian *Ligo*, the Ukrainian Ivan Kupala and the Russian Holiday of the Birch. They have been adapted to Soviet sensibilites by extirpating or neutralizing their magical elements as well as interspersing them with contemporary Soviet ritual and custom. It is noteworthy that holidays of pagan origin are considered more amenable to redefinition and, therefore, more acceptable for inclusion in the Soviet ritual–festive complex than those with Christian or Islamic content.

Most of the holidays in this group had been proscribed during Stalin's time and had fallen almost into oblivion until, during the sixties, they were resurrected in the general drive to merge new ritual

content with old and familiar ritual forms and symbols. Once redis-
covered, many people began to value them as a rich depository of folk
culture of a regional or national population rather than just as a means
to an end. While there is some evidence that these resurrected seasonal
holidays and their ritual have gained a certain amount of popularity,
particularly in new industrial towns (Rudnev 1967: 19), other evidence
throws doubt on the notion of a general successful resurrection. It is
also not at all clear whether efforts to inject them with new Soviet
meaning have been successful, or whether they have merely remained
occasions to mark the change in the seasons in a colourful, enjoyable
and culturally distinctive way.

SEEING-OFF OF WINTER OR ''MASLENITSA''

The revival of *Maslenitsa* or Shrovetide in recent decades is an example
of a deliberate elimination of the relatively short Christian interval in
the history of a holiday. *Maslenitsa* started as a pagan holiday in ancient
Rus. Its ritual tried to influence the coming of spring, and it was notable
for its cult of the sun (hence the *blinis*, a kind of pancake, as the
traditional food of this holiday). In Christianized Russia, the Church
tried to control this holiday by absorbing it into its holy calendar.
Maslenitsa became celebrated in anticipation of the ascetic life during
the Orthodox Great Fast. Shrovetide never became thoroughly Christianized and has always been distinguished by its focus on pagan ritual
as well as on physical pleasure and popular entertainment. To free it
completely from its Christian associations, attempts have been made
to change its name to "Seeing-off of Winter" (*Provody Zimy*), albeit
with limited success (Kampars and Zakovich 1967: 115). The extensive
colourful ritual and folkways have been adapted to the present ideological requirements by purging them completely of any remaining
pagan magic, as well as by inserting a socialist reference into some of
the traditional ritual actions.

In pre-revolutionary Russia the pagan associations had already been
lost to a large extent, and *Maslenitsa* had become a popular communal,
jolly celebration dedicated to the seeing-off of winter (*Nashi prazdniki*
1977: 152). It was celebrated in various ways in the different regions of
Russia and contained some or all of the following elements: a ritual
dramatization of the meeting of Winter and Spring and their help-
mates; a carnival parade on sleighs of the main characters of this
dramatic encounter, such as Grandfather Frost, Snow Maiden, Little

Mother Winter, Fair Spring; mummers as well as effigies of the spirits people wanted to exorcise; a big bonfire on which the straw effigies were burnt; and the taking of a snow fortress. Allied to these were songs by Slavic bards, performances by buffoons, winter games, sledge and troika rides, special food (particularly *blinis*) and the general atmosphere of a funfair.

At the present time, most of the traditional elements have been retained. According to the description of the troikas in the carnival procession today, it does not differ much in appearance from that of old times: "The manes of the horses and their harness are decorated, under the shaft bows are little bells. The coachmen are dressed in sheepskin coats, belted with coloured sashes. On every troika is an accordionist surrounded by fairytale characters" (*Massovye prazdniki* . . . 1961: 213). One of the changes in the substance of the holiday has been the replacement of the bad spirits with negative social types of the present time, such as drunkards, hooligans, bureaucrats; or allegorical depictions of such negative events as war. (In Leningrad during one holiday, for example, the Cold War was represented by a Snowman.) A socialist element has been inserted into the holiday by turning the Meeting of Winter and Spring "into a review of readiness (for new labour) of farms and enterprises, . . . into a handing over of the relay staff of labour" (Kampars and Zakovich 1967: 133ff), or, in some areas, of the "torch of peace" (Nagirnyak *et al.* 1970: 99). On this occasion production reports are made, good workers are honoured and the fairytale characters may be seen to interact with the leading members of collective farms. Sometimes the floats in the carnival procession are not only on traditional themes but may also be on distinctly Soviet ones, such as a juxtaposition of pre- and post-revolutionary technology (Brudnyi 1968: 88). The troika and sledge rides, in many areas, are reserved for the village's "best people", that is for the shock workers and veterans of labour. These political elements are present in varying degrees in different areas, and in many places they are kept so unobtrusive that the popular focus of the holiday is not affected (see *Massouye prazdniki* . . . 1961: 212ff). Another contemporary element is the prominence of competitions in the various modern winter sports.

But the biggest change has occurred in the general spirit of the holiday. While it was once a holiday organized by the small community for itself, it is now being celebrated in big towns as well as in villages, and impersonal organizations rather than the community itself stage the holiday. In the large towns it is held in one of the big Parks of Culture and Rest or in a stadium. The bulk of the organization, unlike on other mass holidays, is being carried by Houses of Culture and Houses of Popular Creativity. Consequently this traditional folk holiday, although colourful and offering plenty of entertainment, has not been easily reaccepted, has not got a fixed date and is not being celebrated universally in the Russian areas. Nor does it attract widespread participation in those big towns where it is staged regularly. The recommendation by Nagirnyak *et al.* (1970: 94) to advertise the holiday extensively with enticing preludes by the main characters supports this impression and shows that it is no longer a genuine popular holiday. The question of whether such a traditional popular holiday can effectively reassume this status in the conditions of the large industrial town is, surprisingly, never raised in the Soviet literature.

HOLIDAY OF THE BIRCH

Ritual centring on the birch tree was already popular among the ancient Slavs who, on their holiday *Semik*, associated the birch with fertility. They tried to influence the spirits of fertility and of their forefathers to help them achieve a good harvest by such means as decorating birch trees, tying together their tops, cutting young birch trees and sinking them in the river and giving sacrifices (*Nashi prazdniki* 1977: 155). The Orthodox Church, it is claimed (*ibid.*), tried to oust these rituals by putting Whitsun in their place.

During the first half of the sixties a new version of this holiday, utilizing the central position of the birch tree in Russian national symbolism, was being instituted in many places to oust Whitsun and to celebrate the beginning of the summer. The above pagan connections are, of course, discounted in the new holiday scenario, and the birch is now regarded as a symbol of the flowering of nature and is utilized to evoke a lyrical and patriotic mood (Brudnyi 1968: 97ff). There are conflicting reports on the degree of success of this new holiday (*ibid.*). Some authors (*ibid.*; *Nashi prazdniki* 1977: 156) state that this new holiday has not yet developed a clear scenario and its own ritual forms and, although attracting some support, has been unsuccessful in ousting the Christian holiday of Whitsun. Nagirnyak *et al.* (1970: 101ff), in contrast, suggest that the Holiday of the Birch has won great popularity and even love with the people, and they ascribe to the holiday a much more definite, though somewhat diffuse, character than do the other sources. For them it is:

a holiday of a green friend – it inculcates a relation of love towards the timber resources of the native country. It is a holiday of youth, merriment, of the beauty of character of Soviet man who is full of love of life, of optimism, and to whom is given the great happiness to build a new society. (*ibid*.: 101)

It is thus a wide-ranging holiday with three different foci: it is dedicated to the conservation of nature, to the glory of labour and to that of Soviet man, the builder of communism. Its ritual actions and attributes, although specific and original in their focus on the birch tree, appear to be imitative of other Soviet holidays and their ritual. For example, the procession with its chief characters of Birch, Granddad Heat and little Grandson Rain seems to be a straight copy of that central to *Maslenitsa*.

If the holiday has acquired some popularity it is no doubt due to the popularity of its central symbol – the birch tree, and its connection with poetry, nature and patriotism, as well as to the related emphasis on the conservation of nature, a concern becoming increasingly more important to the Soviet intelligentsia.

''LIGO'' AND IVAN KUPALA

The Latvian *Ligo* or Yanov Day and the Ukrainian and Belorussian Holiday of Ivan Kupala are both ancient celebrations of the summer solstice, sharing many elements in common. Both have traditionally been devoted to an extremely rich pagan magic, designed to both protect and bring about health and general well-being. The media of fire, water and plant life have traditionally played central parts in it (Drazheva 1973: 109).

Today *Ligo* is still one of the major Latvian holidays and is celebrated fairly universally there. It is a genuinely popular holiday with several days' preparation preceding it in every family (*Nashi prazdniki* 1977: 157ff). Although the rituals have lost their magic quality, many of the very romantic ritual forms have been faithfully preserved. Everywhere there are huge bonfires, lit-up oil barrels on the hills and on the banks of rivers, lakes and the shores of the Baltic; singing and dancing by the bonfires; many oak wreaths and flowers; and generous regaling of all visitors with home-brewed beer and specially prepared ''Yanov'' cheese (*ibid*.: 158). Today *Ligo* is seen as a holiday which ''poeticises summer when it comes into its full strength and nature achieves the peak of it flowering and splendour" (*ibid.*: 159), but its popularity must also be due to the fact that it enables the Latvians to assert their own tradition against the general Soviet one.

Inevitably attempts have been made to attach to this holiday some Soviet socialist elements of ritual, to turn it into a holiday of labour and of collectivism. These attempts have obviously not met with much success. At the very most they have had the result of adding a public organized side to a holiday which, in the past, had been very much a spontaneously evolving local community affair.

The Holiday of Ivan Kupala in the Ukraine, unlike *Ligo*, had almost fallen into oblivion (*ibid.*: 158) and was only revived during the sixties in the general drive to fill traditional ritual forms with new Soviet socialist content. Consequently many old traditions have been lost, and at the present time it is not celebrated as enthusiastically and as universally as the Latvian *Ligo*. Some clumsy attempts to introduce into this romantic and poetic holiday elements of Soviet labour ritual (see chapter 12) have done nothing to further its re-establishment.

"NOVRUZ" OR HOLIDAY OF SPRING

A similar example from the Islamic tradition has been the revival of an ancient holiday which combined pagan, Islamic and national elements – the Central Asian *Novruz* or *Nauruz*. Traditionally this holiday has been celebrated all over Central Asia to mark the beginning of the Islamic New Year and of spring. Dating from pre-Islamic times it was eventually absorbed by the Muslim religion and merged with the religious practice of worshipping Islamic saints (*Nashi prazdniki* 1977: 160). It had been proscribed as a public holiday during the Stalin era and had almost fallen into oblivion. In 1967, the year of the fiftieth Anniversary of the Revolution, the Party Committee of Azerbaid-zhan's capital Baku decided to resurrect the ancient holiday as part of the jubilee celebrations. The Party wanted to make this revived holiday as authentic and colourful as possible and drew in as advisers and designers of the new scenario ethnologists, creative artists and dramatists. Similar developments have taken place in Uzbekistan and Tadzhikistan. One of the basic ideas of the holiday, the celebration of the arrival of spring, has been retained, as well as many of the ritual forms, such as lighting fires and carrying spring green. The idea that the holiday marks the beginning of a new Islamic year seems to have been quietly dropped. The name *Nauruz* has been changed to Holiday of Spring to prevent the encouragement of religious associations. The main measure to Sovietize this holiday has consisted in turning it from a private family- and *meheta*-based holiday into an occasion for the collective, celebrated in public places (based on Eberpi 1969: 72ff).

THE NEW YEAR CELEBRATIONS

The all-Soviet New Year holiday today occupies a prominent and secure place among the revived, traditional folk holidays with a sometime religious element. The New Year celebrations combine the pagan elements, formerly associated with the Christian Christmas, and the Slavic folk ritual of revelling (*shchedrovanie*, derived from *shchedrost'* – generosity, or, in some areas, *kolyadovanie*, presumed to be derived from the Latin *kalenda*, first day of the month) with the general jollities of private celebrations with family and friends to greet the incoming new year. The celebrations also include the inevitable doses of political propaganda.

Whereas in ancient *Rus* there were only pagan New Year celebrations (performed in March and merged with *Maslenitsa*), in Christianized Russia the New Year and Christmas festivities became merged by the Church into a period of celebration called "Holy Days". In 1918 the militantly atheist regime no longer recognized Christmas as a public holiday, and the general deprivation and chaos made the traditional New Year celebrations seem inappropriate. The Soviet people in one stroke had lost two major occasions of general rejoicing. This was soon realized with regret by some of the political leaders. In 1918 Lenin himself introduced a Soviet New Year holiday and transferred to it the rituals of lighting a "Christmas" tree (*elka*) and giving children presents. The reintroduction of the traditional figures of Grandfather Frost, symbolizing kindness and generosity and of Snow Maiden (*Snegurochka*) standing for joy and gaiety, further enhanced the child appeal of this ritual. Lenin personally took part in several such New Year celebrations, despite much criticism against this revival inspired by the Proletkul't movement (*Nashi prazdniki* 1977: 149). At first these celebrations were public and were staged by various collectives. But gradually they also became private, and today they are a firmly established part of Soviet family life. The New Year is celebrated in the home in much the same way as Christmas is in an English family without

137

New Year's party with Grandfather Frost

strong Christian commitments, even including the card-sending ritual.

The public aspect of the New Year holiday is to review "what has already been done in the name of communism and what is still to come" (Nagirnyak *et al.* 1970: 76). The three top political organs – the Central Committee of the CPSU, the Presidium of the Supreme Soviet and the Soviet of Ministers of the USSR – address the Soviet people on the radio and on television at twelve o'clock midnight with greetings, give a progress report about the past year and announce plans for the following year. In conclusion, they wish the Soviet people success in their work, and happiness in their personal life. Similar addresses to their employees are made by the management of every enterprise and collective farm.

The original New Year's Eve ritual of revelling was revived only during the sixties, when the general preoccupation with new ritual also led to a renewed interest in traditional folk ritual. Up to then, revelling had been proscribed by the authorities on the grounds that it was a type of charitable activity and that there were no needy groups in Soviet society requiring such charity. The New Year ritual of revelling is as yet performed only in some areas, being particularly well established in the Ukraine, Belorussia and in the Kuban area of the RSFSR (Kikilo 1969: 137). It has been adapted to the demands of the socialist present and, although having undergone significant changes in both content and form, it has not lost its basic character.

In pre-revolutionary times revelling consisted of neighbourhood groups of dressed-up children or young people going from door to door, blessing the household, singing traditional songs and performing funny sketches suited to the occasion. In return they received small edible gifts. If no gifts were forthcoming, blessing would turn into jocular abuse. At the present time, similar groups perform before deserving collectives, such as the residents of orphanages, hospitals, large blocks of flats or those who work the night shift in an enterprise. They may also visit selected individuals, such as outstanding production workers or honorary citizens. Rather than being spontaneously constituted neighbourhood groups, the revellers (*shchedrivki* or *kolyadki*) are now chiefly members of amateur art circles, mobilized by Houses of Culture or Workers' Clubs. In rural areas these groups often drive through the village in colourful procession. Everywhere they wear traditional costumes, such as that of a bear, hare, goat, fox or of Grandfather Frost, or they may be dressed in drag. They wish those they visit a good new year, good health and success in their labour. Gifts are no longer received by the revellers themselves. They are demanded from the chairman of a collective farm on behalf of the whole collective, and pleas have been reported to be for a palace of culture or the provision of gas for the village (*Nashi prazdniki* 1977: 152). More often, gifts are presented to members of deserving collectives or to individuals who have excelled in their labour. In the Kuban, for example, it is customary to decorate outstanding farm workers with laurel or fir wreaths, decorated with a red ribbon (Kikilo 1969: 137). Songs, sketches and dances are mainly traditional popular ones, but some new Soviet ones have been created (Kampars and Zakovich 1967: 153ff; Kikilo 1969: 137; Nagirnyak *et al.* 1970: 82). Some of those quoted by Kikilo successfully combine the lighthearted jocular spirit of the occasion with political elements. In rural areas the evening may be concluded with a general meeting around the New Year's tree (*elka*), where the Old Year gives the New Year the relay staff of good works (*dela*) with the wish to see them increased (Kikilo 1969: 139).

9

vʊvʊvʊvʊvʊvʊvʊvʊvʊvʊvʊvʊvʊvʊvʊvʊvʊvʊvʊvʊvʊvʊvʊvʊvʊvʊvʊvʊvʊvʊvʊvʊvʊvʊvʊvʊvʊvʊvʊvʊ

Ritual of the military–patriotic tradition

The notion of patriotism became very suspect after the Revolution, which was dedicated to internationalism, and disappeared from official ideology until the beginning of the thirties. When the Revolution failed to extend beyond the borders of the Soviet Union and Stalin saw himself compelled to build "socialism in one country", the notion of patriotism began again to serve a useful political purpose. Since then it has gradually increased in importance as a component of the official ideology but gained its biggest impetus during and after the Second World War. Although the patriotic tradition is thus the youngest of the three "holy" traditions it is without doubt the most influential, being, in the words of Smith (1976: 371), "the most unifying force in Soviet society, the most vital element in the amalgam of loyalties that cements Soviet society".

Soviet patriotism contains many diverse strands. The first is the deep, and almost proverbial, love of Russians for their *Rodina* or Motherland which long antedates the Soviet patriotic tradition. Smith describes it as follows:

Rodina to Russians has the ring of "My Country 'Tis of Thee" – that singing devotion to country, unreasoning, unquestioning, unstinting, the way a mother loves her smallest child and the child blindly returns that love, a constancy and homage that makes the individual forget all the petty nuisances, harassments, inefficiences and entanglements of daily life, and proclaim his loyalty, take pride in it, merge himself somehow with the nation and find there comfort, confidence and a sense of community that nowadays eludes Americans and many other Westerners. (*ibid.*: 373)

The devastation of land and life by the Germans during the Second World War mortally offended these feelings of love and pride and, in the process, not only further deepened this patriotism but also widened it in significant directions. It was no longer just the patriotic feeling of ethnic Russians for Mother Russia but a devotion to the

140

Soviet Motherland of citizens of all nationalities. Whereas before it had entailed loyalty only to a geographic–cultural unit, it now became translated into loyalty to the political unit and its social system, the Soviet socialist state. Pride in the various achievements of the Soviet Motherland – in the fields of economic development and science and technology as well as in its international political role – is consciously fostered and is focussed on the Soviet Union both as a country and as a political system.

The genuine deep feelings aroused by the Second World War have been utilized ever since by the Soviet propaganda machine to blurr distinctions between various kinds of loyalties. In the process patriotism has been transformed from a narrow into a wider kind, and an attempt has been made to create a sense of political community transcending all internal diversity. This transformation has, of course, not been perfect, and the danger that the old, divisive nationalistic patriotism will reassert itself, either among ethnic Russians or among one of the smaller nationality groups, is constantly lurking in the background. It is to ensure that distinctions remain blurred and that this danger does not become acute that a host of patriotic holidays and ritual have been developed, all keeping alive the memory of the Second World War. This concentration on the war, according to Smith (*ibid.*: 386), has become even more pronounced in the last decade. It has acquired a fresh urgency now that there is a new generation coming to adulthood which has no personal memory of the war and consequently lacks the strong feeling about it which the parent generation still nourishes (Kampars and Zakovich 1967: 180–1).

NATIONALISM VERSUS SOCIALIST INTERNATIONALISM

This new all-inclusive patriotism, it is suggested in Soviet writing, is not based on an introverted narrow nationalism but on socialist internationalism. Internationalism in this context has not got the traditional socialist meaning of friendship and political support between the Soviet working class and those of other non-Soviet nations, but refers to the friendship between the different nationality groups making up Soviet society. This socialist internationalism, it is further claimed, can be combined with a nationalism focussing on the local national group. But the form such local nationalism is permitted to take is strictly circumscribed. It must remain an expressive cultural nationalism which eschews chauvinism and exclusivity and never comes into conflict with the notion of socialist internationalism. It is thus meant to be a nationalism which expresses Soviet socialist ideology in traditional local national form. It is obvious, however, that although such a clear distinction is possible in theory, in practice a national and a nationalistic orientation are very close, and the first is always liable to change into the second. Soviet political leaders are very aware of this danger and extremely worried about any nationalistic tendencies. When the system of new socialist rituals was created in the sixties the question of nationalism versus socialist internationalism was a very important issue in the general theoretical discussions. It was realized that, on the one hand, the new ritual could become a powerful tool in developing a socialist internationalism but that, on the other hand, it could be used to stimulate divisive nationalism among the constituent nationality groups.

An orientation of socialist internationalism has been fostered in two different ways by the new ritual. The first and as yet fairly marginal method has consisted of creating ritual specifically expressing the values of socialist internationalism and Soviet patriotism in areas where different nationality groups live in close proximity and thus can perform these rituals together. The second and by far the most important way in which the new ritual fosters socialist internationalism does not flow from any particular rite explicitly devoted to this value complex, but from the very existence of an all-Soviet, relatively uniform and homogeneous system of rituals. Such a system, being the same for all the nationality groups, attempts to create a unified Soviet culture in place of the many diverse religions which previously divided the various nationality groups and led to frictions or even to conflict. The new system of socialist rituals is thus an ideal instrument of nation-building. Besides uniting the various nationalities within the whole Union it can also become a factor of cohesion within republics which have a multi-national composition and where intermarriage between the various groups is common. There the existence of socialist life-cycle rites avoids the conflict-laden choice between the different religious rites for marriage partners from different nationality groups.

But ritual specialists soon realized that there is a limit to the degree of homogenization of the new system of rituals and that the traditional local holidays, ritual and symbolism of the various nationality groups cannot be totally ignored if the people are to accept the new ritual. Thus many concessions to local traditional culture have been made but such concessions, it must be stressed, have always been on the *form* and never on the *content* of ritual. The slogan of nationality politics in general, "socialist in content, national in form" was also applied to the field of socialist ritual. There still remains, however, the danger that the old forms cannot become wedded to the new content and that instead they continue to keep alive old associations of a national kind. These, in the long run, might strengthen national awareness, rather than evoke the intended socialist internationalism. Also, the creation of *new* music and poetry for the three main *rites de passage* has been made a local concern and may become a focus for the expression of national sentiment. This has already occurred to some extent in the Baltic republics, where the annual Holiday of Song has become an extremely popular occasion on which the population expresses its national identity through the medium of the folksong. Also in Estonia, the republic of the minority nationality group most opposed to Russianization (Aspaturian 1968: 174), the creative intelligentsia has become involved in developing the aesthetic side of the new ritual, whereas in the RSFSR, the republic of the national majority, no such co-operation has been secured.

In areas inhabited in close proximity by a great number of different nationality groups, such as the Caucasus, holidays and rites of international friendship have become a specific expression of the norms and values of socialist internationalism (Khachirov *et al.* 1973: 56ff). But generally, as I pointed out above, Socialist internationalism is seen as a component of Soviet patriotism and therefore receives expression mainly in ritual of the patriotic tradition, either implicitly or by symbolizing the international orientation in the common performance of a patriotic rite by representatives of several national groups.

VICTORY DAY

Whereas the Anniversary of October and May Day are the chief ritual manifestations of the revolutionary and the labour tradition respectively, Victory Day is the chief holiday dedicated to the affirmation of the patriotic–military tradition. Victory Day differs from the other two mass political holidays in two significant and related ways. The formal side of the holiday, the public rituals, are more decentralized and occur on a much more modest scale than do the other two and, in comparison, appear almost restrained. The informal activity, the visiting of the graves of the fallen by individual Soviet families, is strongly developed, and spontaneous expressions of deep feelings about the war are frequently encountered. These two features are conspicuously lacking in the other two mass holidays. The comparative modesty of the ritual of Victory Day and its much shorter historical existence mean that little descriptive material can be found in the literature on Soviet holidays and their ritual. Consequently my own description, based on these sources and on observation in Leningrad in 1978, will have to be short and without great historical depth.

Victory Day was first celebrated in 1945 when the Second World War or, as the Soviets call it, the Great Patriotic War, was won. After the announcement of victory people spontaneously started to celebrate, singing and dancing in the streets. There was also a "tremendous" victory parade in Red Square, bringing together a regiment each from every Soviet front as well as navy and air force units. Each regiment had its favourite march performed for it. The high point of this official celebration came when the two hundred captured Fascist banners, which had been brought to Lenin's mausoleum, were ceremoniously dashed down by veterans (*Massovye prazdniki* . . . 1961: 23). The Red Flag, hoisted onto the Reichstag building in Berlin, was brought back especially for the occasion.

Besides the all-Union Victory Day on 9 May there are also local Victory Days or Days of Liberation from the Fascists on other dates, celebrating the "crushing defeat" of the latter in a particular town or locality. These are celebrated in a similar way as the national holiday but may have some local specificity. The popular feeling and public ritual reach a pitch during jubilees.

A high point in the history of such local Victory Days, which are at the same time the concern of the whole nation, was given by the twenty-fifth anniversary of the decisive battle for Moscow. On that occasion an Unknown Soldier, a defender of Moscow, was given a hero's funeral in the place near the Kremlin wall, and the "fire of glory and immortality" was lit on his grave (*Nashi prazdniki* 1977: 28). This place is now widely known as "The Grave of the Unknown Soldier with the Eternal Flame". The state funeral, in which the whole nation participated via television, has been described as follows:

Quietly sounds the command. Soldiers of the escort stand stock-still with their rifles at the present-arms position. (There follows) a solemn and strict minute's silence for those fallen for Moscow. And into this mournful silence is inserted Chopin's Funeral March. An artillery gun carriage with the ashes of an Unknown Soldier, taken from the Brotherly Grave 41 km from Moscow, slowly moves to the place of its new burial. The funeral cortège moves slowly through

144

the main streets to the centre . . . Under the salvo of an artillery salute the coffin is lowered into the grave. (Blinova 1968: 356)

The large sheet of red polished granite put onto the grave bears the inscription:

> Your name is unknown,
> Your deed is immortal.
> To those fallen for the Motherland
> 1941–45.

The Eternal Flame lit over the grave has since become a national symbol, and its importance in the ritual system is indicated by the following words:

This is the fire of millions of hearts who have not faltered in battle; the fire of burning hatred towards the enemy and of boundless love towards the Motherland; the fire of faith in the great cause of Lenin which led our people to victory. (*Nashi prazdniki* 1977: 28)

Since 1945 Victory Day has been a national holiday and has been celebrated every year on 9 May in every town and village of the Soviet Union. In 1965 it became a public holiday. On the eve of the holiday every collective, in a small-scale internal ceremony, gathers around a place of remembrance and honours both its living war veterans (who come to the ceremony bedecked in their medals) and its fallen heroes, laying a wreath in their memory. On the day itself, in the early morning solemn public ceremonies are held in every town and many villages near the war memorials that can be found all over the Soviet Union. At the memorial place there is usually a guard of honour of three generations of Soviet people and/or of soldiers. These ceremonies consist of some or all of the following elements: short memorial speeches, stories about heroic deeds and solemn oaths to repeat them, music, declamation of verse, a minute's silence for the fallen and the laying of wreaths. In some areas it has become customary to begin the ceremony with a solemn roll-call from the Book of Eternal Glory of heroic individuals or collectives. Often Pioneers take part in it. Whenever a name is read out, a Pioneer steps forward, says, "He died the death of the brave", and places flowers at the bottom of the monument (El'chenko 1976a: 17). Many war memorials have been erected in areas where several republics border on each other, and here memorial ceremonies underline the values of socialist internationalism, of multi-national defence of these areas and of solidarity in war

Veterans' procession on Victory Day

and peace. One such memorial is placed on the Hill of Friendship, situated where the RSFSR, the Latvian SSR and the Belorussian SSR meet, and is reached by Avenues of Friendship from each republic (Kampars and Zakovich 1967: 47).

These ceremonies are all devoted to honouring the living and the dead war heroes and war victims in general. They are also designed to keep alive the memory of the war: of the suffering, the heroism, the community spirit and the eventual triumph of the Soviet people and of the social system that inspired them to, and sustained them in, their battle. Lastly, these ceremonies are directed towards developing a determination to prevent the repetition of such a holocaust by strengthening the vigilance and defence readiness of every Soviet citizen against the capitalist West.

In addition to such memorial ceremonies there may also take place a military parade, and/or a march of war veterans through a town's central streets. In the evening there are usually a festive artillery salute and fireworks in the Union's capital, in the republican capitals, the "hero" towns and in the Siberian and Far Eastern towns of Novosibirsk, Murmansk, Khabarovsk and Vladivostok. In many places popular entertainment on the theme of the war is being offered on that night.

Besides such publicly organized ceremonial occasions there also occur spontaneous private remembrances. The large majority of Soviet families – of which most have lost at least one member during the war – visit the war memorials and/or cemeteries to show their respect, to place flowers and, quite frequently, various kinds of food and children's toys. When I visited Leningrad's Piskarevska cemetery (where the thousands of victims of the blockade are buried in unnamed mass graves) on the bitterly cold Victory Day of 1978 I saw an endless stream of people entering its gates. The countless bunches of flowers (which are very expensive at this time of the year in this northern town) on the gravestones to the unknown dead showed that large crowds of people had visited earlier. On approaching the memorial at the far end of the cemetery, I saw a long queue of people patiently and silently filing past the many wreaths from one side of the war memorial to the other. The closing words of the poem inscribed on the memorial "Nothing and none shall be forgotten" seemed as true then as they were when the memorial was erected.

Remembrance ceremonies for fallen heroes are not conducted only on Victory Day but on many other days all through the year. Of these the following two are particularly distinctive in their choice of symbolism. In the Leningrad area a remembrance ceremony is performed annually on the Peter and Paul Fortress just outside Leningrad where, during the war, particularly fierce battles took place. Of the many wreaths that are brought some are thrown into the River Neva. As they float towards Leningrad and the Gulf of Finland they are greeted by the populations of all the settlements on the river banks, and the ships which pass them sound their hooters in salute (Rudnev 1974: 124). In Latvia the Remembrance Day is celebrated with a torchlight procession. Gerodnik (1970: 116) describes it like this:

Evening. By the flickering Eternal Flame on the Brotherly Grave a long column of torch bearers has formed. Young men and young girls in national dress, at the front – a stately, grey-haired man, the Elder . . .
Fanfares sound the signal, the spiritual orchestra plays the "Requiem". In the ensuing silence the Elder raises his torch high and, with a majestic gesture, lowers it and lights it from the Eternal Flame. A solemn pause: the Elder holds high his flickering torch, and then lights with his torch the torches of those standing in the first row of the column. These pass on the fire to the second row and so forth . . . The Elder again lifts up his torch. On this conventional sign three young men and three young girls leave the column and stand by the

Eternal Flame as sentries. Another such gesture – and a youth and girl leave the column and stand on either side of the Elder. He lightly draws a semi-circle with his torch and indicates the direction in which the column must go. The solemn procession towards the town centre begins.

War memorials are focal features of all towns and of many villages. Tremendous resources have been expended to make them impressive, and in some places they are show-pieces of modern architecture on a grand scale. A prime example here is "the majestic memorial complex" of Volgograd (formerly Stalingrad), including a burial mound, a museum, a pantheon and picture galleries, all designed on a large scale. War memorials are as frequent a sight in the Soviet landscape as shrines were in the Western European countries at the height of the Catholic Church's influence. Every year their number is again increased. In the Ukrainian republic alone there are 27,000 war memorials of various kinds (*Nashi prazdniki* 1977: 90). Not only are they places where solemn rituals of various kinds are conducted, and centres for national pilgrimage, but they are also shown off to foreign tourists with the same pride with which a Western European would show off a Gothic cathedral. The villages are not left out either. In many villages of Voronezh region, for example, collective farms have put up granite obelisks and marble boards bearing in golden letters all the names of the villages' fallen heroes (Teplyakov 1972: 93). Being a guard of honour on special days at these memorials is considered a distinction by the children selected for this task and an effective measure of patriotic education by those who select them. In addition to the grand memorial complexes and modest obelisks and stones, some of the battlefields themselves have been turned into places of remembrance, with every trench, commanding post and dug-out faithfully preserved.

While the solemn memorial ceremonies involve and touch mainly the older people who remember the war, another patriotic activity of a ritual nature, allied to Victory Day, has successfully involved young Soviet people. This is given by the All-Union Hiking Tours of Places of Military Glory by the so-called "Red Pathfinders". This organization first developed in 1965 and assumed a mass character during the year of the fiftieth Anniversary of the Revolution. It has since gone from strength to strength. More than thirty million young people are said to participate in the tours at the present time (*Nashi prazdniki* 1977: 114). They are organized jointly by the Komsomol, the Voluntary Society for Assisting the Armed Forces, the political departments of army units

and by activists of the Defence Society. Members of the latter organization work out the routes of these tours and organize the necessary
visits and meetings. On these hiking tours, Komsomols and young
people in general visit all the "places of military glory" in a given
geographic area. They collect memorial relics and documents and note
down eyewitness accounts of the military events. Sometimes they
reconstruct from these by painstaking research the course of the battle
and identify by name the hitherto unknown soldiers and partisans,
fallen in the battle or skirmish. They follow up their field visits by
creating small museums of military glory, erecting obelisks and memorial boards to those identified through their research, and they put into
order "Brotherly Graves". The success of these tours can be attributed
to the fact that the mixture of adventure and serious research are in the
foreground and disguise the ritual and didactic character of these
activities. Writers reporting on such tours testify to the strong educational effect they have on their young participants (e.g. Kikilo 1969:
53).

Additional ways to keep the memory of the war alive and to honour
fallen heroes are to enter their names into so-called "Books of Eternal
Glory" (Rudnev 1974: 124ff), a kind of socialist *Who's Who*, or to turn
their former work-place in an enterprise into a place of remembrance
and of special honour, to be occupied only by a Hero of Labour
(Kampars and Zakovich 1967: 86).

In addition to these rituals with a predominantly patriotic orientation there are related rituals which put more emphasis on the military
aspect of this tradition. There is a number of military holidays devoted
to the different sections of the Soviet armed forces. On these occasions
celebrations are designed to both honour them and to carry on propaganda on their behalf. Efforts are made to involve wide sections of the
civilian populations in the festivities and to demonstrate, through
ritual, that "the army and the people are one" (*Nashi prazdniki* 1977:
75ff). Of these holidays, the oldest and most popular holiday is the Day
of the Soviet Army and Navy, celebrated every year on 23 February.

Other military–patriotic rituals and ceremonies are performed
throughout the year. "Evenings of Military Glory" are occasions where
several generations of fighters impart their experience to the young
generation. Such evenings are organized jointly by the Komsomol, the
trade union organization, sections of the Knowledge Society (an atheist
organization), and committees of the Voluntary Society for Assisting
Army, Air Force and Navy, aided by military commissariats and

military units. Their aim is to inspire the young generation to be worthy successors of these heroes and to continue the heroic traditions of the Soviet people (*ibid.*: 111). These evenings are either conducted as solemn occasions, according to the pattern familiar from many other political rituals, or as "thematical" evenings. The latter are dedicated to the overtly instrumental activity of uncovering the details of one aspect of the heroic past by various kinds of documentation, such as eyewitness reports, film clips, lectures and relevant music. Some other military activities with a strong ritual component are specifically organized for the young. These are the All-Union competitions called "Summer Lightning" (*Zarnitsa*) and "Eaglet" (*Orlenok*) which both glorify the military tradition and serve as recruitment grounds for the armed forces. But military ritual, as has been shown throughout part II, is by no means confined to these military holidays. Some military ritual act, such as marching, parading, bearing the banners, changing guard, is part of nearly every rite, regardless of the tradition to which a ritual belongs.

LOCAL PATRIOTIC RITUAL

Local patriotism is not as ardently fostered as national patriotism, but local patriotic rituals are sometimes encouraged as stepping-stones to the development of a broader patriotism. They usually ally their local orientation to a celebration of the universally shared revolutionary, patriotic and labour traditions. They serve to enhance the latter by utilizing the greater emotional impact of locally significant symbols.

One such ceremony is the declaration of Honorary Citizens. In the Kazakh town of Syryanovsk, for example, such diverse "heroes" as a partisan of the Civil War who took part in the liberation of the local area, an esteemed Party worker, a hereditary miner with more than thirty years' service in one combine and the long-serving chief doctor of the town's maternity hospital were chosen as Honorary Citizens. During a solemn ceremony they were decorated with a ribbon in the colours of the Kazakh flag and received a diploma and an emblem of the town. The best Pioneer detachment brought in a Book of Honorary Citizens into which their names were entered. After several congratulatory speeches the ceremony was concluded with the rendering of both the Kazakh and the Soviet anthem (Novopistsev 1970: 48).

A totally different ritual is performed by celebrating what is called a "Holiday of the Street". According to Nagirnyak *et al.* (1970: 137), such holidays are now becoming widely established. They have no fixed date or ritual and express their local specificity in the choice of them, but they are all oriented towards developing national as well as local patriotism. The wider focus of this local community ritual is emphasized by one author: "Native street, native district, native town – it is thus that a young person entering life becomes conscious of his belonging to that large community, the name of which is the Soviet people" (Mel'nikova 1976: 106).

In Volgograd (formerly Stalingrad) this holiday was celebrated in the following way (the account is based on Mel'nikova 1976: 102ff). Inhabitants of blocks of flats forming two or three streets bring to life the history of their area. They investigate what the area looked like before the war, what war events took place there (Volgograd has a very eventful, tragic and heroic history), or what significant people lived in these streets. The holiday is preceded by many months of research, and the results of that work are revealed on the day in exhibitions, film shows and dramatic re-enactment, or the history of the area is told by surviving witnesses to earlier periods.

In another area of the country this holiday tries to involve both the local residential and the industrial community. Holiday activities, such as competitions to establish the best balcony or the cleanest yard, try to draw in that part of the Soviet population which is "unorganized" and thus difficult to mobilize politically – housewives and pensioners (Kikilo 1969: 142). Workers from the various local industries and representatives of three generations talk about their experiences, linking local efforts to national concerns. An attraction for both "organized" and "unorganized" people of the area is the illustrated talk by a local architect–planner, showing the development of the area during Soviet times and outlining future plans in this direction. It is designed to develop both civic pride and political loyalty. The holiday is concluded by a concert and various popular amusements.

In other Holidays of the Street, as described by Nagirnyak *et al.* (1970: 138ff), the development of local identity appears to be of only tenuous importance. It serves only as a pretext for a holiday devoted to the adulation of Lenin and, indirectly, to the propagation of some of the values of Soviet Marxism–Leninism. The two holidays described by the above authors are both centred on the small towns' Lenin Road and celebrate the memory of Lenin in a variety of ways.

Thus, to sum up this chapter, the ritual of the patriotic–military tradition differs from other ritual described in important ways. It is generally less developed, less standardized and more decentralized. In it are united officially devised ritual sequences and some evolved by the people themselves. Popular participation in the main holiday of this tradition, Victory Day, is both more widespread and more spontaneous than is usually the case. In its celebration, unlike in the other mass holidays, Geertz's "model of" appears to have for once equal weight with the "model for" aspect of ritual performance of a valued social relationship.

vwv

The mass political holidays of the revolutionary tradition: a historical review 1918–78

Mass political holidays and their ritual involve the whole of Soviet society and keep alive the memory of important transitions in its life. Like the rites of transition and incorporation described earlier, the ritual of these holidays also models by symbolic means exemplary relations between individuals and the collective and between leaders and led. Its foremost role is to both demonstrate and consolidate the unity and strength of the whole society and to inspire future effort towards perfecting the social system. The rites performed during these mass holidays do not just focus on present strength, but they are what Durkheim called "commemorative" rites which present the past to the present and justify and strengthen the one by reference to the other.

Although the scale and continuity of these holidays are unique in modern industrial society they are not unique in history. They were prominent in other historical societies which raised the *polis* to supreme importance, such as the ancient Greek city states and French society after its great Revolution. It is obvious that those involved in staging and perpetuating the Soviet mass political holidays were greatly influenced by these historical precursors, particularly by the ceremonial forms adopted by the French revolutionary rulers (Genkin 1975: 25ff). More immediate origins of the ritual and symbolism of the Soviet holidays lie in the international revolutionary movement of the late nineteenth and early twentieth century. Many of the central ritual forms of these holidays entered the life of the Russian working class already before 1917, particularly during the Revolution of 1905 (see Shiryaeva 1975). As regularly recurring holidays with a specific character, however, the mass political holidays became established only from 1917 onwards. As such they have become unique to the Soviet Union and its satellite states and have by now acquired a long and rich history. Although one of these holidays, May Day, is also celebrated in many Western societies, the Soviet version is quite distinct from its Western counterparts.

Soon after the Revolution, in February 1918, a new Red Calendar was introduced with the dual aim of ousting the holidays connected with the old regime and social order and of building a new Soviet culture. In the early post-revolutionary years there were a great number of annually recurring mass holidays, but from the late twenties onwards some of these were abandoned again. Among the latter were some relating to international socialist events (e.g. Anniversary of the Second International) or to internal events preceding Bolshevik supremacy (e.g. the anniversaries of Bloody Sunday (22 Jan) and of the February Revolution (12 March)). May Day and the Anniversary of the Great October Socialist Revolution became the main holidays. After Lenin's death in 1924, Lenin Day was added to these. This was first an occasion to mark the anniversary of his death but, after Stalin's death, was changed to celebrate the anniversary of his birth (22 April). Lenin's Birthday, differing in character from the other two holidays in the revolutionary tradition and being poorly documented, will be briefly referred to in chapter 11, dealing with the cult of Lenin. Stalin's birthday was only celebrated during Stalin's lifetime. Victory Day, already discussed in chapter 9, became the fourth major mass political holiday after 1945. In addition, there are a number of other recurring mass holidays (see the ritual calendar, appendix B). Some are well established in Soviet life, others have mainly an official character. Besides those already mentioned in a previous section, notable ones are International Women's Day on 8 March (Mother's Day in the family) and Day of the Constitution (since 1977 on 7 October). I shall not consider the latter in this book.

The two most important mass political holidays in the revolutionary tradition are well established in the ritual calendar and have by now a long and eventful history. They have greatly expanded in scale over the years, but have not basically changed their character. Timoshin (1966: 148), a Soviet writer on the subject of mass political holidays, outlines the following four basic roles which the revolutionary political holidays have performed over the years:

(a) to remind the working class of its victories and to honour, and render glory to, the heroes of revolutionary events (*b*) to create unity and solidarity among the workers for the further continuation of the cause of previous generations

(*c*) to demonstrate the successes and achievements of the new generation and to honour and glorify the heroes who have successfully taken up the cause of their forebears

(*d*) to express through definite actions, customs, and rituals the relations of the popular masses to the surrounding reality. Spelled out in more concrete terms, this involves "the demonstration of unity of purpose of the people, the Party and the State; it is a demonstration of love of the Motherland, the social system, and the ideas of communism". (*ibid.*: 154)

Despite continuity in the performance of these basic roles, over the sixty-odd years of Soviet history there have been many minor changes and shifts in emphasis expressed in differing ritual forms and content as well as in basic mood. A detailed historical examination of these changes can show how the ceremonial of a society reflects both the level of its material and cultural resources and the central concerns of its leaders in the economic, political and general social field, as well as being something of a barometer of the popular political mood. An assessment of the degree of mass involvement over the years can attempt to gauge the changing balance between spontaneous and directed participation by the masses and thus gain some idea of the nature of popular political opinion. In what follows I shall first outline the permanent and common features of the two oldest mass political holidays and then proceed to a historical review of their unique and changing characteristics during different periods, referring to the four basic roles as outlined above.

Mass political holidays of the Soviet type comprise festivities of a public and ritual kind and private celebrations, which consist of individualized entertainment and of feasting with relatives and friends in the family home. Surveys have shown that the overwhelming majority of people celebrate these mass political holidays privately in a similar way as people in Western Christian countries, who are without strong religious commitment, would celebrate Christmas (Kampars and Zakovich 1967: 45–6; Ivanov 1968: 154). These celebrations in the home have not acquired a ritual character. The only elements distinguishing them from other festive occasions are the singing by members of the older generation, in some families, of songs of the revolutionary period and the sending of cards to friends with revolutionary slogans and emblems (Ivanov, *ibid.*). The public side of the holidays consists of a complex of activities in which ritual is intermingled with dramatic and political activities and decorative–political art in such a close way that the boundaries between the various types of activity become fuzzy. In the following, therefore, this whole complex will be referred to by the short-hand term "ceremonial".

Genkin (1975: 6ff), a specialist deeply involved with the "staging" of mass holidays and their ceremonial, distinguishes between three basic forms of activity employed separately or together to express the role of these mass holidays. Among the oldest and most widely used form is:

(1) The festive procession or demonstration, in which march in unison a very large number of people as representatives of the multitude of social, political and work collectives which make up Soviet society. Each delegation represents by various means the central theme of the holiday as well as bringing out the distinctive contribution of its particular collective to the whole society. The means employed include dramatized scenes, sketches, symbolic objects, figures or settings, decorated panels, slogans, banners, emblems, flowers and greenery. Since May 1921 detachments of the various divisions of the Armed Forces have headed the demonstration, displaying the latest weapons and other equipment. Participants in the demonstration assemble at various points on the outskirts of the town and march via various key routes to the centre, converging at a large central square for the culminating events.

The most important demonstration takes place, of course, in Moscow. In Red Square the national political leaders stand on an elevated platform on Lenin's mausoleum, while various lesser political figures and foreign guests sit on lower tribunes erected on two sides of the square. The massed procession, headed by detachments from the Armed Forces, files through the square. The members of these detachments give a solemn oath of allegiance to the political leaders. The other delegations salute the leaders and are, in turn, greeted by them before all leave the square at the opposite end. People become involved in their own local demonstrations and later, through television, in the procession in the capital which brings together people and national leaders. The festive procession is considered an ideal means "to express the unity of the Soviet people around the Communist Party and the Soviet state" (*ibid.*: 6), as well as giving a maximum number of people an opportunity to become actively involved in expressing their personal relation to the solemn events in Soviet society (*ibid.*).

(2) The dramatized meeting, mass dramatic presentation or mass spectacle is also a traditional basic form used in conjunction with, or

separately from, the procession–demonstration. This form evolved out of the political meeting (indoors) or demonstration (outdoors) of the pre-revolutionary and early post-revolutionary years. It replaced the rather prosaic and dull spoken words of political propaganda speeches with the more vivid and rousing use of dramatic speech, supplemented by movement, music and poetry. In more recent times greater variety has been introduced through two variants of this form, namely a "dramatized concert" and a *Son et lumière* spectacle, where the dramatic situation is expressed through the media of music and sound and light respectively. These three forms of conveying a given message differ from traditional theatre or opera in that they do not develop a plot but string together a number of loosely connected episodes. They fuse them by employing the medium of the massed choir. This links the episodes and drives the action forward, as well as forging a link between the actors and the spectators. The episodes presented are based on topical political scenes or on scenes from Soviet history close to the Soviet people. Identification is achieved by presenting the big national events in their local manifestations, evoking memories, associations and feelings of local patriotism. The emphasis is on vivid immediate effect rather than subtle development of a theme, and images and symbols are chosen accordingly. All the three forms outlined combine the documentary with the artistic approach and are the dramatic equivalent of a cross between a poster and a collage. They are therefore flexible, lending themselves to infinite variety. The mass holidays and their ceremonial have thus given rise to a new genre of popular art, part theatre, part ritual. Each such dramatic presentation has its own scriptwriter and producer who are usually artists of national standing.

The staging of these events is regarded as an opportunity to bring art out of its ivory tower and into the streets and has contributed to the fusion between theatre and ritual. These mass spectacles have usually been performed in a town's largest square, in a scenic place or, later, in Parks of Culture. There is no traditional stage or curtain, and the action is continuous. Performances are given to very large audiences, in some cases of up to 10,000 people. The number of actors is also on a mass scale, having been as high as 6000 in some productions. In this way wide popular involvement is achieved, and occasionally, particularly in the early years, the boundaries between actors and audience have become very blurred.

While the producers and directors have usually been professional artists the actors have mainly been amateurs. The great majority of the actors have formed a "massed choir" of workers, soldiers and revolutionaries, acting and singing or talking in their own working-clothes without any theatrical apparel. In addition, there has been a small group of costumed actors, wearing the masks of enemies of the people and appearing as theatrical symbolic or buffoon-type figures in opposition to the mass of the people's choir. While the former are meant to attract derision, the latter should incite audience identification or even active participation (see Piotrovskii 1926: 59–61).

(3) Another important component of the mass political holidays are the works of representative art of various kinds and, in later years, the more decorative art adorning important public places and buildings, complementing and enhancing the political messages of the ceremonial activities. These have usually been executed by professional artists who, in the early post-revolutionary years, were stimulated to inventiveness and high levels of creativity.

The ritual of the holiday proper is usually preceded by a host of minor rituals which both enhance, and are enhanced by, the central events of the holiday. These satellite rituals may be the recurring rituals of initiation into social and political collectives, such as the Young Pioneers, or they may be such singular important events as the opening or naming of a new factory, school, club or hospital. These, it must be remembered, were great achievements in the early decades of Soviet power. Another type of achievement or sacrifice to be celebrated ceremoniously on the eve of a mass holiday has been the completion by workers, with either their own (collected) money or in their own time, of new tanks, aeroplanes etc. (Tsekhnovitser 1931: 93).

Besides the ceremonial designed to demonstrate and reaffirm the loyalty of the people to State and Party and the unity between them there are also separate ceremonies that precede the Anniversary of the Revolution to express and strengthen the unity of purpose between the political elites. Thus a few days before the Anniversary proper a joint Festive Session of the national political elites takes place – of the Central Committee of the CPSU, the Supreme Soviet of the USSR and of the Supreme Soviet of the RSFSR – at which past political successes and future concerns are outlined in a keynote speech by the political leaders of the country. This is communicated to the entire population in the newspaper *Pravda* on the following day. Similar Festive Sessions of the local elites of Party and soviet take place. The choice of principal and supporting speakers on such occasions usually indicates the *de facto* political status hierarchy. Unlike the events for the general population on the holiday proper, these Festive Sessions are devoid of elaborate ceremonial and utilize mainly verbal means to indicate that they have a ritual as well as an instrumental political purpose.

Similar Festive Sessions take place in all social and political collectives on the days preceding the major holidays. Particular emphasis is given to preparations for the holidays proper in the work of schools. Several weeks before the major holidays a good deal of school work becomes related to the holiday and to the ideas of which it is an expression. Special stories, songs and art work for the procession, or the festive decoration of the school, focus the children's attention on the significance of the holidays.

While all these different aspects of the mass holidays have been developed most extensively and strikingly in the two capitals (Leningrad remained a ceremonial capital long after it ceased to be a political one), they were also duplicated in other Soviet towns, though on a more modest level. Some of the towns, particularly those with a revolutionary tradition before 1917, have enacted very impressive ritual–dramatic presentations during the first post-revolutionary decade. Although the pattern of the holidays is basically the same all over the Soviet Union, some towns attempt to give it a special local colour. Thus a naval port like Sevastopol, for example, will include in its holiday events armed salutes, naval parades, illumination of warships etc. (Fursin 1973: 59). The mass holidays and their ceremonial have remained largely an urban phenomenon, and rural inhabitants often make these holidays an occasion to visit their urban relations and to watch some of the spectacles.

The scale of these mass holidays has increased from year to year. While at the beginning there were the procession, the mass meeting and the revolutionary funeral, in the following years all kinds of spectacles and ceremonies (e.g. erection of monuments, opening of new factories) became included in the ceremonial. This variety decreased again after 1928, and the increase in scale then became expressed in the steadily rising number of people who participated actively or passively in the events.

Although the ceremonial of the mass political holiday had been organized from the beginning, like a military operation, in a strict and centralized way, organizers in the early years left also plenty of scope to individual and group spontaneity and creativity. Over the years the

increasing concentration of organization and design in a few specialized hands gradually eliminated spontaneity and creativity of the small
collectives, let alone that of individuals.

The mass political holidays each started out with a distinct focus of
their own. Over the years May Day and the Anniversary of the Great
October Socialist Revolution have become very similar in content and
form and are, with a few exceptions, almost indistinguishable at the
present time. The first Anniversary of the October Revolution was
celebrated in 1918 and was meant to commemorate a *national* revolutionary triumph of the proletariat as well as to remember those who
died in the struggle for it. May Day, in contrast, originated outside the
Soviet Union as an *international* holiday, "a day of militant review of
the strength of the workers of all countries" (Genkin 1975: 33). This
holiday had been instituted in 1889 at the Paris Congress of the Second
International with the aim of uniting the international proletariat, and
it quickly became established all over Europe. It was keenly accepted
by the Russian Social Democrats before the Revolution, where it
served as a rallying means for the repressed workers' movement and
became the scene for militant confrontations with the autocracy. After
the Revolution, when capitalism had been abolished, the original
foundations for May Day protest were removed. The first few May Day
celebrations after the Revolution were, like the Anniversaries of the
Revolution, devoted to rejoicing in the victory of the proletariat as well
as being focussed on the necessity to strive for the development of
socialism. In addition, though, the first few May Days, particularly in
1919, still focussed on the international significance of May Day and
expressed their hope for revolution in Western Europe. Very soon
though this international orientation and focus on the working class as
the revolutionary agent receded. Thus the first two roles of the holidays, as outlined by Timoshin, receded in importance, and the last two
received greater emphasis. Both May Day and the Anniversary of the
Revolution alike came to concentrate on the task of building a new
society, on reviewing past successes and encouraging future endeavour. In recent decades, the holidays have also become important
as the means of reminding the young generation that their society is
not "just given" but is founded on revolutionary struggle by people
with "revolutionary passion, deep communist conviction, devotion to
the great cause of the Party" and to revive that generation's "fiery
romanticism and hatred towards enemies of revolution" (*Nashi
prazdniki* 1977: 14).

This communality of general purpose and particular short-term goals, expressed in common forms, would make a separate historical review of each holiday rather repetitive. Consequently, they will be reviewed together in the following pages. There is, however, one difference between the two which needs to be brought out now. This contrast is manifest in a difference in mood among participants, conditioned by the differing seasons in which the two holidays fall. Whereas the May Day procession shows people in their light and bright spring clothing, carrying greenery and multi-coloured decorations, the October celebrations see them in dark clothing, and displays and decorations are dominated by the colour red. All this makes the October celebrations stern and sombre and May Day comparatively light and gay. Over the years, the latter has become as much a holiday of spring as a political holiday (Rudnev 1974: 111).

Having explored the relatively constant forms of the two most important mass holidays I will examine their unique nature during different periods of Soviet history between 1918–78 and relate them to changes in the general society. To highlight the fact that the various roles of these holidays were given varying emphasis during different periods, from time to time I shall refer back to the four basic roles assigned to them by Timoshin (see p. 154).

1918–1922

The first few ceremonial celebrations of revolutionary victory were planned by a Central Bureau under the Executive Committee of the then Petrograd soviet with the assistance, on artistic matters, of the department of fine arts under the People Commissariat for Education and Culture. But they evolved with a large degree of spontaneity out of the widespread enthusiasm generated by the revolutionary events. Workers, soldiers and intellectuals all made their own distinctive contribution. The participation of the workers during the first two years took the forms they were used to from their previous political activities – demonstrations and mass meetings. In addition there were the occasional revolutionary funeral and the ceremonial unveiling of monuments to revolutionary heroes. The holidays in those early years were celebrated on a grander scale in Petrograd (after 1924 Leningrad) than in Moscow. They were more decentralized, with a large variety of events being spread over three days and taking place in different parts of the town. The political demonstration in Petrograd in November

161

1918, unlike in later years, has as its central points two places intimately connected with the Revolution – the Smolny Institute and the Mars Field. The culminating event at the Smolny was the unveiling of a monument to Marx. At the conclusion of the demonstration the columns filed past the monument and placed at its foot ribbons with proletarian slogans (*Agitatsionno-massovoe iskusstvo* . . . 1971: 43). In Moscow, in November 1918, the culminating events were the opening ceremony for a monument to Marx and Engels, attended by Lenin, and the unveiling of a plaque in memory of the fallen heroes of the Revolution in Red Square (Rudnev 1979). Otherwise the procession–demonstration was relatively modest and colourless. It was enlivened only by the various revolutionary banners and by the singing of revolutionary songs. These latter were by then traditional songs which had been created for, or had been adopted by, the Russian revolutionary movement of the 1890s, such as "Boldly, Comrades, in Step", The *Varshavyanka*, and The International.

In May 1919 the demonstrating marchers in Leningrad enlivened the ceremonial a little by introducing the following symbolic action: the leaders of the columns, passing through the field of Victims of the Revolution, struck a specially erected anvil to denote a symbolic oath (Piotrovskii 1926: 56). Another symbolic gesture to liven up the demonstration was the showering of marchers, from an aeroplane, with Red Stars, the emblem of the Red Army. The slogans of these years were taken from The International and from communist classics, particularly from the Communist Manifesto. The necessity to secure the initial revolutionary victory gave the demonstrations a stern military character all through the period of War Communism (Brudnyi 1968: 64). But besides the military mood there was, from the first year onwards, an awareness of the necessity to build up a strong economy. A basic theme of the demonstration was therefore the parading of economic achievement in order to boost confidence in the capabilities of the new system.

In 1920, when the first wave of revolutionary enthusiasm had been dampened by the gravity of the internal military and economic situation, the ceremonial core of the mass holidays – the workers' demonstration – became temporarily replaced by a ritual activity with a strong instrumental component to it. May Day in 1920 became a general holiday of labour, a so-called *Subbotnik* (Saturday), on which people gave their labour free during their normal hours of rest. The revolutionary enthusiasm of workers and of some sections of the intelligentsia was harnessed towards efforts to bring the disrupted economy back to normal. To the constant sound of revolutionary music and the reading of revolutionary poetry working parties performed such tasks as breaking down the fence around the Tsar's Winter Palace, cleaning canals, covering dams with earth and loading railway carriages. The work accomplished was very often of a poor standard. But as the activities were as much symbolic as they were instrumental this did not detract from their value (Piotrovskii 1926: 74). This *Subbotnik* turned out to be the trail blazer for many more such activities in years to come, independent of the mass holidays. (For further details on *Subbotniks* see chapters 7 and 11.) May Day in 1921, which coincided with the Orthodox Easter, went off very quietly with very little activity of note.

This mood of stern restraint and the unimaginative appearance of the demonstration were not paralleled in the decoration of the towns. Whereas the visual effects of the demonstration were mainly produced by the workers themselves, the designs decorating the towns were almost exclusively the work of professional artists in the early years (Gushchin 1930: 5). Around 170 artists of various artistic backgrounds and organizational affiliations participated in the decoration of Petrograd in November 1918 (*Agitatsionno-massovoe iskusstvo . . .* 1971: 15). The artists who worked on the decoration of Petrograd from 1918–20 did not follow any unified plan and consequently offered a great variety of designs, individualistic in form and content (Nemiro 1973: 8–12). The call to decorate the towns for the holidays in those early years evoked an enthusiastic response from artists and gave rise to a burst of creativity, the scope and high level of which has few parallels in modern history. Among the artists were many of the big names of both the Futurist and the Proletkul't (advocating proletarian art forms c. 1917–32) movements; the latter often organized workers' brigades of amateur artists to participate. A second group of artists was more traditionalist and drew its artistic forms mainly from the classicist tradition. In their work, obelisks and gates and arches of triumph in classical and baroque styles predominated. The poster and wall paintings, although also depicting such traditionalist subjects as *bogatyrs* (Russian folk heroes) with swords, beautiful youths blowing fanfares and victory chariots, showed them in new ways. The subject matter, the style of painting and the grandiose designs, according to Nemiro (1973: 10–20), exude vitality and optimism and express hope for material and spiritual progress. Soviet authors of later periods describe the group of Futurist and Proletkul't artists as "leftist" and the more

163

traditionalist group as "rightist" (Gushchin 1930: 13). The one significant innovation of those years in the content of symbolic work was the creation in 1918 of the symbol of Hammer and Sickle, which soon became widely used and adopted as the State emblem (*Agitatsionno-massovoe iskusstvo . . .* 1971: 68). The Red Star, another newly adopted symbol of more ancient origin, changed in the same way.

In the early years, symbolism in ceremonial art showed attempts to merge the old and the new. A striking example was the decoration of a public building with the Imperial Double-Headed Eagle which held in its clutches the Hammer and Sickle. It was adorned with a Red Star in place of the crown and bore the inscription RSFSR across its chest.

An equally high level of revolutionary enthusiasm and creativity was manifested in the mass dramatic presentations of the early years. Although the dramatic art was mainly amateur and therefore much cruder than the visual art, it was innovative and gave scope to the spontaneous expression of revolutionary enthusiasm. In Petrograd in November 1918 seventeen open-air productions were staged in the town's squares on various themes of the Russian and international workers' movement. In the first two years, these spectacles were staged by a Red Army workshop with soldiers taking the actors' roles and improvising freely a lot of the time (Tsekhnovitser 1931: 17). Producers and directors, however, were professionals of high standing in the theatre of the time. A second group involved in staging spectacles was associated with the Proletkul't movement. Among the spectacles produced by this latter group were "The Taking of the Bastille", "The Legend of the Communard", and Meyerhold's production of Mayakovskii's "Mystery Bouffe".

In 1920 mass spectacles on military themes ruled the day. Not only were the actors chiefly soldiers and sailors, but the whole organization of the productions had a military character and reflected the mood of the period of War Communism. According to Piotrovskii (1926: 66), ". . . the discipline of the holidays of the year 1920 was immaculate. Several thousand participants constructed their festivities with such a unified will and with an enthusiasm held in check by military discipline which were common to the year 1920." Even after the Red Army workshop ceased to take the central role in the organization of the mass spectacles after 1920, the military organization remained. Of the productions in 1920, "The Storming of the Winter Palace", directed by Vinogradov, became the trail blazer for the dramatic style and content of mass presentations in years to come (*ibid.*: 57–9). During this performance audience involvement became so strong that the spectators spontaneously joined the actors in the "storming of the Palace" scene, and the whole performance ended with actors and audience rendering The International in unison.

In 1921 a new development in mass dramatic presentation gained full effect. In that year "the cultural and creative cells of the young revolutionary classes", the amateur clubs of industrial workers, assumed the central part in the organization and presentation of the mass spectacles (*ibid.*: 76). Their work was guided by a group known as "The Studio" and, in later years, as the "*Agit* theatre". Instead of one massive central performance they now staged several in different districts of Petrograd. The spectacles tended to merge into political mass meetings, concluded by a massed rendering of The International. The plays staged under The Studio's guidance developed the forms and techniques of the earlier years in significant ways and set the pattern for future years. While all the basic features of the earlier productions were retained, the various elements of the composition became more controlled and concentrated, and a shift of emphasis occurred. Whereas the elementary earlier spectacles abounded with fighting and shouting, choir singing and reading became the main element of the productions after 1920 (*ibid.*: 78).

The ceremonial of the mass political holidays during the years of War Communism evolved with great spontaneity and reflected the fighting spirit and revolutionary enthusiasm of its participants. During the first two years enthusiasm was somewhat unbridled, and diversity in both representative and dramatic ceremonial art indicated the absence of a consistent new orientation and of a clear focus. But it also indicated the lively search of the people, particularly of the creative intelligentsia, for appropriate forms through which to express their relation to the revolutionary events and to the new society. During the following two years the seriousness of the political and economic situation dampened the general exuberance, as well as making ceremonial activity more disciplined and purposeful. The positive side of this spontaneity and diversity was the high level of creativity among theatrical and artistic professionals. The workers themselves during this period did not enliven the demonstration by the creation of new symbolic forms to express their changed relation to society. Towards the end of the period, however, they were drawn into the creative process by the theatre workshops. These helped them to express their new status in society through dramatic–ritual activity and thus laid the foundations for the generation of future, more independent expressive ritual activity.

During the first four post-revolutionary years the ceremonial of the mass political holidays only performed the first two of Timoshin's four functions. With the experience of the Revolution still vivid in people's minds they did not need much reminding but joined spontaneously and enthusiastically in the festivities. Ritual in those years served as much to express emotions as to mould attitudes. Lunacharskii's (1924: 62) hope that the demonstration would enable the people to express "the essence of their ideas, their hopes, curses and all kinds of other emotions . . . to demonstrate to itself its soul" did not seem too unrealistic in those early days.

1922–1927

The new phase in the Soviet Union's internal development from 1922 onwards became manifested also in important changes in the nature of the mass holidays. Their stern military character under War Communism gave way to a more festive and varied appearance during the politically and economically relatively free and diverse period of the New Economic Policy (NEP), which began to have effects in 1922. The predominant focus of the ceremonial shifted onto the plane of economic construction and onto the task of mobilizing labour enthusiasm. In addition to the usual procession–demonstration and grand spectacle as a means to restructure social identity a new form was introduced in 1922. This was a solemn ceremony of renaming all the big enterprises, bestowing high-sounding socialist names on them. Of all the forms utilized during the NEP period, the demonstration became by far the most important one and has remained so ever since.

In the mass demonstration of the first four years symbolic activity and attributes were weakly developed and were, in the main, separated from other types of activity and objects. From 1922 onwards, they became more frequent and diverse, and symbolic activity became closely entwined with instrumental and expressive activity. These various developments were in practice closely connected. Whereas before the workers, soldiers and members of sports and political youth organizations had merely carried banners and placards with political slogans and sung revolutionary songs, they now widened the range of their symbolic attributes and activities, both evolving directly out of their everyday work life.

They proudly displayed the products of their labour or models thereof, particularly the new powerful industrial and agricultural machinery, as well as demonstrating the actual process of production in the form of charts and diagrams or by going through the real actions. The first tractor or electro-motor that an enterprise had produced were exciting enough to form the sole exhibit of a float. Some enterprises made more imaginative use of their products and aimed to convey a more complex message. For example, in 1924, a float by a cork-producing enterprise carried a reproduction in cork of Lenin's mausoleum surrounded by capitalist emblems, which were ceremoniously burnt at the high point of the demonstration.

The official slogans for the mass holidays suggested a dual focus on an economic and a political theme for the demonstration. In 1924, for example, the slogans were on the raising of labour productivity and on the political alliance of town and country. The great majority of the floats in the procession that year (44 per cent) illustrated the first theme, while the theme of the political slogan was taken up by only 15 per cent of the floats. Another 27 per cent had exhibits or spectacles referring to various other national and international political and social concerns, but only 6 per cent of these were in a satirical vein. Lenin, in 1924, formed the subject matter of only 2 per cent of the floats (Avdeev 1926: 98) which, according to Gushchin (1930: 19), was a higher-than-usual proportion on this first Anniversary celebration since Lenin's death. In 1925, the proportion of floats with an economic theme stayed equally high at 46.6 per cent (Lastochkin 1926: 163). A more detailed analysis of the relative importance of various economic and political themes represented in the demonstrations was made for May 1925 and is produced in the table (taken from N. P. Izvekov 1926: 118).

Themes illustrated	No.	%
Connected with production	147	42.0
Struggle with capitalism and imperialism	86	24.5
Centred on the tasks, goals and achievements of the state	66	17.5
Culture and education	21	6.0
Co-operative enterprise	20	5.5
May Day	11	3.0
Trade Union matters	5	1.5

As far as the use of colour was concerned, red predominated, but several other colours were also used with significant frequency (*ibid.*: 116).

Themes, relying on political satire, directed against internal and external enemies of the new society, increased markedly during this period (*ibid*.: 115). The targets of satirical attacks during the years from 1922–7 remained fairly constant. Among the external targets were the world bourgeoisie, ministers of capitalist governments, the League of Nations and the Treaty of Locarno. The internal enemies, besides the remaining capitalists, the Church and the White Terror, comprised a colourful assortment of undesirable social types, such as the bourgeois, the bureaucrat, the *kulak*, the speculator, the shirker or truant, the drunkard, the loafer and the "eyewasher". On many floats economic and political satirical themes achieved an imaginative synthesis by making the product or production process of an enterprise engage in an allegorical fight with internal or external enemies. Examples of such syntheses were designs, such as a mill grinding up capitalists, a giant pair of scissors cutting up speculators, a primus stove heating a frying-pan in which is squirming a White Guard or a giant sledge-hammer dealing blows to the bourgeois and the conciliator. Another way to attack enemies through ridicule, which also greatly enhanced the carnival atmosphere of the procession, was the practice of having enemies allegorically represented by live zoo animals marching in the parade (Tsekhnovitser 1931: 92). Allegorical depictions of world political relations were also popular, particularly compositions showing the superiority of socialism over capitalism as, for example, a pair of scales showing a great imbalance between capitalism and socialism. Turning from the visual to the audial element in the ceremonial, one might note that two indigenous Russian revolutionary songs "Marsh Budenyi" and "Pesnya Provody" were sung most frequently, while The International was sung relatively little (Lastochkin 1926: 177).

Themes were presented either in static or dynamic form, the former predominating during this period. Dynamic displays consisted of demonstrations of labour processes, of short humorous sketches or playlets, of symbolic actions or of political speeches. The preparation of the material exhibits and, mostly, of the dramatic activities for the floats were financed by the enterprises and conducted by the workers themselves under the guidance of a club instructor. Only rarely was outside professional advice sought (*ibid*.: 168). The demonstrators were on foot, or horseback, on all sorts of vehicles or, increasingly from 1922, on motorized floats.

On its route through the town to the central square the procession

often came to a standstill, and time was whiled away with both prepared and impromptu sketches, games, songs, dances and jocular
shouting matches between participants and spectators. In those years
there occurred a lively interaction between those on the floats and
those participating more passively. Shouted comments and jokes were
attracted mainly by the villains portrayed in satirical designs or dramatically in the "masks" of the playlets. Even in those early years the
positive characters (workers, peasants, members of co-operatives)
communicated only in the dull idiom of slogans or political speeches
and incited little reaction (Avdeev 1926: 101). The procession in those
years, according to Piotrovskii (1926: 83), has become a political carnival
which, "with its noisy jolly platforms, symbolic figures, metaphorical
groups, was the direct development of amateur art, was a vast production, put on wheels". This was particularly the case in 1924 and
1925.

Participation in the demonstration in those years was entirely voluntary, but the turn-out of people was very good. It is estimated that in
May 1925 in Leningrad around 200,000 people or 21 per cent of the town's
population took part in the demonstration. The turn-out was biggest
in districts which were predominantly working class (N. P. Izvekov
1926: 118). Those who participated in 1924 and 1925 in the preparation of the demonstration and in the demonstration itself were, according to surveys conducted in those years, to an overwhelming extent
young (19–25 years old), politically active men. Manual workers made
up 60 per cent, 25 per cent were white-collar workers (*sluzhashchie*), 5
per cent were Red Armists, 6 per cent were students or pupils and 4 per
cent came from professional bodies (Lastochkin 1926: 168).

The spectacles continued to be produced by workers' amateur dramatic circles. The production in November 1922 in Leningrad, devoted
to the preceding five years of history, was significant for introducing
for the first time on a large scale the media of light and fire to express
meaning. To express expectations of the international significance of
the October Revolution a small fire was lit which grew into a gigantic
blaze and gradually kindled bonfires everywhere in the environment
(Nemiro 1973: 36). Another feature of this spectacle was the arrival in
the square of a solemn torchlight procession of the delegates to the
Fourth Communist International.

During the first half of the twenties spectacles were not only performed in the two capitals but also in many other large towns all over
the Soviet Union (*Rezhissura* . . . 1973: 75ff). A notable mass spectacle

in the provinces was one devoted to the ritual recreation of history in Ivanovo-Voznesensk. There the general strike of the town's workers in 1915 was reproduced with great faithfulness to historical detail and engulfed the whole town in revolutionary fervour. Just as on the strike day in 1915, tools were laid down in all the factories at 4.0 p.m., and the town's 20,000 workers again took to the streets and attended a mass demonstration. The day ended with the massed singing of a funeral march for those killed in the general strike, followed by a rendering of The International.

The festive decoration of the streets and fronts of buildings, although more plentiful as a result of the improved economic situation, did not maintain the same level of lively and colourful originality as the other two aspects of the mass holiday, particularly after 1923. Many of the talented professional artists who had worked on them up to then had become disillusioned by the narrow-minded response to their work. According to Gushchin (1930: 13) and others, workers and Party men had accused the artists of "abstractness which was minimally accessible to the understanding of the very working masses to which they (the artists) had been addressing themselves, and (this) almost completely devalued their work on the tasks of art of the Revolution". After 1923 artists either withdrew completely or went over to providing decorative, rather than original creative, designs. Their efforts were not replaced, as in the other two fields of ceremonial art, by that of amateur artists from among the workers (*ibid*.: 7). Houses and shopwindows were now being decorated with portraits and busts of Lenin, Red Stars, State emblems, flags, buntings and slogans. A detailed analysis of the decorations of house fronts and shopwindows in one of Leningrad's main squares during the May Day celebrations of 1925 showed that portraits and busts of Lenin were by far the most popular means of decoration, being used in 86 out of 150 cases (N. P. Izvekov 1926: 108–9). Only in 1927, on the occasion of the tenth Anniversary, historical retrospection led to a temporary reversal of this trend. Turning to the use of colour in those decorations, it is notable that the colour red predominated, appearing in nearly half the designs. White, presumably as a background colour, and green were also used frequently, but other colours were applied only infrequently (*ibid*.).

In 1927, the year of the tenth Anniversary of the Revolution, there were noticeable beginnings of a new phase in the mass holidays. These were, however, obscured by a revival and creative extension of all the best developments of the preceding years, particularly of the two first

170

years. The tenth Anniversary was prepared by a special commission at the expense of much time and money. It was particularly brilliantly staged in Leningrad, still the ceremonial capital. Here the most striking aspects of the holiday were the mass spectacle and the artistic decorations of streets and buildings. The latter were being created by talented professional artists of the "leftist" Proletkul't movement who, on this occasion, made their last contribution to ceremonial art (Gushchin 1930: 46). The evening spectacle, a recreation of the last decade of Soviet history, was notable for the skilful use of the symbolism of light and fire. The progress of Socialism, for example, was symbolized by a gradually increasing number of men with lighted torches climbing higher and higher up the walls of the Peter and Paul Fortress, a symbol of the old order. The struggle of the new against the old social order also found skilful symbolic expression through the music of this spectacle. By counterposing revolutionary and Tsarist music and making them struggle for supremacy, the class struggle was indicated. Such mass spectacles, recreating revolutionary history, were performed in towns all over the USSR in that year. The most popular topic for these spectacles was the Storming of the Winter Palace, but revolutionary episodes of local importance were also being produced quite frequently (see Tsekhnovitser 1931: 22ff).

The tenth Anniversary was the first occasion on which the celebration of Lenin's memory became a central motif of a holiday. The most notable decorative/symbolic device of that year in Leningrad was an illuminated globe rotating in the sky. Above this globe appeared, in illuminated letters, the first of a long chain of slogans building up Lenin as a superhuman being: "Everywhere, always, whole-heartedly (*bezrazdel'no*) with us is Lenin."

The ceremonial art of the demonstration was not as lively and original as that of the town's festive decoration. Although the bulk of the work on the floats and on other decorative/ceremonial devices was still being carried out by the workers themselves (Gushchin 1930: 26), the number of original and striking floats had greatly diminished in comparison with previous years. In the demonstration of that year there figured for the first time the theme of militarization of the civilian population. Detachments of the armed forces, who had always headed the parade, marched together with the workers of the enterprise which had assumed patronship over them. This was intended to demonstrate both the close ties between workers and soldiers and to propagate the idea of the militarization of the civilian population.

The period between 1922 and 1927, characterized by gradual economic recovery, social and political diversity, and by widespread political
idealism and enthusiasm, was a time when the mass holidays had the
greatest vitality. All three aspects – the procession–demonstration, the
mass spectacles and, to a lesser degree, the ceremonial decoration of
the towns – were well developed and lively and varied in both content
and form. Although the dramatic activity up to 1922 was usually on a
higher intellectual level, the work produced between 1922 and 1927
had more crude vitality. The ceremonial decoration of the towns,
however, although increased in volume, had deteriorated after 1922,
and had lost both artistic merit and symbolic value.

In comparison with the first period, participants in the ceremonial
between 1922 and 1927 were more actively involved in its preparation,
and grassroots amateur activity far outweighed any involvement of the
professional artists. Towards the end of this period, between 1926 and
1927, the general popular enthusiasm began to wane. One writer
(Zhemchuzhnyi 1927: 5–7) remarks that the demonstration was losing
its spirit and that habit rather than interest motivated those who
participated. The fresh impetus gained from the historical retrospection of the tenth Anniversary of the Revolution partly reversed this
mood for a short while and obscured the general trend. The year 1927
thus bridged two stages in the history of mass holidays and their
ceremonial. While it still displayed the lively variety and exciting
creativity of the earlier years it already possessed an indication of
developments to come – of single-minded political purpose, greater
constraint on ceremonial art, greater professionalization and an increasing loss of interest among rank-and-file participants. Thus, to
characterize this period in terms of the nature of its ritual, in the early
years the "model of" and the "model for" aspects of the ritual of these
holidays were still well balanced. In the closing years, there were
indications that the "model for" aspect would soon come to dominate.

Looking at the holidays and their ceremonial in terms of Timoshin's
four basic functions, it is clear that the first function had been largely
abandoned. The first flush of victory was over, and retrospection had
given way to a forward-looking activism in which all energies had been
harnessed to economic reconstruction. Instead, the second and third
functions became more important. The people demonstrated to themselves the successes of the present to stimulate further effort for future
tasks. Only towards the end of this period, on the tenth Anniversary of
the Revolution, when enthusiasm began to wane and energies became

exhausted, did historical retrospection again become important to rekindle fresh impetus. Timoshin's fourth function, which is essentially concerned with consolidating the existing power structure, was not very developed during this period.

1928–1940

In the period that followed, the gradually decreasing diversity in social and political life and the greater expansion of the sphere of Party control, as well as the increase in political coercion, became reflected in the mass holidays. Variety and crude vitality began to give way to uniformity and standardization in form and content, particularly from 1930 onwards. But the early years of this period were not just characterized by governmental coercion but also by a still widespread popular enthusiasm and idealism in the face of the challenge of industrialization. These feelings were also expressed symbolically in the ceremonial of the demonstration and account for the fact that the demonstration was still enlivened by flashes of colourful originality. Centralized mass spectacles were becoming rare, little effort was being invested in the ceremonial decoration of the town, and the demonstration became the focal part of the holidays. The many political and economic crises in the early years of this period – intra-Party struggle and the problems encountered in mass industrialization and collectivization, particularly the confrontation with the peasantry – all found expression in the ceremonial of the mass political holidays.

Although mass spectacles on a giant scale became phased out of the two mass political holidays, they were still occasionally performed for less regularly recurring occasions. Also, new and more decentralized types of dramatic presentations became prominent – the dramatized meeting and the thematical fête. These were staged in the new Parks of Culture and Rest and mixed the dramatic with the straightforwardly political or agitational form of presentation (Pisarevskii 1940). Besides changes in form there were also changes in content in these mass spectacles. Whereas during the twenties their themes had been the class struggle of the proletariat, the events of October 1917 and of the Civil War, during the thirties productions reflected industrialization and the fulfilment of the first Five-Year Plan, the threat posed by the capitalist West and the necessity to strengthen defence capacity, and tended towards anti-religious themes (*Rezhissura . . .* 1973: 11).

Concerning the ceremonial decoration of the towns, the trend

173

towards mere adornment, begun in 1923, became even more dominant during these years (Gushchin 1930: 7). In addition to the standardized flags, garlands, posters and slogans there appeared also "naturalistic, naive" works of collage on economic topics, "overladen with technical details, such as graphs and diagrams" (Nemiro 1973: 54). This latter feature both expressed the great pride about the industrial achievements of the first planned economy and the increasing interpenetration of the symbolic and the instrumental. The colour red is said to have become even more dominant than in earlier years (*ibid*.: 58).

Most of the human and material resources now became diverted to the demonstration, which became even more massive in scale. Of the demonstrations of that period the one in 1929 was particularly noteworthy as it combined in a novel way the mass spectacle with the demonstration. It made more explicit the relationship between political leaders and the working masses than had been the case in earlier years. The mass spectacle–demonstration was called "Account of the Giants for the First Year of the Five-Year Plan". As the name suggests, it was an attempt to commit the workers of the giant factories to the goals of industrialization by means of a centrally planned and controlled economy, as well as to mobilize them to work-enthusiasm. This took the form of a carefully planned roll-call of the major enterprises, during which they demonstrated their production process and expressed their commitment to fulfil the Plan before time in a dramatized procession past the country's political leaders. Whereas in previous years there had occurred merely an exchange of greetings between political leaders on the tribune and the working masses filing past, in this demonstration a more complex exchange took place. When questioned by members of the government, workers of the different enterprises gave accounts of their efforts for fulfilment of the plan by showing lit-up statistics and diagrams. At the end massed workers gave a solemn promise to fulfil the plan, repeating words transmitted to them by radio (Tsekhnovitser 1931: 32ff). This planned and directed declaration of political loyalty well expressed the growing political regimentation in Soviet society from 1929 onwards.

But the procession–demonstration still retained some of its carnival-type character, expressed through satirical posters and little sketches employing the device of "enemy masks". The assortment of internal enemies of the new society steadily increased during these years, and satirical attacks became directed towards more specific groups of enemies. Thus in 1928 the set included ministers of the Provisional Government, Cadets, Socialist Revolutionaries, Mensheviks and factory owners (Nemiro 1973: 59), and in 1930 members of the right-wing opposition, Trotsky and members of the Industrial Party (a group comprised mainly of engineers who were given a show trial for alleged industrial sabotage) were added to these. These satirical attacks indicated that, although Stalin's faction had eliminated all organized political opposition, its members were still wary of their enemies. It also showed that they needed public legitimation of this move towards political monism.

In addition to the list of the politically harmful, there was also an enlarged list of the socially harmful, exposed to public ridicule by means of the demonstration. In 1928 this included the saboteur, the philistine, the fashionable *petit-bourgeois* (*meshchanin-modnik*), the trouble-maker (*sklochnik*) and the informer (*sheptun*) (*ibid.*). In 1929, political satire was employed to agitate for the continuous working-week. This was done by professionals who portrayed Saturday as a backward (and religious) old woman and Sunday as a drunkard. But amateur work on satirical and agitational themes was less original, and there were complaints about repetitiveness and cliché, such as the symbol of the coffin to signify the dying out of all manner of undesirable characters and activities (Gushchin 1930: 54). Later on these socially harmful characters became skilfully amalgamated in an allegorical figure called "The Old Way of Life".

But one of the so-called "harmful" social phenomena, from 1929 onwards, was singled out for frequent satirical attack, both in the demonstration and in the festive decoration of the buildings, as well as in a mass spectacle, namely religion. Being religious was being equated with being a class enemy and an opponent of the Revolution. This strong emphasis on satire against religion was the ceremonial mirror of events in Soviet society at that time. In the year 1929, a relatively tolerant stance on religion, based on Lenin's 1918 Law on religion, gave way to a new and harsher set of laws and to a wave of religious persecution, culminating in the show trials of 1929 and 1930. Attacks were also directed against religion outside the Soviet Union, mainly against international Catholicism (Shchukin and Magidson 1932: 40ff). Particularly aggressive was the anti-religious play on the theme of inquisition, staged at midnight before the Orthodox Easter Day of 1929. Having the medieval Inquisition as the epitome of the evil of religion as its basic theme, the spectacle concluded with a switch to the contemporary Soviet period. It portrayed the victory of atheism over

175

religion by having a group of Young Pioneers chase the members of the Inquisition from the stage (*Rezhissura . . .* 1973: 87).

Satirical attacks and other methods of agitation also focussed on the chief social and political concerns of political leaders of that period. Between 1928 and 1930 both collectivization and industrialization were important themes, the former becoming the prime focus in 1930. Ceremonial built around the theme of collectivization was designed to both win support for the policy of collectivization and to shift the blame for its disastrous consequences from the political leaders to a scapegoat group – the *kulaks* or strong peasants. The improvement of industrial production became a particularly urgent concern, and a new method of agitation was adopted towards this end. Whereas in previous years the demonstration had been a parade of industrial achievement, in 1930 it became a means to publicly reward good, and reprimand bad, work performances by individual enterprises. Thus a contingent from the giant Leningrad Baltic Works, which had fallen behind in its fulfilment of the Plan, had to march at the front with a placard urging "Let us declare war on an antiquated pace of work!" All the enterprises which were behind in the fulfilment of the Plan had their names chalked up on a special blackboard. When filing past the political leaders in Red Square, their delegations were greeted with shouts to "pull their socks up". Shock workers were especially honoured by having their portraits carried at the front of the parade. (In May 1931 one of the five thus honoured was comrade Stalin.) A confrontation between the good and the bad characters of production was staged, during which shock workers were shooting down effigies of characters harmful to production (Tsekhnovitser 1931: 154ff).

A perennial concern of foreign policy, the relations between the socialist Soviet Union and the capitalist West, became expressed with new sharpness between 1928–9. Late in 1927 a part-real, part-manipulated fear of foreign intervention led to the development of a siege mentality. During that time the theme of conflict and possible military confrontation became expressed in various forms in the ceremonial of the two holidays. Displays and activities around this theme demonstrated the defence capacity and readiness of the USSR and of its population, as well as the latest achievements in industrial technology (*ibid.*: 116-17). The events put on in the Parks of Culture and Rest during the mass political holidays tried to mobilize the civilian population around these issues (Pisarevskii 1940: 99ff). Particularly noteworthy was a spectacle in the summer of 1929 with the title

"War on War". It expressed the concern that the imperialist and capitalist West would attack the peaceful, industrializing USSR, and tried to rally workers in the West to the cause of revolution. Towards the end of the play fiction and fact became merged. When it was announced to the audience that news had been received of Britain breaking its agreement with the USSR on Far East policy, spectators broke the police cordon and stormed the square to express their protest at this action. Individual orators from the audience made impromptu speeches on the subject and led a protest march through the streets, its participants singing revolutionary songs (*Rezhissura . . .* 1973: 88). The necessity for a militarization of the civilian population was also expressed in the demonstration of the mass holidays through such devices as mingling soldiers with workers, forming Komsomol regiments and having members of detachments of the *Osoaviakhima* (a voluntary society for the defence of the conquests of the Revolution) march, wearing gas masks. In 1930 additional drama was created by an air display over Red Square during the demonstration (Tsekhnovitser 1931: 82ff).

Later on in the thirties, other concerns and priorities assumed temporary importance and became expressed in the ceremonial and ritual of those years. For the eighteenth Anniversary, for example, the building of the Moscow–Volga canal became the central topic for the ceremonial decoration in Moscow. As it was a gigantic project which would not only further the economic power of the Soviet Union, but would also bear witness to the might of its human and technical resources and to the victory of human ingenuity over natural forces, the celebration of its completion was ideally suited to ritual elaboration.

Another theme, which has remained important up to the present, first became ritualized in the second half of the thirties, namely the notion of friendship between the peoples of the USSR. From that time onwards people in national dress began to form part of the procession. This development coincided with a distinct shift during the middle thirties in Stalin's nationalities policy, from exercising positive discrimination against non-Russian national groups, to favouring the Great Russian group (Utechin 1961: 372). Later, between 1936 and 1938, this policy change became more drastic, and the country was purged of the "federal deviationists", that is those who wanted a greater amount of independence and power for the non-Russian republics (Kolarz 1952: 11). Thus a deterioration in actual nationality relations became disguised by a ritual presentation of harmonious relations between the different national groups of the Soviet Union.

Another concern that emerged, which has become progressively strengthened over the years and has given rise to a new form of symbolic action (see p. 225) was with physical education and sport. Not only were special holidays dedicated to sport, for example the Festival of Gymnasts and Athletes (*Fizkul'turniki*), but we also get for the first time the mass "living pictures" of gymnasts, the symbolic use of body movement in a disciplined, carefully co-ordinated mass display. During the thirties there was shown not only a strong concern with physical fitness and discipline, but great efforts were also invested in raising the general cultural level of the population. One instrument to achieve the "cultural revolution" was the demonstration of the mass political holidays which, with its agitational posters, floats, playlets etc., frequently focussed on this theme.

On the international front, the great practical and moral support given by the Soviet Union to the Spanish Communists during the Civil War found its reflection in the ceremonial of the mass holidays. Songs, poems, posters and slogans in support of the Spanish Communists took a prominent place in the October celebrations of 1937 (Glyaser 1938: 8–9).

Turning from a description of the forms and content of the ceremonial of the mass holidays to their preparation and general organization, significant changes occurred after 1928 and more so after 1930. Whereas in the preceding six years the bulk of the preparations had been carried out by workers' amateur artist circles, they hardly figured after 1928. According to Gushchin (1930: 38), in Leningrad their number had fallen from eighty-four in 1925–6 to fifteen in 1929. What "ceremonial art" was produced by workers was done haphazardly and hurriedly by inexperienced men, assigned to the job from above. In 1929 professional artists were brought back in on a large scale. It is, however, emphasized in the literature of the time that their part had to be that of the professional organizer and helping comrade who should, on no account, stifle or regiment workers' creativity (*ibid*.: 39–40). The year 1929 is also the first in which vigilance about political deviation of the left and the right in professional and amateur art work is advocated (*ibid*.). There are indications that the loss of enthusiasm by those who used to prepare the ceremonial attributes of the holidays is paralleled by a greatly lowered degree of audience involvement during the festivities. Such indications are given by recommendations in the literature on the holidays to incite audience participation (e.g. shouting "hurrah" in the appropriate places) by the careful positioning in the crowd of professional instigators of positive reaction (Tsekhnovitser 1931: 54), and to distribute song sheets, because the revolutionary songs were no longer generally known (*ibid.*: 98).

After 1930, the centralized co-ordination and standardization of the activities of the mass holidays proceeded a lot further. It becomes clear from the literature that the ceremonial art and the ritual of the mass holidays had become the result of a careful process of sifting and elimination according to political criteria, and had ceased to be the expression of any popular mood. This was due to the creation from 1930–1 in Moscow of a Central Staff for the Conducting of Holidays, which introduced political censorship over design and eliminated local and grassroots initiative. The formation in 1932 of a "United Artists' Front" on the position of Socialist Realism and the organization of artists in unions also gave the state a greater control over them and led to a further reduction of creative individualism. The Central Staff was subordinated to the urban soviet and had on it representatives from the Party, the Komsomol, the trades unions, central sports organizations and from departments concerned with the economy at local level. It was divided into sub-sections, the most important of which was the political one. Its duties were defined as follows: "(It) carries out the political leadership of the festivities, it works out their general aim, (and) conducts and carries out all tasks in accordance with the Party and general social line" (quoted *ibid.*: 183). The Central Staff had subordinated to itself a number of District Committees, which issued to all factories and enterprises plans and orders about the conducting of the mass holidays, laying down the themes and slogans for each. These plans were then discussed by a "leading group" at the enterprise, which adjusted them to local conditions and capabilities and distributed the execution of various tasks to different groups in the enterprise (Shchukin and Magidson 1932: 8ff). Members of these "leading groups" came from the enterprise's cultural–educational organizations, its clubs, Red Corners or works committees (Tsekhnovitser 1931: 185). These "leading groups" planned the workers' participation in the demonstration down to the smallest detail and left no room for any spontaneous activity. Special marshals were selected to see that directives were followed and to maintain order and discipline (*Massovoe* . . . 1932 9ff).

The dull uniformity and low level of creativity in ceremonial art and ritual activity resulting from these developments is described in harsh words by a contemporary Soviet author: "It happened that the creative invention, the living fantasy became substituted by a pseudo-pathos, cheerless greyness, or by coarse picturesqueness" (Nemiro 1973: 67).

Even in these years of ever-increasing political regimentation and standardization there was still an awareness that these developments might completely kill the spirit of these holidays. Thus Tsekhnovitser (1931: 204, 206) closes his book with the following words:

We want to warn the organizers of the holidays about superfluous regimentation and petty tutelage of the masses. Owing to the latter we have already managed to generate a well-known stereotyped pattern, a cliché, a commonplace . . . We must not give the masses slogans, caricatures etc. and expect them to be nothing more than carriers of them.

But it is clear from the description of the ceremonial of this period that the above warning was not being heeded. During these years of the most basic social and economic transformation of Soviet society the mass political holidays were unequivocally used to mobilize the population to effect these transformations. The ritual of the holidays was structured in such a way as to offer mainly "models for" the new social relations that were required to successfully complete the social and cultural revolution of that period. But the "model of" aspect of ritual was not completely lost, particularly during the years of the First Five-Year Plan. Although the ceremonial was now extensively State-managed, the goals, aspirations and emotions of many people still overlapped to some extent with those that were officially encouraged. During the late twenties and early thirties the government and Party could still generate enthusiasm, excitement, optimism and altruism for the tasks of industrialization and technological development in many sections of the population. The ceremonial of the mass political holidays was an excellent vehicle for the people to give expression to these sentiments.

As in the previous period, all energies were concentrated on the present and the future, and the mass political holidays, looked at in terms of the four basic roles attributed to them by Timoshin (1966), were neither devoted to revolutionary retrospection nor to consolidation of achievement but concentrated instead with great intensity on functions (*b*) and (*c*) to create unity among the workers (of hand and brain), to evoke optimism and a willingness for sacrifice and to continue the achievements of the present with new successes.

THE WAR AND POST-WAR YEARS

During the war years, there were no mass political holidays involving the whole population, but some elements of their ritual were performed at certain crucial stages of the war. These were, of course, concentrated on both demonstrating and strengthening the power of the Soviet State, of its defence capacity and the people's faith in victory. A notable mass ritual was performed at the beginning of the war in October 1941 which featured a full military parade in Red Square. The impact of this military display was greatly increased by making it an activity combining symbolic and instrumental aspects. The participants of the parade went from the holiday military display straight off to the front, ensuring that the eyes and the hearts of the nation went with them. Another notable celebration was that of the twenty-fifth Anniversary in blockaded Leningrad. Its staging in the face of great material want and of a real threat to freedom and life became an act of defiance and of the assertion of hope against great odds, and must have greatly strengthened the morale of Leningraders. From 1944 onwards solemn salutes were fired every time the Soviet army had achieved a victory (*Massovye Prazdniki* . . . 1961: 23).

In the war years the beginnings were laid for the development of a third "holy" tradition – the patriotic tradition, and from that time dates a first batch of new symbolic devices which have steadily increased in both number and potency ever since. I am referring to the Eternal Flame, boards of honour, war monuments and the creation of heroes on a large scale. It is significant that among these heroes were not only Soviet citizens but, for the first time, figures from the Russian historical past, such as Alexander Nevsky, Suvorov and Kutuzov.

After the war the celebration of the mass political holidays was again resumed. The trend towards greater dullness and uniformity in the ritual and artistic attributes and activities continued, and was further aggravated by the general material deprivation and greyness of life. While in earlier years creative impulses had triumphed over material adversity, this did not occur in the post-war years. Not only were the decorations of the towns taken solely from the limited repertoire of established emblematic devices (flags, banners, slogans, portraits, emblems), but the procession–demonstration became dull and colourless. The dramatic or visual illustration and celebration of themes by decorated floats had become a rarity, and there is no mention in the literature of the use of political satire. Mass dramatic presentations are

181

no longer referred to. Only in key years (e.g. the thirtieth Anniversary in 1947) were energies aroused to provide some more memorable holiday scenarios. The only development of note in the early post-war years was a further refinement, due to technical innovation, of the powerful drive to project illuminated objects or portraits of people into the sky. In 1947, illuminated portraits were held in the sky by aeroplanes. (Names are not mentioned, but it is certain that one of them must have been Stalin's.)

The scarcity of information on the nature of the mass political holidays in the post-war years and their suspension during the war years makes it impossible to draw any general conclusions about the nature of their ritual and about which of Timoshin's (1966) four roles were most strongly emphasized at that time.

THE POST-STALIN ERA

Although the trend towards a general ossification of all aspects of the mass holidays has continued during this period there have been a few changes in the form and content of ceremonial, and on some aspects a reversal of this trend has been attempted. As might be expected, the continually growing economic and political strength of the Soviet Union has been expressed in the emergence of new national concerns as well as in a general perfecting of techniques in the design of ceremonial forms. The staging of the mass holidays received a further degree of professionalization during this period by instituting training courses in Institutes of Culture to create specialists in this area (*Rezhissura* . . . 1973: 17). It would be repetitive to give year-by-year accounts of the mass holidays of this period. Instead I shall outline very briefly a few of the more constant preoccupations and the ways in which they have been expressed, and give a more detailed description of the one crucial holiday of this period – the fiftieth Anniversary of the October Revolution.

During the late fifties and the sixties, years distinguished by great achievements in space research as well as by the threat of another world war, the national concerns with science and advanced technology on the one side, and for prevention of such a war on the other, were also dominant on the ceremonial plane. A lot of rockets, sputniks and cosmonauts appeared in the demonstrations. Among the officially minted symbols of this time were a white dove on a stretched-out hand and a flying rocket against the background of a globe, emblazoned

Display of rockets during the May Day parade in 1966

with the Hammer and Sickle. Of the established symbols, that of Lenin requires a special mention. In these years Lenin-worship reached a higher peak.

In 1967, the fiftieth Anniversary of the October Revolution was celebrated with fitting splendour. Events were staged on a fantastic scale and at phenomenal expense to create a holiday worthy of the occasion (Nemiro 1973: 83). The great day was heralded by a number of preparatory events. The celebrations both on the day itself and in the preparation for it were distinguished by the unprecedented amount of faithful historical reconstruction of all aspects of the Revolution itself and of the whole revolutionary period. Although the recreation of significant historical events had always formed an important part of the Soviet ritual repertoire, previously it had remained confined within the bounds of discreet dramatic presentations. In 1967, in contrast, not only were the various dramatic presentations carefully co-ordinated to form a historical sequence, but efforts to enliven history spilled over into all aspects of life, affecting the smallest details.

The Anniversary itself was preceded by the re-enactment on the appropriate days of such events as the workers' first free May Day, or Lenin's return from exile and his arrival at the Finland Station. Events were staged in their original setting, clothes and uniforms of the period

183

were brought out, old posters and slogans were rehung and the old picturesque notice-boards reannounced the exciting events of that time. In addition, the period spirit was recreated by exhibitions that played old sound-tracks and showed films, photographs, posters and objects of the time, and by special performances rendering the songs and the poetry of 1917. In Moscow, history was evoked by decorating all the important squares and streets in accordance with the event or personality that had given them their name.

In Leningrad, the sequence of events constituting the October Revolution was faithfully re-enacted at the same times and places, starting with the first shot from the cruiser *Aurora*. In the procession decorated floats, giving dramatic presentations, re-emerged for the festivities. The procession was divided into five sections, the floats of each portraying one of the significant periods of Soviet history. Each period was recreated both by a heroic–pathetic (adj. of "pathos") and by a satirical sub-section. Music and light were used to complement and enhance the scenes created. Also reminiscent of the early post-revolutionary political holidays was the effort to create interaction between participants and spectators (*Rezhissura* . . . 1973: 126ff).

The chief elements to express meaning in the ceremonial of this important jubilee were fire and light, using the most advanced techniques to create stunning effects with the latter. It was also used to great effect in the Lenin cult which reached a new pitch in 1967 in both Moscow and Leningrad. In Moscow, for example, a huge portrait of Lenin (26 m by 50 m) was suspended in the sky with the aid of a giant balloon. The portrait was lit up by powerful projectors which created the impression that Lenin was in the middle of a huge star.

The events of the Revolution were not only recreated visually on an unprecedented scale, but they were also brought to life in print at all levels. For example, a study of a Soviet children's magazine all through the Soviet period (O'Dell 1978: 161ff) emphasizes that, whereas the October issue of 1928 carries only one commemorative article, those of the times of the jubilees are replete with such articles.

THE MASS POLITICAL HOLIDAYS AT THE PRESENT TIME

To conclude this account of the historical development of the two main mass political holidays I shall give detailed descriptions of both October and May Day celebrations that I observed in 1977 and 1978 in Moscow and Leningrad respectively.

Both May Day and the October celebrations are still universally accepted as important Soviet holidays, celebrated not only publicly but also at home with flowers, presents, cards and a festive table. Long before the actual holiday, factory workers are encouraged to engage in "socialist competition" in honour of it, and the results of that competition are proudly displayed on the day. Since the late sixties, Tours of Places of Revolutionary Glory (see p. 168) by groups of young people have also become customary. Celebrations start on the eve of the holiday. Everywhere there are cultural events, and amateur activities on revolutionary themes are encouraged (Rudnev 1974). It has also become customary to enact rituals of initiation, such as Reception into the Pioneers, on the eve of the holidays, utilizing their atmosphere to enhance the solemnity of these rituals.

Turning to the holidays themselves, the following general observations are of interest. The overwhelming impression now is that of a demonstration of military and economic might. Only the ample use of the colour red and portraits of revolutionary leaders still remind the viewer of the holidays' original intent. The events are on a very grand scale, totally professionalized, and give little scope to individual enthusiasm and popular creativity. The participation in the demonstration is bureaucratically organized, and the ritual attributes displayed are mass-produced and standardized. Even committed communists (e.g. Timoshin 1966: 165; Aliev 1968: 160) admit that the demonstration has become a "mere ritual" which is no longer apt to evoke strong sentiments among its participants. Words like "stereotyped", "regimentation", "banality" sum up the widespread disenchantment with this central Soviet mass ceremony. It is also suggested that professionals concerned with drama regard the dramatic–ritual activity of the mass political holidays as being of secondary importance and do not give them the necessary artistic care (Genkin 1975: 81).

Watching part of the October procession on the occasion of the sixtieth Anniversary of the Revolution in 1977 coming towards Red Square along one of the main feeder roads, I noted that the ritual attributes consisted mainly of red banners and flags, red artificial carnations, large red panels inscribed either with slogans or with declarations related to the current Five-Year Plan, larger than life-sized portraits of Marx, Engels and, more frequently, of Lenin, Brezhnev and other members of the Politbureau (the latter two usually together). In addition there was the customary military contingent. Gay multi-coloured balloons, another standard issue, appeared somewhat incongruous in this sea of red political formality. Except for one float with a copy of the cruiser *Aurora*, I noted no other distinctive political symbolism nor any carnival-type floats of political satire with live performers, which had been common in the early years. The general impression of unimaginative uniformity was further reinforced by the prevalence of canned music. (There were only two live bands and no singing in the procession, which took over an hour to file past my vantage point in Gorky Street.) The people in the procession at no time gave any display of spontaneous revolutionary enthusiasm. (The only outburst of this kind I witnessed during my stay came from the visiting Italian communists in my hotel.) The street decorations, too, were standardized and uninspiring. The slogans and figurative decorations were on various political and economic themes and gave no feeling of any overriding concerns as on some historic anniversaries. Yet despite the large extent of uninspired State management of the demonstration, its sheer volume made it nevertheless impressive, not only for the foreign observers but also for the Soviet people who had turned out in great numbers to witness it with interest. On the other hand, I spoke to many people who could no longer work up any interest for the events of this day and preferred to stay at home.

The high point of the demonstration is reached when the procession files past, and greets, the political leaders standing on top of Lenin's mausoleum in Red Square. The demonstration in Red Square starts with the military parade of the Moscow garrison. The beginning is heralded by the chimes of the Kremlin bells. The Soviet Minister of Defence receives the report from the commander of the parade. Then both inspect the troops and wish them a happy holiday. The fanfares sound "Listen all!" The Minister of Defence delivers a speech from the tribune. The hymn of State is played, and the parade of the troops proceeds. The troops are succeeded by large groups of athletes and gymnasts in their bright costumes. Then some children take bunches of flowers to the leaders of the government and the Party. The columns of demonstrators described above are headed by the following: the red banner of the Soviet Union, the flags of all the Union republics, the flags of all the friendly socialist countries. The victors of the pre-October socialist competition take the place of honour at the head of all the columns (*Nashi prazdniki* 1977: 19).

For the many people who miss the high point of the demonstration there is an opportunity to see the full coverage on television at night. While during the daytime events Lenin's presence is only indicated by

186

the central place in the demonstration of his mausoleum, the televised revival of the day's events imposes Lenin's presence more directly on the viewers. For what seemed to me the duration of many seconds, a large close-up of Lenin's face with his eyes focussed directly on the viewer, accompanied by a reading in his own voice of one of his famous speeches, arrested my attention in a startling way. (My Soviet friends around the festive table, however, carried on drinking and talking in the usual way.)

Turning to the celebration of May Day in Leningrad in 1978, the street decorations for the occasion were the same standardized and unimaginative red flags, portraits and panels with slogans as for October, but on a more modest scale. It was notable that of the four huge posters of Lenin, Marx, Engels and Brezhnev which decorated the main square, Brezhnev's was placed at a considerable distance both from the other three and from the tribunes. Watching the whole demonstration for about three hours as it filed past my vantage point on one of the tribunes in Leningrad's main square, I received the following impressions: instead of the predominance of the colour red of the October demonstration, colours in the procession were very varied and deliberately gay and spring-like – artificial flowers of many colours and shapes, balloons, different-coloured flags and clothes of sportsmen. But within this variety there was organized uniformity. The most notable difference from the October demonstration was the absence of any military displays and personnel. The demonstration was headed by a huge portrait of Lenin inscribed "Let the banner of Lenin always fly!" This was followed by the State emblem and the portraits of Brezhnev and of all the members of the Politbureau. Behind these marched the town's newly honoured heroes of labour. Several contingents of brightly and uniformly dressed groups of sportsmen, giving simple displays during their march past the tribunes, separated this first section of the demonstration from the second, more bulky and complex latter half.

In this section marched representative contingents from the major industrial, commercial, political, cultural and educational institutions of five of Leningrad's urban districts, each with their float(s), banners, flags, slogans and portraits. The floats were neither very original nor very striking. Most were of a geometrical design that depicted the collective's product or basic activity in some kind of synthesis with the State symbols of Hammer and Sickle, national emblem, Red Star etc. Of the portraits carried by these organizations, Lenin's was by far the most predominant. Brezhnev's portrait on its own appeared fairly rarely, but the portraits of the whole Politbureau relatively frequently. Those of Marx and Engels could be seen only three or four times during the three-hour-long demonstration. During all this time, a commentary was being delivered with great pathos by a voice over the loudspeaker. Each collective was greeted with the words "Long live the glorious . . . (name of collective)! Hurrah!" In between, more abstract social and political groupings, such as the working class, the peasantry, the native intelligentsia, the union between them, the Party, the Komsomol, women and youth were honoured in this same way. Groupings singled out in this way were mainly internal Soviet ones, and the international proletariat and workers in the West received only a few mentions. At regular intervals the two slogans of this May Day were repeated. Reactions from the marching columns were not very notable. Shouts of "Hurrah!" by the loudspeaker voice were taken up but without much strength or spirit. No other verbalization or singing was produced.

To sum up, in my observation of the ceremonial of the two major Soviet holidays in the revolutionary tradition the following impressions were paramount: the gigantic scale of the events; the State-managed nature and dull uniformity of the procession; the lack of spirit and passivity of the participants in the demonstration.

The ritual of the mass political holidays in recent decades has been devoted only to providing for the masses a "model for" social relations and has ceased to be a vehicle for the expression of popular feelings and mood. It is thus ritual in name only. As concerns the main functions of the holidays, there has occurred a definite shift to Timoshin's fourth function, to a concern with the consolidation of the political and social *status quo*. Although Soviet society has by no means come to the end of its planned developmental road, it appears as if the goal of a communist society remains too vague and distant to provide a future-oriented impetus which could return some life to the ossified ceremonial of the holidays. Instead of seeking fresh impetus in posing the challenge of a communist future, a rekindling of inspiration and enthusiasm is sought by concentrating on function (*a*) that is retrospection to the revolutionary past. Particularly during the jubilee years, the mass political holidays became commemorative rites *par excellence*. Although they probably fulfilled their purpose for the time of their duration, it is clear that this historical retrospection has brought no lasting changes in the nature of the mass political holidays and their ceremonial.

Part III

vvvvvvvvvvvvvvvvvvvvvvvvvvvvvvvvvvvvvvvvvvvvvvvvvvvvvvvvvvvvvvvvvvvvvvvvvvvvvvvvvvvvvvvvvvv

Selected theoretical issues in Soviet ritual

11

vvvvvvvvvvvvvvvvvvvvvvvvvvvvvvvvvvvvvvvvvvvvvvvvvvvvvvvvvvvvvvvvvvvvvvvvvvvvvvvvvvvv

Analysis of Soviet ritual symbolism

Previous chapters have focussed on the problematic realities of Soviet society which are being represented symbolically, and on the value orientations which, it is hoped, will be effected by such ritualization. In chapter 1 I investigated how ritual in general accomplishes such a restructuring of basic attitudes. In the present chapter I shall make an analysis of how Soviet ritual employs symbolism to achieve this task. Symbolism, I said earlier, is what distinguishes ritual from other types of social action and is therefore the nucleus in its structure. The impact of ritual rises and falls with the quality of the symbolism employed, and a careful analysis of Soviet symbolism becomes therefore particularly pertinent.

The power of the symbol, according to Victor Turner (1967: 20–30), springs from its three basic properties: polarization of meaning, condensation of meaning and multivocality (i.e. the accumulation over time of layer upon layer of meaning). At one pole of the symbol are clustered significata which refer to components of the moral and social order, while at the other pole significata are usually natural or physiological and arouse basic emotions. At this sensory pole a whole number of disparate elements can be united and evoke multiple references and meanings. Between the two poles of meaning occurs an interchange of qualities, and in the interaction they strengthen and enhance each other. The social norms and values acquire greater force through saturation with emotion and the basic emotions evoked by the sensory significata are ennobled through contact with social values.

While this basic structure of symbols is also characteristic of those embedded in Soviet rituals, there appears to be an important difference in the significata at the sensory pole. In many cases, emotions are aroused not by the direct inclusion of elements of man's natural environment or physiological make-up, but by utilizing significata from Soviet history, particularly from its "heroic periods". It is perhaps not surprising that a ritual symbolism, developed in a modern industrial society which is characterized by its remoteness from the "natural" and by its disdain of the "physiological", should seek its significata elsewhere. A knowledge of the collective and individual traumas and triumphs of the first thirty years of Soviet history makes the latter a very plausible source of symbolic forms that are able to arouse strong emotions. Taking symbols from a common historical past also ensures that they can be shared by the highly heterogeneous population of a modern industrial society, while a common relation to natural symbols can no longer be taken for granted. This reliance on symbolism supplied by history is least developed as far as concrete objects are concerned, but is strong in most other kinds of symbolism. A more detailed discussion of this characteristic of Soviet ritual symbolism is given later in this chapter.

Ritual symbols can take a great variety of forms. They can be objects, activities, body movements, persons, relationships, events, spatial units, words or sounds. Some of these forms can be conveyed by a number of different media. Both the basic forms and the media through which they are given shape differ between types of society. In modern industrial society they have become more diverse, more technically sophisticated but also more abstract and remote. While in earlier societies the concrete and immediate was dominant, in modern industrial society the emphasis has shifted to a greater use of words, sounds, graphic depictions and light in all their various forms and combinations. In Soviet contemporary ritual, in addition, there has occurred an increasing reliance on the technically produced and preserved, rather than the immediate human product, as in soundtracks, films, sound- and light-effects as well as in the utilization of historical "relics". While such a shift gives greater variety and, more importantly, allows for the creation of greater historical depth in ritual, it loses in impact through a lack of concreteness and immediacy.

The fact that ritual in Soviet society has been consciously designed by ritual specialists during a relatively short period has greatly affected the development of its symbolism. Seeing Soviet society as a new type of society, ritual specialists have thought it inappropriate to borrow its ritual symbolism to any great extent from Tsarist Russia. Consequently, the new ritual has little historical depth and, with a few exceptions, has lacked proper models to copy (I am referring to the ritual of the French Revolution and to the ritual forms of the international and pre-revolutionary Russian labour movement). Having been designed by ritual specialists in a relatively hasty manner (between 1960 and 1970) rather than having evolved slowly through the gradual accumulation of new layers of meaning, the new ritual symbolism also lacks emotional depth. In contrast to popular ritual, where a large variety of associations and meanings reflect the variety of popular contribution to the shaping of ritual symbolism, the new Soviet ritual has not benefited from such a democratic process to the same extent and has drawn on a too-confined and uniform pool of creativity. The consequence of all this is that either the symbolism of many rituals is so underdeveloped that some rituals are rituals in name only; or the symbols developed have not yet acquired that multivocality, that is reference to a wide and disparate number of phenomena and meanings, which give them their special power. Consequently, it then becomes difficult to distinguish between what are claimed to be symbols and what are merely signs. The shortage of fitting symbols has also led to the practice of overextending the application of some symbols by inserting them into unrelated ritual contexts. This has cheapened and debased them (*Nauka i religiya* 1973, 4: 41) and has introduced uniformity into the rituals affected. The lack of concrete, vivid symbolic objects has led instead to a strong reliance on verbal communication. The general underdevelopment of symbolism is acknowledged by many writers in the field and is rightly related to the weak impact of some of the rituals (see Filatov 1967: 20, 63; Kampars and Zakovich 1967: 103; Brudnyi 1968: 183; Fursin 1972: 164; Ugrinovich 1975: 133).

The anxiety felt by many ritual specialists about the insufficient impact of the new ritual on people's attitudes may account for what appears to be a compensatory activity in Soviet ritual. I am referring to the pronounced tendency in most rituals either to give ritual participants a keepsake reminder of their ritually formulated obligations in the shape of badges, letters, albums etc., or to make them state their commitment in writing in an attempt to secure a more lasting attachment to the norms and values expressed in the various rituals.

But weak development of symbolism is not a feature of all Soviet rituals. In general, symbolism is stronger and more unified in the rituals initiating individuals into a socio-political collective. It is weaker and more haphazardly developed in the rituals of the life cycle and of the calendric cycle, that is rites not organically connected to a distinctly Soviet culture but adapted and grafted onto it at a relatively late stage in its development. Ritual specialists have also shown a differential mastery of the various forms of symbolism. While they have not been very successful in expressing meaning through concrete objects, words or sounds, they have more skilfully employed such forms as spatial configurations, body movements, activities and personification. This is probably due to the fact that the latter are readily supplied by history, while the former demand a greater degree of either elite or popular creativity. Whereas popular creativity has been excluded to a large extent by the Soviet approach to the creation of ritual, help from the creative intelligentsia has not been sufficiently forthcoming in recent years, to the sorrow of ritual specialists (e.g. Brudnyi 1968: 187). This state of affairs is in marked contrast to the situation in the first post-revolutionary decade, when the new ritual of the mass holidays excited a great burst of elite and popular creativity.

To establish to what extent symbolism, as defined by Soviet ritual specialists, has been accepted and integrated as such into general Soviet culture it is useful to subject it to an analysis that makes use of Ortner's (1973) typology of symbols. Ortner identifies as key symbols those which attract much cultural interest. Such interest is indicated when:

(1) the natives tell us that X is culturally important
(2) the natives seem positively or negatively aroused by it
(3) X comes up in many different contexts, either behavioural or systemic or in many symbolic domains
(4) there is greater cultural elaboration surrounding X compared with similar phenomena in the culture
(5) there are greater cultural restrictions either in number or severity of restriction against misuse. (*ibid.*: 1339)

Ortner distinguishes between two ideal types of symbol, each at the ends of a continuum. Summarizing symbols "sum up, express, represent for the participants in an emotionally powerful and relatively undifferentiated way what the system means to them" (*ibid.*). These symbols belong to the category of sacred symbols in the broadest sense. They encourage an all-or-nothing allegiance for a diverse cluster of ideas, values, but do not invite reflection on the relation between values (*ibid.*: 1338). Elaborating symbols, in contrast, order experience and help translate undifferentiated feelings into action. They provide orientations or strategies for action. Those which predominantly perform the first are called "root metaphors" and those which provide the second are "key scenarios". Ortner emphasizes that summarizing and elaborating symbols are only analytically separate. She calls them

194

"key" symbols because they occupy a key status in the system of cultural meaning. This consists, for summarizing symbols, in their property to shed light on, and make sense of, other meanings, and for elaborating symbols in their capacity to organize relationships between a wide range of culturally diverse elements (*ibid.*: 1343).

In previous chapters I have described symbolism and signs as they are embedded in the various rituals. I have offered partial interpretations based on their context and on background information. Here I shall detach them from their context and group them together, according to their form, with other symbols and then attempt to analyse their special properties and the meanings they convey. Lastly I will examine their degree of integration into, and congruence with, Soviet ideology and culture.

Ortner's ideas about key symbols implicitly contain the same suggestions on the method of analysis as are made explicit by V. Turner (1966: 172ff). He recommends that an analysis of symbolism must be conducted at three interpretative levels of meaning: the exegetical, the operational and the positional. Of these three only the first is problematic in the context of the present research, as indigenous exegesis is predominantly interpretation by ritual specialists, that is those who devised the rituals and their symbolism, as given in the literature of the field. Analysis of symbolism by other knowledgeable informants could not be considered, because traditional methods of fieldwork employed by social anthropologists to elicit such information cannot be practised by Western researchers in the Soviet Union. But my observation of moods expressed non-verbally in relation to some of the symbols covers the gap at the exegetical level to some extent.

CONCRETE OBJECTS AS SYMBOLS

Turning to symbols and signs in the form of concrete objects, one is immediately struck by three features: their small number, the lack of unity in their field of reference and their lack of multivocality. While all the rituals are claimed to be part of one unified system with a socialist and secular thrust, the symbols employed do not mirror this unity. About half of them reflect in their content this underlying world view and have forms which originated mainly in Soviet or international revolutionary and military history. The other half refer scarcely, or not at all, to these basic orientations and, like traditional symbolism, have taken their forms from the realm of nature.

195

In the first group are the Hammer and Sickle, the Red Banner, the Red Star, the Red Kerchief, the Eternal Flame and the Blazing Torch. The latter two should be seen as part of a more diffuse concern in Soviet socialist ritual with the symbolism of fire and light, which will be examined separately below. Some of the former lack multivocality and have an unambiguous relationship between a message and message-bearing entity. They are, therefore, signs rather than symbols.

An exception is the Red Banner of a collective which is not part of everyday life but is brought out only on ritual occasions. Attitudes towards it, inculcated in Soviet citizens from childhood, are a mixture of reverence, love and pride. The Banner is regarded as a holy object. It lends special significance to solemn occasions, and the privilege of carrying it is reserved for a small number of carefully chosen people, "the best of the best", as the Soviets call them. Whether these stipulated attitudes are actually held outside the milieu of political activists it is impossible to ascertain. In many collectives the Red Banner also has a connection with significant historical events and may therefore evoke a number of associations and emotions not immediately obvious to the observer. The banner also has the capacity to fuse the three holy Soviet traditions. It has a clear revolutionary association originating with the Paris communards, being taken up by the international revolutionary movement and, later, by the Russian Bolshevik movement. It has a military association in that it is connected with blood spilled in battle, with sacrifice for the political cause and for the Motherland during the Great Patriotic War. Lastly, it has become connected with the labour tradition, with every labouring collective according its Banner the same special place it would have had in a military collective. The Red Kerchief of Pioneers is a symbol closely related to the Red Banner. It is regarded as "a small part of the Red Banner, steeped in the blood of fathers and grandfathers – of fighters for the present happiness of millions of Soviet children" (*Nashi-prazdniki* 1977: 96).

The symbol of the torch has a long history and was particularly prominent in Greek antiquity, expressing the humanist orientation of that culture. It had also a central place in the ritual of Hitler's National Socialism, where it was meant to evoke the pagan Germanic heroic heritage as well as lending drama and making an impact on the young. The Eternal Flame, in contrast, is of more recent origin and has acquired many of its meanings only in Soviet times. Both symbols have at the sensory pole significata with a double association: with a natural

phenomenon – fire – and with significant historical events – the revolutionary movement and the Great Patriotic War. Both link the
elementary power of fire with the political power of the Soviet State,
albeit with different aspects of it. The Blazing Torch has become
connected with the power of labour, with its view as an elementary
and creative force in society. In this context, the torch is a symbol of
immortality in a secular sense, the intensity of its glow expressing the
lasting influence on other men of great human works (Whittick 1971:
334). It is also associated with revolutionary vigour, the latter being
closely connected with labour (Brudnyi 1968: 129). The often-cited
phrase that the "Blazing Torch of labour glory . . . is being carried
forward to communism" underlines this fusion as well as bringing out
the dynamic property of this symbol. Not only is the power of labour
fused with revolutionary power in the symbol itself, but also it is
connected with patriotism by symbolic transference of power, as when
torches are lit from the Eternal Flame. In recent years, the symbol of the
torch, lit from the Eternal Flame, has even been inserted into life-cycle
rituals (e.g. the wedding rite in the Ukraine). Here it is not only meant
to symbolize the transference of the three "holy" traditions to the new
generation, but it is also said to act as a traditional popular symbol of
warmth, light and life (*Nashi prazdniki* 1977: 140, 142).

The Eternal Flame, once associated solely with honouring the memory of fallen heroes, has now acquired a much wider and deeper
significance in the Soviet Union. It symbolizes not only the sacrifice of
the fallen soldier during the Great Patriotic War but the sacrifices of
the Soviet people, the eventual triumph which arose from the sacrifices and the love of, and pride in, the Motherland in whose name they
were endured. The Eternal Flame also rekindles feelings, experienced
in the war, of unity among the people, of solidarity between leaders
and led as well as the sensation of invincible power after victory (see
also Smith 1976). Beyond this it has become a symbol of timelessness
and of a general sacred power, supplying the religious dimension in an
ideological system, rejecting the traditional religious definition of
sacred power. As pointed out above, this sacred power is transferred
onto other symbols and other ritual occasions through contact. Soviet
people seek to experience this sacred power not only on those public
occasions that celebrate the patriotic tradition, but also on joyful or
serious significant occasions in their private lives, such as a wedding,
conscription into the army or the beginning of a new school year. It is
highly significant that this most powerful and most spontaneously

accepted symbolic object originates from the patriotic rather than the revolutionary or labour tradition.

Both the Torch and, more strongly, the Eternal Flame can be regarded as summarizing or sacred symbols demanding an all-or-nothing allegiance to a spectrum of values and linking them in the process. They are well established in Soviet culture and can be said to have "key" status in Ortner's sense.

The other group of symbolic objects mentioned above is comprised of a young tree, the birch tree, clumps of earth, lighted candles and rings. These symbols are mostly traditional ones, found and interpreted in similar ways in the whole Western cultural area. The association of soil with sweat and blood, with fertility and patriotism, is so common as to be almost trite to Western sensibilities. (In the Soviet context, however, where patriotism is strong, this symbol is probably still quite powerful.) Equally trite and sentimental to us is the association of the wedding ring, in the words of a ritual specialist, "with bright and endless love" (Veselev 1973: 71).

The symbol of a lighted candle is also known in many cultures but has various meanings in different ideological contexts, depending on whether the transcendent principles are pagan, Christian or secular. Whereas in the pagan context the lighting of candles had magical connotations, being intended to ward off spirits, in a Christian environment the burning candle at baptisms is a symbol of the light of Christ, meant to guide the baptized child. In Soviet birth ritual, in contrast, a candle only symbolizes the beginning of a new life. At socialist funerals candles are not meant to be symbols but are merely utilized to create a solemn mood. But one needs only to remember the important part candles play in the Russian Orthodox church service to realize that the (church) religious association cannot be eliminated at will in the minds of those who perform the rites.

The symbol of a young tree, familiar in many cultures as denoting the start of a new life, has in the Soviet ritual context become a vehicle to express its secularist thrust. In the words of one author, it has become a symbol of "all-triumphant life, of its eternal rejuvenation in new generations, a symbol of the relay staff taken up by those who fought for our present happiness" (Rudnev 1974: 101). This symbol is thus utilized in an attempt to overcome the meaninglessness and hopelessness implied by a secularist interpretation of human existence with a promise of timelessness through constant renewal and of a triumph of life over death. Another aspect of this symbol is that it is used to stress sex-role differentiation. Planting a fruit tree for a baby girl still focusses on the traditional child-bearing role of the female, while a chestnut or a maple tree for a boy emphasizes male vigour.

The symbol of the birch tree, in contrast, is an indigenous ancient Russian symbol, deeply embedded both in popular and high culture. Thus Nagirnyak *et al.* (1970: 110ff), when reviewing established music and poetry for their suitability for the scenario of the Holiday of the Birch, come up with about fifteen items of each. Originally the birch was connected with a pagan fertility cult. In the new ritual, of course, this association has been discounted, and the birch is now no more than an image evoking a lyrical and patriotic mood. Not surprisingly, none of the symbols in this group have assumed "key" status.

LIGHT, HEIGHT AND FIRE

Light is traditionally regarded as one of the most important religious symbols, indicating deity and, by association, the qualities of knowledge and wisdom, truth and goodness (Whittick 1971: 132–3). The religious thrust of this symbol is made even stronger when it is used in combination with the symbolism of height, indicating heaven and God in or above the sky. It is no coincidence that from the early post-revolutionary years onwards there has been a strong drive in Soviet ritual to express meaning through the media of light and height, as well as through fire. While the symbolic use of these media does not indicate the presence of a well-defined deity in the traditional religious sense, they have nevertheless been used to invoke in a diffuse way the qualities and perspectives usually associated with a divine presence.

A utilization of light, height and fire has been particularly strong in the ritual of the mass political holidays. It is true that often light has either a functional or a decorative purpose rather than being expressive of a message. The same usually applies to fire when used in fireworks. As in the staging of theatrical productions, light was frequently used dramatically to turn an otherwise ordinary occasion into an extraordinary event, or to catch attention in the hours of darkness. But very often light, height and fire assume a more primary significance expressing meaning in a distinctive way. Electric light as, for example, in the lit-up globe rotating in the sky with Lenin's name above it came to symbolize both the brightness or joy and the enlightenment brought about by the Revolution. The propensity to project lit-up objects or names into the sky must be seen as an effort to achieve permanence, to become like one of the timeless stars in the sky.

The symbolism of fire, in contrast, has more divergent meanings, having been used both in religious and in secular humanist contexts, the latter focus being probably more general. It has been a very popular and central symbolic device in such different secular cultures as ancient Greece and Nazi Germany (for the latter see Gamm 1962: 195ff). Fire represents life, light and eternity. Being a primary element, it is also a symbol of power and is conceived of as a means towards man's mastery over nature. In the context of Soviet socialist ritual fire, both in general and in the more specific forms of the Blazing Torch and the Eternal Flame, has been used extensively from the early days of Soviet power. It expresses well the secular intent of the new value system but at the same time leaves room to develop impulses for sacralization.

Fire, in the form of figurative fireworks, bonfires and torches, has been used to express both the destructive and the creative force of revolution as well as the continuity of the revolutionary endeavour and its dynamic property. The destructive force of revolution was expressed in 1917 and 1918 when such relics of the monarchy as portraits, emblems and crowns were burnt on huge bonfires. Similarly, on the tenth Anniversary of the Revolution fireworks were used to bombard and destroy effigies of men personifying the foreign intervention of the early twenties. On the fifth Anniversary, when one big bonfire – the Revolution – sparked off a number of smaller fires all over the place, the dynamic property of revolution and the hope for world revolution were given expression.

COLOUR SYMBOLISM

Colour is used in many cultures to symbolize sentiment and/or categories. Victor Turner's (1967) famous analysis of colour symbolism shows that it can refer with great subtlety to a wide variety of meanings, particularly when colour contrasts are involved. In Soviet ritual the colour red or scarlet has always been of paramount importance. It was taken over by the Russian Social-Democratic movement from their revolutionary forebears, the Paris communards, where it stood for blood and revolution. It remained the chief colour when this movement became transformed into the new government in 1917. It had also been a popular colour in pre-revolutionary Russian society, the

Russian word for it (*krasnyi*) also meaning "beautiful". While in the first post-revolutionary years the contrast of red (the Bolshevik revolutionary forces) with other colours symbolized a greater social and political diversity in the Soviet society of that time, in the following decades the near monopoly of red has expressed the development of monolithic political power and lack of social diversity. The warning of Meyerhold (famous avant garde theatre director) in 1932 that red would lose its impact unless a greater variety of colours was introduced (Nemiro 1973: 58) can be interpreted not only as a plea for greater diversity in the theatrical world but also in the Soviet society of the early thirties in general. Such a warning was also frequently issued during the late sixties, when the fiftieth Anniversary of the Revolution induced much historical work on this holiday and comparisons were inevitably made. This plea for a greater variety of colour on ritual and ceremonial occasions has been heeded to some extent, but at the present time the colour red is still the dominant colour. It does not symbolize a bundle of significata but is merely used to signal an ideological direction. It is one of the few means of giving an instant revolutionary aspect to a ritual occasion. Thus the October celebrations differ from those of May Day mainly by the ample use of red.

VERBAL SYMBOLISM

Words can be used to evoke associations in a variety of ways: as speeches, declamations, slogans, poems, images or in the form of oaths, to give only a few examples. They can be spoken or written, live or recorded. To create symbolism from words is a very difficult task and requires great restraint and imagination. To become symbolic, a verbal construction must propel its listeners into action. Notwithstanding this difficulty, verbal forms are most extensively used in attempts to express norms and values symbolically. Not surprisingly, the attempts often fail.

The strong reliance on long, didactic speeches gives many so-called ritual performances the character of political meetings. A good example of this are some of the birth rituals described above. At these, representatives of all the institutions which touch on the new child's life make speeches to lay a claim on the new citizen. One exception to this rule of speeches destroying ritual is the sparing use of the most famous recorded speeches of Lenin. Here the spoken words combine with the pre-eminence of the speaker to evoke pride in, and reverence

201

for, the revolutionary past, adulation for Lenin and fresh enthusiasm for the political tasks of the present.

Words can also be used to create images which, through vivid and economic use of language, impress themselves on the mind and in time assume a symbolic quality. One such verbal image found in one form or another in many Soviet rituals is the notion of a baton used in relay races. The baton represents the heroic Soviet traditions which are being passed on from generation to generation (Brudnyi 1968: 153). This symbol of the baton and relay race is an old Soviet one which was first used during the Cultural Revolution of the early thirties, when the baton of culture, that is knowledge and skill, was being passed on from experienced workers to new recruits from the peasantry (Fitzpatrick 1978: 35). Sometimes the idea of the baton and race is given concrete form, as when some object, usually a torch, is passed from representatives of one generation to those of the next. The tendency to have representatives from several generations take part is common to a majority of rituals and implies this "relay race" through history even when the verbal image is not utilized explicitly. Likening the building of communism to a relay race brings out both the competitive urgency of the task and the spirit of collective endeavour in which it is being accomplished. This verbal symbol or some concrete expression of it is inserted into a wide range of rituals and serves two important functions. It is one of the ways to evoke the more heroic past to ennoble the present. It also provides a secular belief system with a means to abrogate biological time and to transcend history, thus creating a feeling of collective continuity and purpose. This verbal symbol has some of the characteristics of a key symbol of the elaborating type, although the "scenario for action" it implies remains at a fairly abstract level. Another verbal symbol is the term "Workers' Dynasty". Descriptive terms of the feudal historical past are fused with a modern industrial category, as when Rudnev (1974: 58) describes Workers' Dynasties "as genuine representatives of His Highness the Working Class". This symbolic fusion is meant to express the honour accorded to labour and manual workers in the ideology of Marxism–Leninism.

A way of using verbal symbolism that is widely employed is the insertion of oaths of loyalty into rituals of initiation. This reflects the manner in which Soviet life is deeply ingrained with military traditions. The military association is further strengthened by the fact that oaths are usually sworn in front of a collective's Red Banner. This imitative practice is designed to invoke the same sense of holy obligation and total commitment that is demanded from military recruits. Such an oath, if it is kept short and simple, can be the effective centrepiece of a ritual, as in the Leningrad ritual of initiation of young workers (see p. 110). Or it can appear contrived and theatrical, as when it comprises as many as eleven different promises, each formulated in high-flown language (see the initiation ritual described on p. 122). It then puts into question the aptness of transferring the oath from the military to the civilian context, and destroys the ritual intent.

The poetic word, skilfully employed, can also assume a symbolic quality. Poetry provides man with images through which he can emotionally conceive his environment, and it evokes moods in those who listen to it. Sometimes these moods express the sentiments of a whole generation or historical period and, if read at a later time, call forth associations focussing on that period. Such poems in the Soviet context are those written by Mayakovsky and Gorky – two openly propagandist but nevertheless distinguished and popular writers – in the first hopeful and enthusiastic decade of the new Soviet State. The inclusion in the new ritual of lines by these two poets must therefore be considered a skilful move which is bound to have impact. It is surprising that this has been so rarely effected.

More effort appears to be directed at stimulating the creation of new poetry, tailormade for a particular ritual. So far there has been little response from the creative intelligentsia. The few poems which are in use seem to have little artistic merit, and are either devoid of imagery or the images used fail to express the secularist and socialist intention of the rite. The poem read at an Estonian remembrance ceremony (see p. 88), for example, uses the very traditional and trite expression that "the wheel of time rotates eternally". This, in my opinion, runs counter to the intended essence of the new rite, conjuring up thoughts about fate, about its inevitability and man's powerlessness in front of it.

Altogether then, only halting and isolated efforts have been made to create verbal symbolism. Generally speaking, rituals and ceremonies are overloaded with non-symbolic verbal ballast which deadens rather than sensitizes the emotional responses of ritual participants. The padding out of ritual with lengthy verbal constructs is ironic when one considers the fact that ritual was introduced in the first place for its capacity to present things in vivid graphic form which would eliminate the necessity to talk *about* things.

MUSICAL SYMBOLISM

Most of what has been said about the verbal symbolism of poetry also applies to musical symbolism. Although music is prominent in Soviet rituals it rarely has symbolic quality. At best it evokes a general heightened mood, at worst it runs counter to the essence of a given ritual. Thus the custom of interspersing wedding or funeral rites with items of traditional classical music increases the solemnity of the occasion but does nothing to enhance the *new* socialist secular value system. Sometimes the choice of music betrays a complete lack of understanding of the nature of ritual as a solemn social action to be raised above the level of everyday expressive activity. Thus what is called a "Solemn Registration of Marriage" ends with a gay waltz or a polka, or the "set-apart" character of the birth rite is destroyed by starting the performance with a song which is played every morning on the radio to accompany gymnastics. These shortcomings are recognized and deplored by some of the writers in the field (Lisavtsev 1966: 126; Filatov 1967: 57, 63; Brudnyi 1968: 187), but an alternative does not appear to exist. Despite numerous appeals to composers, genuinely artistic expressions of ritual values in music have so far not come to the fore.

The only items reflecting the values of Soviet socialism are revolutionary songs, national anthems and bugle fanfares. The most expressive and effective are probably the classical revolutionary songs, such as "Boldly, comrades, in step", the *Varshavyanka* and The International, rendered by the ritual participants themselves. Given this fact, it is surprising how little use has been made of them in recent years. At demonstrations on recent mass political holidays in Moscow and Leningrad, for example, I did not hear the marchers sing one revolutionary song, although canned music was blared out incessantly. The national anthems of both the Soviet Union and of its constituent Union republics, besides having their obvious uses, are also employed to remind ritual participants that local patriotism always has to be related to national patriotism and must not develop nationalist tendencies. Bugle fanfares are another manifestation of the tendency in Soviet ritual to transfer military modes of action into a non-military context.

SYMBOLIC SIGNIFICANCE OF PERSONIFICATION AND HEROES

Another way to symbolize the presence of public organizations and their claim on ritual participants is to have their representatives perform a role in the ritual. This role is an idealized version of that which they play outside the ritual context. Often representatives from several organizations are present to indicate the different loci of Soviet power and the co-operation between its representatives as posited in the official ideology.

Personification of value orientations is carried one step further in the extremely pervasive Soviet proclivity to create heroes. Heroes have always been a part of Soviet culture and long predate the creation of the system of rituals under discussion in this work. There are several explanations for this great proliferation of heroes. One lies in the Soviet political culture which is strongly conditioned by the Russian tradition of fostering belief in powerful individuals rather than in political structures. Another points to the fact that heroes emerge during times of instability, when rapid change necessitates the creation of models to aid reorientation. Although there is rapid change in most modern industrial societies, few have experienced changes as drastic, quick and constant as the Soviet Union in its first thirty-odd years of existence. These were not just years of change but also of repeated threats to the survival of the new Soviet State and as such were times that offered plenty of scope to heroes of the "avenging" and "delivering" or the "martyr" types. Once such heroes had emerged they were kept alive, or even had new ones fabricated in their image, by the ever-active and all-pervasive Soviet propaganda machine.

What makes a man a hero? There is no agreed definition in the literature, but two basic kinds of hero keep recurring. First, there is the folk hero who has broken through some kind of social or cultural barrier and has achieved something for *himself* which is thought to be both desirable and, after the hero's breakthrough, to have become more tangible for the "ordinary" person. This type of hero, though idealized, still remains as a vivid personality with both strengths and weaknesses of character. He is one of the people. Western examples of this type of hero would be the English Robin Hood, the American Horatio Alger or a contemporary figure like Elvis Presley. Secondly, there is the hero who has achieved something extraordinary for the *common* good, often at great personal sacrifice. Although he inspires other men with his virtue, his achievement is thought to be beyond ordinary men. He is put on a pedestal above his fellow men and becomes, in the public imagination, a man of impeccable character who cannot be touched by the ordinary mortal. A typical example of

205

such a hero in the West would be the American president Abraham Lincoln.

While most cultures distinguish between these two types of hero, Soviet ideology, it seems to me, has attempted to fuse them into one. The Soviet theoretical conception of a hero is, however, nearer to the second type but differs from it in important ways. A hero, according to Sushkov (1969: 10ff), "is an individual or a class who selflessly act in submission to the objective laws of social development, to social progress". Heroism derives from the contradictory character of social development and from the necessity to resolve the contradictions in the interests of progress. A hero thus recognizes social possibilities and, regardless of the cost to himself, translates them into action (*ibid.*: 16). While in capitalist society, therefore, the hero is the revolutionary individual or class, in contemporary socialist society, where no antagonistic contradictions exist, it is the individual or class who is aiding the gradual transition to communist society as defined by the Party. This basic ambiguity in Sushkov's Marxist concept of heroism makes him waver between describing heroism as exclusive original social activity (*ibid.*: 24) and as a fairly common activity "accomplished" in ordinary conditions, without externally expressed signs of the heroic (*ibid.*: 27).

This conception tries to present Soviet heroes (with the exception of Lenin) as folk heroes whose achievement should be imitated. But at the same time, it removes them from the people by making the heroic deed a completely altruistic one and the hero a person of total goodness. While this definition of heroism is shared by Hook (1945: 107ff), who sees heroes as event-making men, that is men who by their intervention change the course of history in some significant way, it tries at the same time to present a hero in Soviet society as someone who maintains the stability of the Soviet system and thus as someone who prevents changes in the course of history.

Expressing value orientations through embodiment in heroic individuals is very effective, particularly in a society where a large proportion of the population have a low level of education. The abstract value achieves a concrete manifestation which therefore has greater emotional appeal. A model of behaviour is more likely to be accepted for imitation if it is presented in a personal relationship. Also, values embodied in a hero enter more deeply into a culture, Warner (1965: 14) points out, "because what is internalized in the form of personal relations in childhood becomes deeply seated and is surrounded by emotion".

The effectiveness of hero symbolism, however, must be somewhat impaired in the Soviet case by the fact that identification with these heroes after childhood is made difficult by their unreality. And the extremely large number of them must reduce their value. Heroes representing the three "holy" traditions appear at every ritual or ceremonial act, in person, recorded on film or depicted in portraits hung in special "heroes' galleries". Heroes are not only immortalized in pictorial form but they also have their names inscribed in Rolls of Honour, and the heroes of war have their memory preserved by often magnificent monuments. Children's literature is full of heroes, both fictional ones and some that are modelled on actual people (see O'Dell 1978).

A hero, according to Warner (1965: 14), "always expresses fundamental and important themes of the culture in which he is found . . . Each theme is a symbolic statement which relates and organizes some of the beliefs and values of a nation to each other and to the group." To put it in the more contemporary sociological language of Ortner (1973), a hero offers a strategy for successful living in a culture. What are these fundamental themes in Soviet culture? They are all related to the three heroic traditions in Soviet history: the revolutionary (including the Civil War), the patriotic and the labour traditions. These three traditions have to do with the creation of Soviet society, with the struggle for its survival and with the triumph over countless adversities. One basic theme common to all three traditions is selfless service or even sacrifice of the individual for the collective good. The heroes personifying this theme are totally selfless men of a fairytale unreality. The greater their sacrifice the more heroic they are considered. This appearance of being unreal, cardboard figures is rather paradoxical when one considers that Soviet ideologists are particularly proud of the fact that their heroes are "real" men in contrast to what they call "the illusory heroes" of religion (Genkin 1975: 97).

Haimson (1970: 105–6), in an analysis of heroism as portrayed in Soviet literature at different periods, finds that the hero in the early Soviet years (up to 1933) differs fundamentally from the hero at the height of Stalinism. In the early period, the hero was a solitary, ascetic Party man who suppressed his own feelings and needs to lead the heroic battles of the Civil War and of the First Five-Year Plan. His loneliness was self-imposed, born out of the necessity to unswervingly lead the anarchic masses. This hero still resembled the hero type of the pre-revolutionary classical intelligentsia. His image slowly changed during the thirties. Having suppressed his feelings too often "he gradually lost the sense of humanity in his followers", he came to view them merely as "detached hands in the building of vast edifices", as cogs in the intricate machine it was his task to direct. While the positive hero, calling the people to selfless sacrifice, is still common in the new Soviet rituals he has almost disappeared from recent works of literature. The young writers of the sixties, according to E. J. Brown (1963: 292), tend to reject positive heroes and programmatic statements. "If one of their characters declaims on . . . heroism of labour the effect is certain to be humorous!"

While heroism based on exceptional political and/or military achievement is common to most cultures, a hero of labour is the specific creation of Soviet ideology. A person who has "endured persistent, highly productive, irreproachable labour", according to Sushkov (1969: 27), must be called a hero. Labour is heroic, he continues, because it is "a battle for man, an overcoming of material and spiritual material" (*ibid.*: 128). By giving equal ranking to a great labour achievement and outstanding deeds in the other two fields or, in the contemporary Soviet context, to achievements in such sports as ice hockey or football, the central importance to society of labour is given expression.

Although this argument is very plausible and worthy, the notion of a hero of labour remains unconvincing. A hero, as I tried to show earlier, is someone who accomplishes a deed which is *qualitatively* different from those of other men, which is held in awe and is rarely duplicated. The achievement of a hero of labour, in contrast, differs only in degree from those of his fellow workers and can be copied. Because it can be imitated it may also be seen as a threat by the less ambitious or less altruistic man and may evoke negative responses. Two facts point to the conclusion that a hero of labour has in fact less status than other heroes, but only empirical research could settle this point conclusively. The fact that the creation of heroes of labour is surrounded by a lot of ritual indicates that a hero does not emerge spontaneously but has to be "made", as in the ubiquitous socialist labour competitions. In contrast, the leading Soviet sports champions or the spacemen, who are spontaneously worshipped as heroes, are not given, and do not need, an official ritual attestation of their hero status. The sizeable material reward a hero of labour receives also implies that he does not receive sufficient honour to raise him above his fellow workers. The impression that heroes of labour do not become genuine heroes is confirmed by Aliev (1968: 73) who says that, although some heroes of labour become genuine popular figures, most appear to be forgotten very quickly.

The honouring of labour achievement started with the Revolution, but the institutionalization of labour heroes coincides neatly with the beginning of the systematic industrialization and of the first Five-Year Plan. Thus the Order of Hero of Labour dates from 1927 (changed to Hero of Socialist Labour in 1938), and the Order of Red Banner of Labour for the whole Union was instituted in 1928 (Nagirnyak *et al.* 1970: 12). To retain their value these orders ought to be awarded fairly sparingly and should honour only outstanding achievement. I have no general figures on the frequency of their distribution to test this for the whole Union, but the figure of 500 Heroes of Socialist Labour out of a population of around 1,400,000 in the autonomous republic of Dagestan suggests that this is indeed the case.

How then does the hero fit into rituals? Heroes do not usually appear singly but mostly as a trinity, one hero for every "holy" tradition. Most of them are not heroes in the sense defined earlier, that is popularly recognized as such throughout the national or local culture. Although they usually have performed an outstanding deed, they derive their heroic status mainly from the fact that they are representing a heroic tradition in a ritual context. Outside such contexts their "heroism" is not widely recognized. Heroes appear in those rituals where young people are initiated into a new collective. They are there as an embodiment of the "holy" traditions which are being brought to the notice of the young people through ritual. By bringing these traditions to life through their mere presence, but also through tales about the "heroic" past, they increase the emotional impact of the message conveyed during the ritual. When they hand over to the initiands the implements vital to their new status (e.g. tools of work, enlistment cards, Komsomol badges) the heroes hand on, at the same time, the traditions they embody. To use their image, the relay baton is being passed from one generation to another, and a feeling of historical roots and of continuity is being evoked. Sometimes the impact on initiands is even more intensified by having the hero and the initiands engage in a common dramatic reconstruction of the heroic event. A hero of the Revolution is raised above other heroes if he can be shown to have had personal contact with Lenin. He can then provide a bridge across the generations to the very source of the holy revolutionary tradition.

The symbolic significance of the dead hero exceeds that of the living, particularly if he died for the nation. While living heroes are revered, dead ones are held in awe. Their collective graves become sacred places of constant pilgrimage.

Among the dead heroes one stands out above all – Lenin. An analysis of the cult of Lenin, focussing on Lenin as an individual rather than on his political theory and strategy, is now in order. In this context Lenin is not so much a historical person but has become a potent symbol which activates positive emotional attachment to the ideas of Soviet Marxism–Leninism. The cult of Lenin is seen as a heterogeneous system of beliefs and practices, designed with varying degrees of consciousness, to both legitimate the Soviet system and the position of its political leaders in it *and* to encourage action conducive to the further perfection of Soviet society.

What forms does the Lenin cult take today? Every visitor to the Soviet Union is aware of the fact that the visual image and the words of Lenin accompany Soviet citizens from the cradle to the grave and that one cannot move about in public places without noticing the omnipresence of Lenin. On mass political holidays, when it's impossible to look up into the sky without being confronted with Lenin's name in blazing letters, this omnipresence becomes a bit oppressive. A slightly more active relation to Lenin is encouraged by the existence of countless Lenin museums, Lenin statues and Lenin memorials. Lenin memorials, to quote Hedrick Smith (1976: 338), "or secular shrines to Lenin, modest or gigantic, are omnipresent in Soviet life, sown like seeds from on high across the full length and breadth of this enormous country". They are visited by groups and individuals all through the year and have become the focus of mass pilgrimage on anniversaries of Lenin's birthday (22 April), when they become submerged in flowers.

Lenin's mausoleum in Red Square fills a very special place in Soviet society. It is the symbolic centre, the "holy shrine" in which the (transcendent) principles of Soviet Marxism–Leninism, the highest layers of significance in the ideological system of Soviet society, are somehow given concrete form. To this ritual centre both individual persons and society (in the form of its representative groups) come to draw moral strength at crisis points, to give heightened significance to important events, to give an account of important missions accomplished, to display and rejoice in successes or just to give homage. Countless examples which illustrate these points come to mind. In

1941 soldiers went there before leaving for the front, and after the war was won the most heroic soldiers from all over the Soviet Union returned there for a victory parade, a triumphant presentation to Lenin of enemy flags. Yurii Gagarin, the first Soviet cosmonaut, is reported to have gone to the mausoleum before his flight to draw strength, and after his successful mission to make a symbolic report. School leavers come here on their last day of school and fall into reverent silence during the changing of the guard. New officers from a Moscow elite training institute receive their diplomas here from Lenin, their Honorary Commander. Pioneers are initiated "in the presence of Lenin" (Abramov 1969: 62ff), and newly married couples come to offer thanks after their wedding. All the important mass political holidays have their culmination in Red Square in front of the mausoleum. There, greetings, reports and displays of economic, cultural or military achievement are not only directed at the living political leaders on the platform erected over the mausoleum but also at the dead leader inside it. The whole nation participates via the television screen. On ordinary days there is a constant queue of patiently waiting pilgrims from all corners of the Soviet Union, as well as from other countries.

Although the cult of Lenin takes place all through the year it reaches a high point on one day, the anniversary of Lenin's birthday, 22 April. On that day, the crowds that visit his mausoleum and other Lenin memorials all over the country greatly increase in size. Individuals come spontaneously to put down a few flowers. Others come as part of a group, for example the Young Pioneers who, in a solemn line-up in front of the mausoleum, report to Ilych their successes and the duties accomplished. The official celebrations on that day, according to one semi-official comment (*Nashi prazdniki* 1977: 29), are deliberately conducted "without splendour and showiness" in trying to take into account Lenin's own wishes in this context. The events organized both in preparation for and on the Anniversary are all designed "to induce the masses to assimilate Lenin's theoretical heritage in some detail and to educate the young generation according to the example of Lenin's life and revolutionary activity" (*ibid.*). To this end, various conferences, lectures, study circles, visits to Lenin museums and other places connected with Lenin's life are organized. Since the jubilee in 1970 research and teaching activities under the heading "Meeting the Anniversary of V. I. Lenin's Birthday" have been directed towards illuminating particular specified phases of Lenin's life, using a large variety of audio-visual material to generate popular appeal.

211

In addition, every working collective engages in a cycle of activities under the heading "The Leninist Watch (*Vakhta*) Reports", all designed to selflessly increase the collective achievement. In Festive Sessions on the eve of the Anniversary, the Party and many other political and social organizations render to Lenin an account of their activities in the preceding year. The institution of socialist *Subbotniks* in honour of Lenin's birthday, already described in detail on pp. 118–19, gave an opportunity to offer up sacrifices to Lenin in the form of presents of labour, carried out in leisure time.

Lenin, I said earlier, has become a symbol embodying selective values and norms of Soviet Marxism–Leninism and activates emotional allegiance to them. When I view Lenin as a symbol I imply that the Lenin cult is not directed towards Lenin as a historical person with a complex personality and a political record that contains both positive and negative features. Instead, I suggest that the cult is oriented towards Lenin as the concrete embodiment of values and norms fundamental to the Soviet system which, although having their base in his actual personality, political ideas and activities, have become gross over-simplifications and are now only tenuously related to them.

Lenin is a very obvious choice for a symbol not only for his association with a *common* positively evaluated historical past but also for his undeniable actual qualities and achievements which, by their wide range, make it possible to endow him with a very general appeal. Building on these actual qualities, Lenin the symbol achieved other, mythical ones, which, in the words of Voronitsyn (1969: 32), made him "an absolute, durable and universally applicable hero". But one set of qualities usually associated with heroism, namely physical strength, daring and military valour, has never been connected with Lenin, while Stalin, in contrast, was commonly presented as "the man of steel". Lenin became endowed with moral superiority and omniscience and, because of these, with supreme and unquestionable authority over a large variety of concerns ranging from ethics, natural science and art to the more applied forms of knowledge in almost every field. He has not only been presented as a mentor for the mentally creative but also was portrayed as the comrade and friend of every worker and peasant, as well as the friend and patron of children, their "Dyadya Lenin". Lenin is thus not just one of many symbols but a key symbol of Soviet culture, in the way Ortner (1973) defined it.

Lenin has become both a summarizing or sacred symbol and an elaborating one, exerting either properties in separate contexts or aspects of both at the same time. When Lenin acts as a sacred symbol he assumes some of the characteristics of a saint, and the expected attitude towards him is one of worship with strong religious overtones (hence the term "cult of Lenin"). In his capacity as an elaborating symbol Lenin is presented as a hero, and people are encouraged not only to admire him but also to be moved by him to action, either in emulation of him or in an attempt to be worthy of him.

An orientation of worship to Lenin as someone with saint-like qualities is well expressed in the well-known Soviet slogan "Lenin lived, Lenin lives, Lenin shall live" and in the attitude to him as someone above human criticism who is worthy of periodic adulation and of the bringing of sacrifice. Any attempt to question the "sacred" nature of Lenin, by either confronting the symbol with the actual historical personality or by destroying one of his many icons, is consequently met by the Soviet regime with the same extreme reaction as was shown to sacrilege by the Catholic Church during the Middle Ages. The following extract from an article in *Izvestiya* (2 February 1966, transl. in *CDSP*), responding to a dissident's attempt to cast doubt on the public image of Lenin, vividly illustrates this reaction: "To what a bottomless morass of abomination must a so-called man of letters sink to desecrate . . . this name that is sacred to us . . . These blasphemous lines alone suffice for the diagnosis that the authors place themselves outside Soviet society". It is noteworthy that one never finds any of the many portraits of Lenin defaced.

Some of the religious overtones of the relation to Lenin by the Soviet people are even recognized by the Soviets themselves, as is made clear in the following despatch, carried by Tass in November 1974, on the occasion of the reopening of the mausoleum after repairs (quoted by Smith 1976: 341):

From early dawn an endless line of people formed up across Red Square from the granite sepulchre held sacred by the working people throughout the world. Over the half century 77 million people [have] passed in a mournful and stern march by the sarcophagus where the genius of humanity lies in state. From this day onwards new thousands and millions of people will be bringing worship to Lenin from all over the world.

But to say that the relation of the Russian people to their dead leader is a religious one still does not tell us what Lenin means to them. Lenin, it seems to me, is not only revered because he was a great revolutionary – the chief inspiration and executioner, and the founding father of the new Soviet society, who exhausted his physical energy prematurely

213

in his selfless struggle for the good of his countrymen. He is also worshipped because his early death in 1924 firmly associates his person with a period in Soviet society when revolutionary *élan* was at its height and idealism and altruism were strong. The notion of a socialist society had not yet become tarnished by the excesses that were to follow under Stalin's rule. The facts that practical policies were not all inspired by high-minded altruism and that many of the later harmful developments had their seeds sown in this early period are, in retrospect, completely obscured by the magnitude of later deviations from the ideal course. This interpretation is supported by the fact that the cult of Lenin assumed a great volume only when Stalin's regime was well established. (For a careful documentation of this statement as concerns the cult of Lenin in children's literature, see O'Dell 1978: 155.) In addition, Lenin also has the great merit of detracting from the conservatism of the existing regime. He can be used to remind people that what may appear as a petrified system is the product of intense and prolonged battles in the past (I am indebted for this idea to G. Hawthorn, personal communication).

An orientation to Lenin as the hero, whose example inspires similar deeds, is developed mainly, though not solely, in children and young people. Not only is children's literature full of stories to foster such imitation, but it is also evoked by the ritual of initiation as Young Pioneers, who are enjoined "to study and work like the great Lenin". This connection is also implied in the Soviet practice to reward outstanding achievement in science, technology or art with the Order of Lenin, the highest and most prestigious in a large collection of Soviet orders. Of these two types of orientation to Lenin the symbol, that worshipping him as a saint has been much more frequently evoked than that of the hero inspiring emulation. This latter function is more prominent in lesser heroes, such as the countless heroes of labour and of the military type.

Looking at the Lenin cult historically, the following developments are of note. Saints arise in the symbolic realm during crises of legitimation, caused either by succession problems or by a weakening or failure of the legitimating ideology. Heroes emerge during times of *general* instability when rapid social and cultural change necessitates the creation of models to aid reorientation, particularly in societies with a low level of education. The Soviet Union has experienced more rapid, drastic and constant change during its first four decades of existence than any other modern society and has inherited, from Tsarist times, a

214

population with a very low level of literacy. Lenin the hero, who inspires by his example, thus became omnipresent during the time of greatest change, the main period of industrialization and collectivization during the thirties, and has never been absent from Soviet life since. The cult of Lenin the saint has shown greater fluctuation and has become most prominent during crises of legitimation. Political power in the USSR, as Barghoorn rightly emphasizes (1972: 29), lacks both the legitimacy derived from custom and kinship in traditional societies and that afforded by competitive political practice and universal suffrage in constitutional democracies. Consequently political leaders since Lenin have had to base their claim to be the rightful rulers of the Soviet State on their alleged custody of Lenin's ideological legacy. It is instructive to reflect when high or low points of the cult were reached, and why these changes took place. A good index of the rises and falls in the intensity of the Lenin cult is gained by an assessment of the amount of Leniniana in the annual demonstration of the October celebrations in Moscow (see pp. 161ff). Another, more impressionistic approach relies on selected direct and indirect historical evidence.

During his lifetime Lenin was already widely loved and revered, and in the critical situation created both for him and for Soviet society by the attempt on his life in 1918 some efforts were made to build him up as a hero. But Lenin himself angrily and resolutely opposed such efforts, as the following remarks made to Bonch-Bruevich, after his recovery, clearly bring out:

What is this? How could you have allowed this? See what they write in the newspapers . . .? It's shameful. They write about me, that I am like this and like that and so on, exaggerating everything, calling me a genius, a kind of extraordinary man – there is an element of mysticism in all this . . . Where does it come from? All our lives we have fought against exalting the individual, against the elevation of the single person, and long ago we were over and done with the business of a hero, and here it comes up again . . . (Bonch-Bruevich reprinted by Deutscher (ed.) 1973: 88)

Although Lenin was worshipped during his lifetime he was still being judged as a historical person and political leader who was not above criticism. The periodic "left deviations" in the Party bear witness to this fact. This state of affairs changed after his death.

In the days and weeks following his death a powerful movement arose to endow Lenin with extraordinary qualities. It sprang from two distinct, though related sources. The leadership Lenin had given in those decisive early years of the new Soviet State had earned him the affection and respect of a very large number of Soviet citizens. His early death threatened to leave a great vacuum which the Soviet people tried to fill by artificially prolonging Lenin's presence in Soviet society. The detailed accounts of the events immediately after Lenin's death by Abramov (1969: 46ff) leave no doubt about the facts that he was genuinely loved and admired by a large proportion of the Soviet population and that the decision to embalm him was to a large extent prompted by spontaneous popular demand. As the people could not do without Lenin, they replaced Lenin the historical person by Lenin the symbol. Lenin had not only the affection and admiration of the simple people but also those of the cultural elite. One concrete manifestation of the latter was the monumental poem *Vladimir Ilyich Lenin*, composed by Mayakovsky in 1924. The closing words of the first verse:

> Lenin
> is now
> the most live of all living,
> Our weapon,
> our knowledge,
> our power
> (translation by Marshall 1945: 84)

combine an attitude of religious awe with a realistic political evaluation, and it is no accident that these words have become a popular slogan.

The other source of a Lenin cult in those weeks following his death was the necessity to consolidate Lenin's image as a charismatic leader and to institutionalize his charisma in the Party in order to secure political continuity in the very young and as yet precariously established Soviet State. This endeavour is very clearly expressed in the following words concluding identical articles in the two most important Soviet newspapers *Pravda* and *Izvestiya* (23 January 1924) two days after Lenin's death.

Lenin lives in the heart of every member of our Party. Every member of our Party is a small part of Lenin. Our whole communist family is a collective embodiment of Lenin . . .

They hope that our Party will fall apart. But the Party will go ahead with iron steps. (This is) because it is a Leninist party . . . because it holds in its hands the testament which comrade Lenin left to it . . .

This was clearly the first attempt to build up Lenin as a superhuman being whose charisma could be institutionalized by attaching it to the organization of his followers, in this case the Communist Party. While the first part of this quotation is written in imagery which is strongly religious, the second is written in the language of realistic politics.

Once the immediate crisis following Lenin's death was resolved and political continuity was assured, the pitch of the Lenin cult fell considerably for a few years. It was revived again only when Stalin had been in power for some time. Then Lenin's charisma became exploited to legitimize and exalt Stalin's position in Soviet society. The following poem (quoted from a 1938 children's magazine by O'Dell 1978: 156) is a typical example of such endeavours:

> *Lenin lived*
> Lenin! Who does not know him?
> From the Kremlin, where he soundly sleeps,
> To the mountain tops of the blue Altai
> The glory of Lenin brightly shines.
>
> Higher than the mountains, wider than every sea,
> Heavier than the very earth
> Was our people's grief
> When he died, our dear one.
>
> Lenin died. But stronger than steel,
> Firmer than the flinty mountain races
> Came his pupil – splendid Stalin.
> He is leading us to victories and happiness.

From then onwards the Soviet population had two heroes to worship. Lenin's and Stalin's portraits appeared everywhere side by side. Although I have seen no sources to document this, it is generally assumed that Lenin gradually receded in importance behind Stalin once the latter was firmly in power. Lenin was usually portrayed as an abstract background figure, while Stalin was shown to be the man of the moment. It is beyond the scope of this work to deal with the Stalin cult, except to say a few words about its end.

Heroes are not only born but they also die, sometimes quickly and violently. The problem of expurgating from a culture a well-established hero who has fallen from official grace was faced by Khrushchev's regime after the public denunciation of Stalin in 1961 at the twenty-second Party Congress. Besides removing Stalin's body from the mausoleum the Soviet leadership also had to remove countless statues, busts and portraits and rename many places (including the "hero" city Stalingrad). But they also had the much more difficult task of changing Stalin from a hero into a historic individual and a political ruler, with a good deal of negative features, in the consciousness of the great majority of the population. There was widespread popular resistance to the abolition of the Stalin cult from people who had preserved a religious faith in him and who were psychologically unable to admit his fallibility (see White 1979: 108ff). Not surprisingly the task of ending the Stalin cult has never been completed. In recent years there have even been attempts to effect a partial rehabilitation of Stalin.

The extreme height of the Lenin cult, it appears, was reached only some years after Stalin's fall from grace during the sixties. This was primarily due to the strenuous efforts to wipe out the memory of Stalin and of the policies which had discredited Soviet Marxism–Leninism and to indicate symbolically a return to Leninist politics. It received an additional impetus from the wave of nostalgia for the "glorious" revolutionary past and the effort to revive the spirit of that time which swept the country during the three big jubilees of 1967, 1970 and 1972. Outstanding among all the anniversaries was, of course, the one-hundredth anniversary of Lenin's birthday in 1970. On that occasion the usual attempts at restraint were abandoned, and there was no moderation in the scale of the organized events nor in the amount of Leniniana produced. From early 1969 onwards every teaching, research and cultural institute in the land was mobilized by the Party to organize some events for the occasion. Although a new pitch was reached in the Lenin cult it remained merely an increase in scale. No new ritual actions, attributes or even slogans were devised to express the Soviet population's relation to their dead leader. Old slogans, such as "Lenin is with us", "Lenin is still more alive than all those living", "Lenin is in our thoughts and in our plans", suggested little change in the nature of that relationship.

Up until the early sixties the cult of Lenin had consisted of a number of unrelated practices. After that it became incorporated into the system of socialist rituals which were being instituted during that time. Thus there are now few places of ritual celebration without their bust of Lenin and few ritual occasions on which the presence of Lenin is not evoked. But besides, and perhaps in spite of, this institutionalization of the Lenin cult there still exists a good deal of spontaneous Lenin-worship.

What then have been the effects of the Lenin cult on Soviet society? Has this form of Leninism been as powerful a contributor to the building of Soviet society as Leninism in its other forms, or has the high pitch of this cult in recent times come to be counter-productive?

Such questions are notoriously difficult to answer as it is impossible to decide to what extent the goals of this cult – the creation of a citizenship loyal to Party and State and constantly endeavouring to improve their individual contribution to the common good – have been reached and, if so, whether successes were due to the cult of Lenin or to other, more rational strategies. The question of whether the cult of Lenin has been counter-productive is also difficult to answer as we have only impressionistic evidence at our disposal. There is certainly still widespread spontaneous expression of admiration and affection for Lenin by many sections of the population and little publicly voiced criticism, even from dissidents. When the taboo on criticism was broken by Solzhenitsyn with his publication in the West of *Gulag Archipelago*, savage retribution followed immediately. But the cult, particularly the activities organized towards it by the Party during the celebrations of Lenin's centenary, assumed such a pitch that it strained rather than enhanced feelings of affection, particularly among the intelligentsia (Churchward 1973: 101). One indication of this strain and of the evolution of a less reverent attitude towards Lenin was the emergence for the first time during that period of jokes about Lenin, a well-known device to release tension. (Example: They are building beds for three now. Why? The answer lies in the well-known Russian slogan "Lenin is always with us".) Though it is notable that, compared with Stalin jokes, there are few Lenin jokes. Moreover, the latter usually poke fun at the Lenin cult, rather than at any of Lenin's policies or actions (see *The Big Red Joke Book*). Voronitsyn (1969: 35) suggests that the Lenin cult has failed as far as Soviet youth is concerned. As evidence for this conclusion he cites the fact (documented by a Soviet survey) that not many young people study the works of Lenin. This conclusion seems unwarranted to me because such rational activity as studying what Lenin *actually* said is not necessary to, or may be even irreconcilable with, cultic adoration.

Finally, I would like to raise the question of whether a leader cult will continue to play a part in Soviet society as it moves closer to the communist stage. The evidence we can call on to answer this question is contradictory. Khrushchev's speech in denunciation of the Stalin cult created a widespread disillusionment with, and awareness of, the harmful consequences of a leader cult in the Soviet population. But ironically the crisis created by the denunciation of one leader cult, causing widespread anomie, made it imperative to revive another leader cult, Leninism, to fill the gap that had been created. At the same time there appeared to be a determination among Party members not to encourage a new cult. Brezhnev, Khrushchev's successor, who holds most of the positions of supreme power in the Soviet Union today, has not yet been built up into a hero or saint in quite the same way as Lenin and Stalin, and initially strenuous efforts were made to avoid a leader cult around his person. To give examples of this effort, in demonstrations on mass political holidays in 1977 and 1978 I observed that Brezhnev's portrait was only infrequently carried on its own but mostly appeared together with those of the other members of the Politbureau. I noticed too, that of the four giant portraits decorating the demonstration square in Leningrad, Brezhnev's was much smaller and further away from the tribune than those of Marx, Engels and Lenin. This impression is also borne out by O'Dell's (1978: 103) analysis of children's literature. Its findings are that, while reference to Stalin was omnipresent in children's literature of the thirties, there has not been a single reference to Brezhnev in the same literature during the early seventies. In recent years, however, there has also been noted a gradually escalating movement towards a cult of Brezhnev by many observers (for a documentation of this developing cult see Brown 1978: 309). It remains to be seen whether it will develop into a full-scale cult. Soviet political culture, as numerous empirical studies have shown (see White 1979: 107), is distinguished by an acceptance of a strong central power and by belief in its infallibility. Such a culture is, of course, fertile soil for the development of a renewed leader cult.

Hollander's (1973: 192) contention that without a living cult figure Soviet secular religion, as he calls it, is bound to decline is untenable. The cult of Lenin seems to be quite sufficient to maintain a religious dimension, and it is a much surer way to secure religious reverence. Not only is Lenin the symbol much more deeply embedded in the Soviet psyche but also it does not entail the risk of becoming devalued through political fallibility, which the cult of a living leader would involve. Also, in the post-Stalin era, the idea of the Party as an infallible body above and divorced from the failings of individuals has once more come into the foreground, whereas previously, Stalin was regarded as almost its embodiment.

SYMBOLIC ACTION

Symbolic action, it was pointed out above, is the very nucleus of ritual and can take two basic forms. The action can be purely symbolic, that is there is no intrinsic means–goal relationship, or the action can be of a mixed nature. If the latter is the case it has a symbolic as well as an instrumental or expressive aspect. Both types are found in the new Soviet ritual, the latter being much more frequent than the former. As might be expected, symbolic action of the mixed type is prevalent in the ritual focussing on areas of social life in which adaptive activity is dominant, such as work, military life, education. Pure symbolic action predominates in ritual dedicated to areas where such activity is minimal, such as changes in the individual life cycle, or focal points in a society's development, like Victory Day or the Anniversary of the October Revolution.

Pure symbolic action is not only very infrequent but also, as a form of action, does not have a unified focus. Thus the Solemn Registration of Birth ritual may include symbolic actions with such diverse origins and referents as lighting a candle to symbolize the creation of new life, on the one side, and presenting parents with a Pioneer scarf to indicate future political obligations, on the other. A secular funeral includes in uneasy coexistence a symbolic action such as throwing three clumps of earth onto the grave with a parting speech giving a secular interpretation of the meaning of life.

In rituals where instrumental action is being endowed with a symbolic aspect symbolism is more congruent with the overall aim of Soviet ritual. In the various rituals of initiation into a new collective the first action of the initiand in his new status or his first encounter with a new mentor and/or with his new tools are given added significance by being separated off from the ordinary run of instrumental activities. This process of "framing" of instrumental activity relates it to a complex of meaning not normally associated with it. Examples which come to mind are acts like pouring the millionth ton of steel, ploughing the first furrow, giving the first military salute or answering the first bell in a new school year. Such symbolic activity, it seems to me, is particularly apt as it makes for an easy transition between ritual and instrumental activity and avoids artificiality, pomposity or sentimentality.

Besides ritualizing otherwise instrumental action by "framing", Soviet ideological cadres have also created various kinds of activity in which the symbolic and the instrumental aspects are of equal importance. These activities, starting with the *Subbotnik* movement in 1919, continuing in the Stakhanovite movement of the 1930s and finding a new interpretation in the movements of socialist competition and for communist labour of the present period, enable people to develop and express a normative commitment through labour, freely given beyond what is required by their work contract. Although the direct economic value of such activities is often doubted by critics, these practices have not only been retained but have become an integral part of Soviet life and can be described, to use Ortner's (1973) term, as a "key scenario".

A third kind of symbolic action results from endowing expressive action with a symbolic aspect. An activity which normally is only expressive – dramatic activity – assumes a symbolic aspect by becoming related to a field laden with evocative significata – Soviet history. The dramatic re-creation of the Soviet past brings history to life and bridges the gap between the present and the past. This dramatic reconstruction of particular heroic episodes, of a group's (a brigade or workers' dynasty) or collective's (factory or town) entire history is performed live either by ordinary participants or, more effectively, by surviving witnesses to the original events and by the use of film and sound-track. Re-creation of history may also be more instrumental in appearance, taking the form of amateur research to establish history, as in the Festival of Our Street (p. 151) or in the activity of young Red Pathfinders (p. 148). But both types of reconstructing history reactivate a host of emotions and effect a transference of emotional energy and ideological fervour onto the tasks of the present. This kind of symbolic activity has appeared most consistently and frequently in Soviet ritual right from the time of the Revolution and this, supported by related symbolic devices, gives it its distinctive character.

This effort to draw out emotional reserves by bringing to life the heroic periods of Soviet history was already evident in the creation of heroes who personify and concretize history. It also forms the motivation for the practice of using historically significant spatial configurations for ritual purposes, as described in the following section. In all these activities history is re-created not as it actually happened but in the way ritual specialists want to believe it happened. Chosen episodes and dramatic emphases, Warner (1965: 107ff) points out, reflect a symbolic choice. History is presented in a way that forges a desired collective identity.

SYMBOLISM OF SPATIAL CONFIGURATIONS

Not only human but also material witnesses of history are widely used as symbolic devices in Soviet ritual. These historical spatial configurations may be buildings, public spaces, monuments and memorials or whole towns that are associated with significant historical events or whole periods – mostly with the Revolution and the Great Patriotic War. Many of them have instrumental as well as symbolic uses, such as the Smolny Institute, the Museum of the Revolution in Moscow or the "hero" towns. Thus the town of Leningrad has become a symbol of both revolutionary and military heroism, of sacrifice and of triumph over great adversity. The Ural town of Magnitogorsk has become a symbol for another set of values. Its large modern industrial complex was created "out of nothing" in the early thirties and initiated Stalin's industrialization programme. It is now seen as a symbol of "labour valour", of industrialization and the political triumph it brought, as well as of technical supremacy and, consequently, of victory in the Great Patriotic War (Grishchenko and Kakonin 1974: 7–8).

Other spatial configurations have purely symbolic significance, having been deliberately created or preserved to keep a historical period alive. Here I refer to monumental art, created on a large scale ever since the Revolution in an effort to express the irresistible might and timeless solidity of the new social system and, under Stalin, of its ruler. Among the many monuments, sculptures and buildings inspired by these sentiments a few have to be singled out for their high saturation with symbolic quality. I am referring to certain war memorials which have assumed a symbolic value far beyond that usually associated with such places, such as the war cemeteries in Leningrad (Piskarevska cemetery) and in Volgograd. While the spatial configurations in the first group bring into play their symbolic quality only *during* ritual performances, those in the second group exude it all the time and to such a strong degree that they have become "holy" or "sacred" places. It is significant that those associated with the Great Patriotic War are more avidly and more consistently endowed with a sacred quality. They have become places of general worship, thanksgiving, inspiration and reflection (see, for example, Fursin 1973: 56).

The spatial configurations in both groups are used to form the setting for the staging of rituals, and their symbolic quality is exploited to set the tone. While towns like Leningrad, Moscow or Volgograd are rich in places of symbolic significance, other towns have to simulate them in the same way as an artistic director designs a stage setting and, in the process, must lose some of that evocative power.

But the "settings" for ritual performances are not only taken from history. Sometimes a contemporary spatial configuration is used to assist the transfer of attachments and resulting moral sentiments from one field of human endeavour to another. This is the case when, for example, the ritual of enlistment into the armed forces is staged in the factory where the young people have worked until call-up. Surrounded by people and sites familiar and dear to them, the young people are made more conscious of what there is to defend.

BODY MOVEMENT AS SYMBOLISM

"The social body", says Douglas (1970: 12, 93), "constrains the way the physical body is perceived . . . The more the social situation exerts pressure on persons involved in it, the more the social demand for conformity tends to be expressed by a demand for physical control." This necessarily becomes reflected in a society's symbolic system in general and in its ritual in particular. An examination of body symbolism in Soviet ritual shows that Douglas's thesis is very apt. So great is the control over the body and disdain of most body processes that the first impression is of body symbolism being non-existent in Soviet ritual. But a closer study reveals that only body movement resulting from a loose control – wild or ecstatic movement, organic processes, trance, unconventional appearance, are excluded from ritual. Body movement expressing careful control and precise co-ordination in the movement of a number of human bodies, in contrast, are highly valued and widely represented. The three most notable examples in Soviet ritual of controlled and precisely co-ordinated symbolic body movement are military modes of action, massed choirs and mass gymnastic displays. Very notable also is the absence of sexual symbolism and the general avoidance (except in the birth rite) of any demarcation of differences between the sexes.

Military modes of action, such as marching, parading, carrying banners, saluting, awarding medals, giving an oath and calling people to attention through bugle fanfares, are a basic ingredient of the ritual of the mass holidays and of the initiation rituals into social and political collectives and occur even in the less political and public familial rites and popular holidays. Ritual movement is often organized in exactly the same precise and detailed way as military movement. The demonstration on mass political holidays, particularly from the thirties onwards, has been organized in every detail. Thus at the beginning of the thirties, according to *Massovoe* . . . (1932: 9ff), the procession was divided into columns and battalions, each separated precisely from the other by a regulation number of paces. Each battalion was given precise specifications of every move, and special people were designated to see to it that the stipulated order was maintained.

The military body movement in Soviet ritual came first both chronologically and logically. Military organization of everyday life, imposed on the new society in 1918 by the necessity to confront internal and external enemies intent on destroying it, naturally found its way into ritual. Later forms of symbolic body movement, although more highly developed, are clearly based on this early foundation. This intrusion of military acts into the ritual of the other two traditions also reflects the predominance and greater intensity in public consciousness of the military–patriotic value complex within the whole ideology of Soviet Marxism–Leninism.

The massed choir, rendering messages both verbally and musically, originated in the mass dramatic presentations or spectacles of the twenties. It links otherwise unconnected episodes and drives the action forward. It is not only a theatrical but also a symbolic device. For both participants and audience it can stand for the elementary power of the people, moving history along by the force of their united, disciplined action. Thus it is not the message but the action of rendering it in unison which makes the choir a powerful symbolic device. Like every activity in which people are united in large numbers, the massed choir can be both an expression of controlled co-ordination and contains the possibility of stimulating spontaneity or even anarchy. In the very early years of the mass holidays, when political control was still relatively loose, this latter characteristic sometimes came to the fore. On one occasion in 1920, when the choir in the mass spectacle had incited participatory responses from the audience, the audience identification with the choir became so strong that spectators with spontaneous enthusiasm joined the choir in storming the Winter Palace (Tsekhnovitser 1931: 17). At the present time, the choir as a dramatic device is rarely used, but a more conventional massed musical choir is very popular. Several republics have annual festivals of song, on the occasion of which thousands of people are organized into one huge powerful choir. Again, it is both the songs rendered and the form of rendering them that symbolize a political relationship between the individual and his society.

The epitome of controlled, carefully co-ordinated body movement is given by the massed gymnastic displays, a cross between sport, entertainment and ritual. They present in both horizontal and vertical form

Mass gymnastic display during May Day celebrations in Red Square

"living pictures", such as a five-cornered star or a dove of peace, verbal political messages, names, or with the help of some attributes, they even develop a theme through several dramatic sequences. This is achieved through the careful co-ordination of music, colour (of dress) and body movement. The successful creation of the whole depends entirely on the disciplined action of each constituent part. The possibilities for social and political education contained in training people for their performance is well expressed in the following extract from a book by a specialist in these mass gymnastic displays:

The success of the mass displays depends a great deal on the accuracy and simultaneity of the execution of the exercises, on the immaculate alignment of participants. To achieve this is impossible without high consciousness, discipline and love of work. These qualities necessarily have to be inculcated during the process of preparing the displays. Mass physical education displays must in every possible way further the strengthening of friendship, self-discipline, collectivism and the inculcation of the feeling of responsibility to one's collective. (Abramyan 1966: 4)

Significantly, these massed gymnastic displays, together with many holidays of sport, have come into prominence only at the height of

Stalinism during the late thirties (for the ritual aspects of Soviet sport in general see Riordan 1977).

All three types of body movement described above point to a striking correspondence between the physical and the social body in Soviet society. Both in symbolic body movement and in socio-political activity the emphasis is on the mobilization of the masses, on the self-control of each constituent individual and on a subjection of the individual to the collective pursuit. Controlled, carefully co-ordinated body movement in Soviet ritual can thus be regarded as a key symbolic activity of the elaborating type providing, in Ortner's words (1973), orientations or strategies for action, "a recipe for living" in the Soviet social context.

The foregoing analysis of the symbolism in the system of Soviet socialist rituals has brought out a number of important points. The paucity of symbols in the form of concrete objects – the most obvious and most visible kind – must not be allowed to obscure the fact that symbolism in general is much better developed than first impressions lead one to believe and that a number of key symbols both of the summarizing and of the elaborating type have emerged. Secondly, the distinctive character of Soviet ritual symbolism is conveyed by the large number of significata taken from Soviet history, particularly from its two "heroic" periods. Thirdly, ritual symbolism occupies the same ambiguous position between a secular and a sacred orientation as is already identified in the system of beliefs and practices in general. On the one side, there is careful avoidance of conventional religious symbolism and of reference to any mystical, supra-empirical powers. On the other side, however, symbolism operates in such a way as to evoke impressions of timelessness and immutability as well as feelings of awe and adoration, together with an attitude of unquestioning acceptance. Fourthly, symbolism is much better developed – in terms of frequency of appearance and horizontal multivocality, as well as in the degree of congruence with the underlying orientations of Soviet political culture and the ritual system – in the *rites de passage*, marking important transitions in the social and political development of individuals or of the whole society than in the less political ritual of both the life cycle and the calendric cycle. But this greater degree of congruence and wider applicability is usually gained at the cost of historical depth and of vertical multivocality, whereas the more disparate and less well-integrated symbolism of the ritual of the life cycle and calendric cycle, often having its roots in ancient popular culture, is strong on both these counts. A judicious mixing of the two kinds of symbolism which, as the following chapter reveals, is as yet rarely accomplished, would therefore seem the best strategy for a future development of Soviet socialist ritual.

12

vvvvvvvvvvvvvvvvvvvvvvvvvvvvvvvvvvvvvvvvvvvvvvvvvvvvvvvvvvvvvvvvvvvvvvvvvv

Syncretism in Soviet symbolism

The creation of the new Soviet ritual during the last twenty years has confronted ritual specialists with a dilemma. On the one hand, the new rituals were intended to indicate a deliberate break with the past, a delineation of the Soviet socialist and secular society from a religious and politically reactionary Tsarist Russia, the assertion of a new value system against an old one. On the other hand, it is recognized that a cutting off of cultural roots goes against the nature of ritual itself. Ritual symbols, it is realized, exert their influence on human emotions because of their multivocality. Whereas ritual specialists working in the early post-revolutionary period completely disavowed the Russian cultural heritage stretching back beyond 1917 and instead sought inspiration in the past of the European revolutionary movement, those working in the present time recognize that multivocality can only be achieved if a symbol is deeply embedded in a people's culture. One Soviet writer goes as far as positing a natural continuity between the rituals of the progresssive exploited classes in Tsarist society and the new ones (Ugrinovich 1975: 110), but evidence in support of this thesis is thin, excepting only the ritual of the mass political holidays. Other writers acknowledge that the old ritual has to be reworked to be acceptable.

Great pains are taken to find elements in the old rites that are congruent with the present value system, and to justify syncretism. The utilization of old rituals is advocated by one influential team of writers in an enthusiastic, almost populist vein:

The more progressive ones . . . express most clearly and distinctively the popular experience accumulated and enriched over thousands of years, their practical wisdom. In them is expressed the character and the soul of a people, the best features of the history of a society's cultural life. The ancient ritual . . . is a highly artistic creation by the people, by its best talents, and in it are concentrated the spiritual strength and mental energy of a people. (Kampars and Zakovich 1967: 94)

To legitimize their attempt to preserve the Russian cultural past many authors (e.g. El'chenko 1977: 56) will point out, with some justification, that this was Lenin's attitude when he rejected the cultural revolution advocated by the Proletkul't movement.

The recognition of the necessity to create continuity between the old and the new has had the consequences of a new submersion into the hitherto rather neglected, or even completely unknown, pre-revolutionary popular cultural past. In some cases this submersion has given rise to an almost lyrical enthusiasm for that past and to inevitable comparisons between the old and the new ritual, which leave the latter in an unfavourable light. The following catalogue by one team of writers (Kampars and Zakovich 1967: 102) of positive features of the old ritual, followed by the concession that these are poorly developed in the new ritual, would be endorsed by many other Soviet specialists in the field:

(*a*) active participation by *all* and no division between participants and audience
(*b*) skilful utilization of symbolism
(*c*) each ritual has its own specific character
(*d*) all-embracing gaiety, life-affirming popular laughter, a connection with the popular humorous (*smekhova*) culture
(*e*) steadfastness and stability.

Lobacheva (1972 and 1977), an ethnographer familiar with traditional popular ritual in the Islamic areas of the Soviet Union, also insistently urges a greater retention of the traditional ritual and more recognition of national peculiarities. Her suggestion of grouping the traditional holidays of the various nationalities under the heading "Soviet national ritual" expresses her wish to see a better balance preserved between the new and the old. Ethnographers, she says, could be most useful as consultants in this area (Lobacheva and Tul'tseva 1977: 43).

The reason for a renewed interest in pre-Soviet rituals and their symbolism does not lie solely in a scientific understanding of cultural processes or in a generous appreciation of the value of the old rituals. It is often based on a more pragmatic realization, taught by experience, that new rituals will be accepted more quickly if they incorporate some of the old symbolic forms (Kampars and Zakovich 1967: 94).

Resolving this problem of the relation between the old and the new in Soviet ritual is seen by many as one of the most important conditions for the success of new ritual. Although in the past there has been much opposition to the viewpoint expressed in the above quotation by Kampars and Zakovich, there is today no ritual specialist who will deny its correctness in principle. In consequence there has occurred in recent years a conscious effort to preserve, and even to resurrect, some of the old rituals or their elements and to create some continuity between the two cultures. Despite agreement in principle and a general recognition of the necessity to approach the selection of elements from the cultural heritage according to strict Marxist criteria of what can be considered acceptable, the practice has been very complicated and controversial.

According to Marxist canons only the progressive elements of the old culture are considered acceptable. Some ritual specialists have clung to a very narrow definition of what is progressive and have wanted to select only such cultural elements that are genuinely of the people's culture and have their origin neither in class exploitation nor in religious domination by the Church. They have further stipulated that their aesthetic and moral tone as well as their practical implications have to be congruent with contemporary life. It soon became evident that such rigid criteria of selection would have to reject nearly all the old rituals and symbols, and some ritual specialists began to advocate a slightly more flexible approach. Spokesmen of this group suggest ignoring the origins of rituals and accepting all those that have changed their content and assumed a new function that corresponds to contemporary aesthetic sensibilities and ideological requirements. It seems that this latter group has won out. The descriptions of holidays and rituals in part II show that a number of those which have been adopted with minor or major modifications would not have passed selection on the criteria advanced by the first group.

A dilemma which usually faces ritual specialists engaged in syncretistic activity in complex societies is demonstrated by the fact that a cultural heritage is not a unitary ideological construct, but contains many diverse strands in the form of class, religious and national sub-cultures. Soviet ritual specialists have shown a keen awareness of the existence of class sub-cultures and have endeavoured, where possible, to select only the ritual of the exploited classes, of the ordinary people. In contrast, they have not faced the problem that the cultural past of imperial Russia was also extremely diverse in terms of ethnic, national and religious groups. They have just tacitly assumed that inspiration for the new ritual must be sought only in the cultural heritage of the Slavic nationalities, and they have borrowed both from their recent Christian and their more remote pagan stage of cultural development. Here it is notable that the remote pagan past is often given preference over the still-living Christian culture.

Thus an important characteristic of syncretism between the new all-Soviet and the old ritual symbolism is an almost complete neglect of the Muslim Islamic past belonging to the very numerous peoples of the Central Asian republics. Consequently, the elements borrowed from ritual in a Slavic Christian tradition are frequently alien to the Muslim national groups, to whom they have often been introduced mechanically. All the socialist *rites de passage* are, in their timing and their structural features, clearly modelled on their Christian counterparts and incorporate their individual symbolic elements.

In the Islamic religious tradition surrounding birth, for example, there is no *one* ritual corresponding to the Christian baptism but a whole complex of ritual actions evolving one out of the other in an established temporal sequence. Also the timing of the Soviet Solemn Registration of the New-Born Child within a month after birth ignores the Islamic prescription of complete seclusion of mother and child during the first forty days after birth. Such a violation of a powerful taboo on human contact evokes deeply ingrained fears in many quarters about supernatural retribution. The Russian popular symbolic action of making guests autograph a bottle of wine to be saved for the next ritual occasion in the child's life, also introduced in Islamic areas, offends against their taboo on drinking alcohol (Lobacheva 1972: 10). Understandably, such lack of sensitivity has led to a low rate of acceptance of the new birth ritual in traditionally Islamic areas (see Lobacheva 1975: 84).

The new wedding rite, too, is difficult to integrate into the much more complex Islamic ritual sequence. Its symbolic actions of exchanging rings and drinking from the common cup have no equivalents in Islamic tradition. Moreover, the latter action is offensive to the sexual moral sentiments of Muslims. The coming-of-age ritual, which was designed to replace the Lutheran confirmation, has also been introduced into some Muslim republics regardless of the fact that transitions at other stages of development have been more significant in their religious culture (*ibid.*: 115). Turning to holidays of the calendric cycle and their ritual symbolism, the introduction into Islamic areas of New Year celebrations with its "Christmas" tree and exchange of presents ignores the Islamic calendar, according to which the New Year, called *Navruz*, is in the spring and has its own traditional ritual (*ibid.*: 134).

A more spontaneous process of cultural borrowing from the European tradition by the Muslim groups has occurred as a result of the shift from a traditional to an urban industrial style of life which has been more advanced among the nationalities in the western part of the Soviet Union. This selective borrowing is thus mainly carried out by the urban educated strata as part of a general process of Europeanization. Examples here are the adjustment of the traditional Islamic wedding ritual to urban living conditions, social relations and sexual morals, or the adoption of celebrating birthdays, a consequence of the greater attention individuals receive in the modern urban nuclear family.

There is an awareness among some writers who are dealing with the new rituals in predominantly Muslim republics (e.g. Aliev 1968; Lobacheva 1975), that this mechanical transference of the new life-cycle rituals from the western republics to their native areas is a harmful process. Some efforts have been made in recent years by local organizations in these Muslim areas to work out their own ritual forms (see Aliev 1968: 207). In some areas of Kazakhstan, in contrast, cultural borrowing has not been as one-sided. There the local version of *Maslenitsa* contains a mixture of Soviet socialist, Russian popular/Orthodox, and Kazakh popular/Islamic elements. Thus in the carnival procession there march both the traditional Russian *Maslenitsa* characters and characters associated with the Kazakh *Novrusa*, and the refreshments sold on this day include both Russian and Kazakh national specialities (Sarsenbaev 1974: 186). Such a development mirrors the greater degree of national integration in Kazakhstan, compared with the other Central Asian republics, due to the fact that the European nationality groups are represented in much bigger proportions in this republic.

The other notable feature of the syncretism between the old and the new is the tendency, shared by Soviet ritual specialists with their Nazi counterparts, to go back to the pagan origins of a ritual and to skip its Christian stage, in the mistaken belief that pagan ritual is less religious than the Christian variety. This tendency is also noted by a Soviet critic of the new ritual who scathingly reminds ritual specialists of the polytheism and of the high level of superstition and magic in pagan religion. He concludes that a preference for pagan ritual could only be made by "a believing pagan but not by an atheist" (Petukhov 1969: 275).

The fact that syncretism of the old and the new often appears awkward or even completely ludicrous is due to a number of factors which will become obvious after an examination of how syncretism is effected. Attempts to fuse the old with the new in Soviet ritual have followed four different, though overlapping, approaches:

(1) Old holidays or rituals have been adopted wholesale, and a few new elements have been grafted onto them.
(2) Old holidays and rituals have been adopted in their entirety, but their main symbolic activities have been given a new content.
(3) Minor symbolic elements have been detached from their old context and have been inserted, with or without modification, into new rituals.
(4) The old holiday and its ritual has been rejected wholesale, but the space it occupied in the calendric cycle is appropriated for a new ritual.

(1) In the first group are mainly holidays of the calendric cycle with either traditional religious or pagan associations and strong national peculiarities, for which there are no equivalents in the new Soviet ritual. Among these are the Slavic Ivan Kupala, the Latvian *Ligo*, the Tatar Sabantui, or the Islamic *Navruz*. They are oriented towards the changes in nature and, to a lesser extent, to the accompanying changes in the cycle of work, and are said to have lost their original religious or pagan content. It is further claimed that they have been given a new content and a new function at the present time. In actual fact they seem to have lost most of their symbolic quality and have become just occasions to mark a change in the seasons and to indulge in general jollity. They are popular for their colourful, vivid and sometimes romantic dramatic form and for the scope they offer for popular creativity. If original symbolic references are still remembered, they are taken as romantic folklore. These occasions of popular gaiety, humour or romantic indulgence do not have any moral or ideological axe to grind. Grafted on to them by ritual specialists have been activities which, because of their dull form and their serious and moralistic content, appear incongruous and contrived and seem unlikely to become integrated into the festivities. They will therefore not achieve their intended purpose and may even be liable to kill the spirit of the festivities and incite counter-productive resentment.

Particularly blatant examples are given by the changes introduced into the colourful old Slavic holiday of Ivan Kupala, a summer solstice focussing on the media of water, fire and plant life and involving Neptune or other water spirits. In one Ukrainian village the newly introduced opening and closing acts of this romantic folkloristic holiday respectively consist of hoisting the Red Banner and of singing a contemporary song of peace. Although tagged on arbitrarily, these additions at least do not destroy the main part of the ritual performance. In other areas, however, the whole ritual is made completely ludicrous. Here the water spirits, when asked permission to swim the river by the young girls of the village, advise the girls to enjoy themselves but also "to be persistent in their work and to storm the cosmic distance" (quoted with strong disapproval by Brudnyi 1968: 96–7). Yet another effort to integrate socialist references into this popular folk holiday also misfires, although it tries to express the new content in a shape that harmonizes with the existing forms of the ritual. In this performance, the candles on the traditional wreaths, to be floated down the river, are lit from the Eternal Flame at the Grave of the Unknown Soldier (quoted with approval by Voina 1976: 81). Such an action exposes the great superficiality of approach to the old holidays and their ritual and makes it quite clear that they are being used, rather than being performed for their intrinsic value.

(2) Efforts to give new content to old ritual forms tackle the problem of syncretism more at its root. They will be successful if the new content harmonizes with the underlying basic mood of the ritual complex expressed in its other symbolic forms. These conditions, in my opinion, are not fulfilled in the changes made to the old Russian Shrovetide, *Maslenitsa*. Here a holiday devoted to the change of seasons has been reinterpreted to become an occasion that focusses on the changes in the cycle of agricultural labour. Although this is quite a subtle change, it nevertheless jars because it is out of tune with the symbolic forms. The romantic, fairytale figures central to *Maslenitsa* just cannot become vehicles for expressing prosaic ideological messages about labour. More successful is the reinterpretation of the symbolic action in the New Year ritual of revelling (*shchedrovanie*) (see p. 139). Here old forms have chiefly been retained, but have subtly changed their content by allying them to a collectivist, rather than an individualist, orientation and by reversing the process of exchange.

(3) A transfer of separate symbolic elements from old to new rituals has been most common in the life-cycle rituals. Here the inability to find new symbolic forms made it imperative to borrow old ones in order to achieve any emotional impact. Although a transference from a religious to a secular context has taken place, a reinterpretation of symbolic content is usually thought unnecessary. Ritual specialists are

at pains to point out that these elements were either annexed by the Church in the first place and have no intrinsic religious meaning or that, if they ever had it, they have completely lost it. Examples mentioned are the institution of godparents, wedding rings, the lighting of candles or the ringing of bells. Sometimes attempts are made to obscure the religious origins by changing names which contain a religious reference, as in the change of *krestnye roditeli* (literal translation "christening parents") to *nazvannye roditeli* (appointed parents) or of *Maslenitsa* to "Seeing-off of Winter".

If the religious content of a symbolic form is thought to be still active, attempts are made to give a new content to this form. A case in point is the act in the funeral rite of throwing three clumps of earth onto the coffin in the open grave, which is now being accompanied by a few words from the ritual specialist indicating the new secular interpretation. Such an attempt, at least in the short run, appears more designed to ease the conscience of the ideologically conscious ritual specialist than to alter deep-seated associations for ritual participants. In either case, the old symbolic element remains poorly integrated. Even if it no longer contradicts the new ideology it refers to, it does nothing to enhance it.

Besides such syncretism in the official part of a rite there is also a lot of spontaneously executed symbolic action of a syncretist nature which the authorities are powerless to control. A most striking example here is the tenacious survival of the Russian Orthodox symbolic action of putting food and even toys on graves, even if the deceased have received a secular State funeral and are buried in such official socialist places as the Mars Field (a memorial place for the victims of the Revolution in Leningrad) or the Piskarevska Cemetery (a national place of remembrance for the victims of the Leningrad blockade and a "socialist shrine").

But even if it is *logically* not very consistent to insert the old symbolic elements into the new ritual, they do *in fact* blend reasonably well into their new context, as the life-cycle rituals are, in general tone, the most personal and the least didactic of all. One must also remember that the early Christian Church, when trying to supersede pagan religion, was faced with a similar problem and solved it in the same way. Although such syncretism was faced by Christian ritual specialists, too, with great misgivings, over the centuries the awkwardness has fallen away and the fact that syncretism has taken place is often no longer recognized.

Old symbols are most easily given a new content if the new ritual complex, into which they have been inserted, is close to the old one in basic intent. Thus the symbols of traditional labour ritual lend themselves fairly easily to a redefinition that is congruent with the ideological direction of the new labour ritual. Examples are the practice of substituting the traditional decorations on a harvest loaf with one denoting the quantity of grain produced by the collective farm, or the reshaping of the traditional wreath of corn ears into a five-cornered star.

(4)   Another attempt to use the old for the creation of new ritual is the practice of filling dates in the calendar that are customarily associated with old religious holidays with new secular ones. Here the general readiness of the people for an event of heightened significance is exploited. Again this tactic is not a new one but was, as Soviet ritual specialists are quick to point out, a customary weapon of the Christian Church in its fight against the hold of pagan religion on the consciousness of the people. The limited evidence suggests that such a tactic can be successful, if the ousted religious holiday had lost its symbolic content and had become merely an occasion for indulging in jollity and hospitality. An example of this is the Russian Saints' Day. This attempt appears to have met with little success if the new holidays try to replace old ones, the symbolic content of which is still relevant to many people, as in the case of the Russian Orthodox Easter or Whitsun. In such cases, the effort can even be counter-productive. It may be misunderstood as giving an ideological sanction to the old holidays and thereby increasing their vitality (see Kampars and Zakovich 1967: 217ff; Sukhanov 1973: 229).

To sum up, syncretism between old and new symbolism in the new Soviet ritual can be regarded as an exercise in deliberate manipulation of symbols. It provides a lesson about the limits set to such an endeavour by the properties of the cultures which come into contact. Lack of success in this endeavour is not only due to hasty, unsophisticated attempts to achieve a fusion but also to a basic irreconcilability between the old and the new ideology and the cultural forms created by each. The old rituals are either of a religious kind or are colourful and light-hearted popular folk rituals, and both their basic mood and their forms do not lend themselves easily to reformulations which express the heavily didactic messages that the ritual specialists are concerned to put across. This seems to be felt by ritual participants who, if given the choice, do not attempt to integrate the old with the new but often perform the old and the new rituals separately. An example of this is the complete absence of integration between the old and the new wedding ritual in the Soviet Islamic areas (see Lobacheva 1972: 12).

Another striking feature of the process of syncretism, I pointed out above, is the Russian chauvinist bias in the process of selecting a suitable cultural past. This selectivity is probably not the result of a conscious choice but is due to the fact that all the initial work on the new ritual was done in the western and European areas of the Soviet Union and that, even if rites were devised in the Central Asian republics, ritual specialists, drawn from Party ideological cadres, were often Russians rather than natives. But whatever the reason for this bias, it is difficult to reconcile with the official ideology's emphasis on equality among the various national groups forming the Soviet Union. It is also bound to hamper the acceptance of the new ritual in Muslim areas and therefore defeat one of the main goals of ritual specialists; it will jeopardize the aim of reaching those groups in Soviet society whose members are as yet ideologically immature and poorly integrated into the socialist collective. Such groups, because of insulation through language and Muslim culture, surely are more prevalent in the Central Asian republics than in any other part of the Soviet Union.

Lastly, it is notable that the selection of a cultural past has frequently been biased in favour of the more remote pagan rather than the Christian stage of cultural development. This preference expresses the dilemma of an atheist ideology which nevertheless needs to introduce a sacred dimension into its beliefs and practice. The absence of a suitable secular symbol system inevitably drove ritual specialists towards pagan symbolism. Such an alliance becomes particularly ironic when one considers that Soviet ideologists consider that their belief system and, by derivation, their system of rituals is the most progressive that history has ever known.

13

vvvvvvvvvvvvvvvvvvvvvvvvvvvvvvvvvvvvvvvvvvvvvvvvvvvvvvvvvvvvvvvvvvvvvvvvvvvvvvv

The impact of Soviet socialist ritual

The question of what impact on Soviet society the system of socialist ritual has had can be approached in two basic ways. First, a very general approach can be made to try to establish what degree of success among the Soviet population it has enjoyed. In this case ritual is judged like drama and is considered successful if it is not a conspicuous failure (see Myerhoff 1974: 59). The researcher merely needs to establish that it seems to be convincing to a reasonably large number of people, but not necessarily to all, and that there is a demand for its continued performance. This approach is relatively straightforward, particularly if statistics on the degree of acceptance are available, as is the case for many of the Soviet rites. This procedure, however, only makes sense if it can be established that participation in the rites is voluntary. As I have already discussed the issue of voluntariness versus coercion in some detail in chapter 4 it is sufficient to say here that although participation in the new rituals is not completely free there is enough voluntarism involved in most of them to make an investigation into the extent of participation meaningful.

The second and more probing way to assess the impact of the new ritual is to enquire about the effects it has had on either the participants' value orientations or on their social behaviour. In this case ritual can be considered successful if it has indeed fulfilled the functions the ritual specialists set out to achieve. To assess the impact of ritual in this way involves dealing with the related problems of establishing what meaning it has for those who perform them and if and how the performance of the ritual has affected their social relations. According to both sociologists and anthropologists this is a very difficult problem which is usually neglected in the analysis of ritual (see Goody 1961: 152; Shils 1969: 744; M. Wilson 1971: 66; Lukes 1975: 291). As Goody (*ibid.*) points out, information about the meaning of ritual and its impact on individual participants is both difficult to obtain and to evaluate, as

239

precise and conscious formulation of such an experience is irreconcilable with the nature of ritual as habitual, non-intellectual activity. Consequently I shall be unable to say much about the meaning of socialist rituals to participants and about how participation has affected their value orientations. Instead I shall concentrate on how participation has influenced their social conduct, in particular their relation to religion. The impact of the socialist life-cycle rites will thus be assessed in terms of the numbers which participate in them in preference to the equivalent conventional religious *rites de passage*. Such a procedure is not ideal, as the performance of a socialist rite is not *always* a genuine choice (see discussion in chapter 4), but it will give us a reasonable indication of the impact of the new rites.

The adoption of either of the outlined approaches will involve a comparison between the new socialist ritual and conventional religious ritual, and here two important facts have to be borne in mind. The firm establishment of new ritual is by its very nature a long and slow process. Both Christian and Islamic ritual have had centuries to lodge themselves in the collective psyche and to develop appropriate ritual forms and symbolism. Soviet socialist ritual, with some exceptions, has only been in existence for between ten and twenty years. On the other hand, however, involvement in religious ritual draws social disapproval or even sanctions, while the performance of socialist ritual receives material and moral support from the State, and participation in it is socially approved.

Turning to our first approach of assessing the impact of the socialist ritual, it is instructive to consider first the evaluation of the ritual made by ritual specialists themselves. There is general agreement among them that the basic foundations for its general acceptance have been laid. But they readily concede that the new ritual is not yet fully established in Soviet life and suffers still from a number of shortcomings which, they are confident, can be eliminated. The reasons given for a lack of full acceptance are varied. Ritual specialists point out problems such as insufficient provision with purpose-built accommodation for the life-cycle rituals, hasty and amateurish work in their staging, undue formalism and a weak utilization of artistic attributes due to lack of support from the creative intelligentsia (Shneidere 1969: 37; Lukacher 1971: 106). Rituals are also said to be too uniform, impersonal, overweighted with speeches and lacking in symbolism (Fursin 1972: 164; Ugrinovich 1975: 133).

These evaluations of the new ritual give a very balanced picture which is largely supported by the available facts. The extensive list of criticisms and self-criticisms in relation to the new ritual is fairly exhaustive. But it is doubtful whether the confidence of Soviet critics that all these shortcomings can be overcome with time is justified. I would suggest that some of the negative features of the new ritual, for example undue formalism, underdevelopment of symbolism and uniformity, are caused by the very structure and organization of the ritual. They can only be eliminated if these two, and thus the basic nature of the new ritual, are altered. These failings are due to the fact that in most of the new rites the "model for social relations" aspect or ideological imperative completely overshadows the "model of" aspect. Therefore, little scope is given to participants to express their feelings about the social transitions which are being ritualized. The fact that the creation of the new rituals is in the hands of ideological cadres and that the people themselves or, at least, their more artistic spokesmen can make few *direct* contributions to the elaboration of ritual scenarios (see chapter 4) has significant consequences. This rather restricted pool of creative ritual talent is not only responsible for uniformity and underdevelopment of symbolism. Not being truly representative of the people, ritual specialists have also ritualized some social relations or transitions which are not perceived as very significant by those who experience them.

My focus on these negative features must, however, not be allowed to obscure the fact that some of the rites have many positive attributes. Some Western writers on the subject, for example Struve 1969 and Unger 1974, eagerly take up Soviet admissions of shortcomings in the performance of the new rites while ignoring, or throwing doubt on, the successes and thus present very biased accounts of the impact of the new ritual.

After this critical review of evaluations of the new rituals by Soviet ritual specialists let us now look at the facts about the degree of their acceptance, as reported in the Soviet literature on the subject. Generally speaking, one can say that nearly all the major rituals are performed now in all the Union republics, and their performance has become a permanent feature of the social life of the population in these areas. This general evaluation needs to be qualified by a more specific analysis, pointing to differential success in different geographical/social areas of the USSR and among different strata of the population, as well as distinguishing between the differential impact of the various rituals. The new ritual is best established in those areas of the USSR which are at the highest levels of both development and secularization. The new ritual has been most successful and can be considered well established in the Baltic republics of Estonia and Latvia, where the Lutheran national churches are in a weak position. A similar, though somewhat lower, rate of success has been achieved in the traditional western outpost of the RSFSR, Leningrad, where the influence of the Orthodox Church is relatively weak. A third area with above-average success in the introduction of the new socialist rituals, the Ukraine, is less easily covered by the above generalization. In the Ukraine the level of religiosity is still relatively high, though much lower in the eastern than in the western parts. Also it is the anti-ritualistic sects, rather than the Orthodox Church, which are strong in this republic. Unfortunately, we have no detailed figures which would allow us to take a more differentiated approach and check whether or not the high level of acceptance is related to such regional or religious specificities. Conversely, the new ritual has had little impact in republics with a strong national church or religion and/or a relatively low level of development. It has had little success in Catholic Lithuania and in the more backward multi-national areas with a strong Islamic influence (we have found no data on the acceptance of the new ritual in Armenia or Georgia). In these areas old religious and/or cultural traditions are still firmly entrenched and serve to preserve national identity.

The second source of variation in the degree of acceptance of the new ritual is given by the nature of the various rites and holidays involved. There is a large degree of difference in this respect not only among the major sub-categories of ritual but even within sub-categories. What then has been the impact of the various rites and holidays?

The two main old mass political holidays seem to be very securely established in terms of continuity and numbers of participants. As participation in them is not entirely voluntary and requires mere physical presence and no explicit gestures of commitment one can conclude little about the motivations for participation. The third and much younger main political holiday, Victory Day, in contrast, attracts a high degree of spontaneous and active involvement. All three holidays are also widely accepted as major family holidays. It must be pointed out that such acceptance has been by no means automatic. Even at the present time there are still religious/national groups which urge their followers to express their rejection of the Soviet order by ignoring its main political holidays (see, for example, the admonitions in the Lithuanian *samizdat* journal *Dievas ir Tevyne* (God and Country), 20–7, quoted in *Radio Liberty Research Bulletin* 192 (1978: 3).

Turning to the adapted seasonal holidays, we have unfortunately no statistical information to judge the degree of their acceptance. Reading between the lines of reports about them, one gains the impression that their acceptance is slow except in areas which have no tradition of genuine popular holidays, such as the new industrial towns of Bratsk and Tol'yatti (Rudnev 1967: 19). One notable exception to this rule of slow acceptance is the wide popularity of the long-established New Year holiday which, significantly, is now predominantly a private family-based holiday.

The slow rate of acceptance of the seasonal revived and adapted popular holidays must be largely due to the fact that they depend more than other holidays on spontaneous participation, while appealing to a rather diffuse social group (e.g. a whole town or urban district), which cannot be mobilized by the usual administrative methods. In other words, their successful celebration depends on the existence of a genuine community, which is no longer the case in the urban areas of modern industrial societies. Curiously, this very considerable obstacle to their success is never even mentioned in the Soviet literature on these holidays.

Initiation rites into social and political collectives, with some exceptions, are still in the phase of being established in most areas. They have been the latest introductions, and most of them have had little more than a decade to gain acceptance. According to Ugrinovich (1975: 132), the Soviet public has recognized the necessity and appropriateness of ritual formulation of these events. However, the ritual scenarios (*ritual'*) of the rites are not yet firmly established, have not "found their face". Ugrinovich's remarks refer only to the more recently introduced rites, such as initiation into the working class, the collective farm peasantry, or into the armed forces, the Passport ritual and initiation into educational establishments. Notwithstanding these teething troubles, the rite of initiation into the working class seems to be widely distributed, both in the geographical centre and in the more peripheral areas. It was being performed in nearly all the areas covered in the Soviet literature on the subject, and the level of ritual participation within factories is usually said to be high. In the large steel combine of the Ural town of Magnitogorsk, for example, virtually every one of the 1800 new young workers recruited every year goes through an initiation rite (Grishchenko and Kakonin 1974: 42).

Some of the older initiation rites seem to be very securely established. Initiation into the Communist youth organizations, particularly into the Pioneers, seems to be universal. Initiation into Citizenship, involving a more diffuse collective, appears to be a resounding success in its older Baltic version for eighteen-year-olds, in striking contrast to the more recent Russian version, the Passport ritual for sixteen-year-olds. Thus the Latvian Day of Maturity and the Estonian Summer Days of Youth have nearly ousted the Lutheran confirmation rite, in competition to which they were initially established (Rudnev 1974: 38). Whereas in 1957 only 36 young people participated in the Day of Maturity and 10,000 were being confirmed in the Lutheran Church, already by 1961 these figures had changed to 7000 and 2730 respectively (these figures are quoted by Alekseeva 1968: 20).

The much greater success of the Baltic versions of initiation into Citizenship, as compared with the Passport rite, may be attributable to the following three reasons. First, the Baltic rites have ritualized a genuine transition in the life of young people which, even in modern industrial society, still introduces youths to very significant changes in many areas of their lives. Even if these changes no longer affect all young people in a uniform way, they are all confronted with a large number of new obligations and rights which create fresh uncertainties. The Passport ritual, in contrast, ritualizes only one small change in the status of young people which, moreover, has only minimal actual effect on their lives. It is doubtful, therefore, whether the latter will be experienced as a genuine transition and as an event of deep social significance. Secondly, the Baltic initiation into Citizenship, unlike the Passport ritual, judiciously mixes symbolic acts with instrumental activity, providing a host of useful information relevant to the transition. Thirdly, it attempts to create a ritual community, transforming the diffuse collective (all those in one age group) by prolonged social interaction into a more or less intimate one. The Passport ritual, in contrast, makes no such attempt.

Yet a different picture is conveyed by the family oriented life-cycle rites. Not only has their impact differed in various regions of the Soviet Union, but also within areas different rites have met with different degrees of acceptance. The wedding rite is accepted by the overwhelming majority of the population. The Solemn Registration of the New-Born Child (or variants of it) has gained acceptance among a large minority of the population of child-bearing age. The funeral rite, with the exception of a few areas, is only beginning to gain acceptance. A large number of figures are quoted in the Soviet literature which document the claims about the steadily rising rate of acceptance of the socialist *rites de passage*. These figures are often made more eloquent by contrasting them with others that show the decline of the equivalent traditional religious life-cycle rites.

It is, of course, obvious that the decline in the number of religious *rites de passage* is due also to other factors, such as the closure of churches in a given area, or to the impact of more general secularizing forces, such as industrialization and urbanization that is experienced in all modern industrial societies. Figures cited by Gazhos (1967), for example, show quite clearly that participation in the socialist *rites de passage* is particularly high in those rural areas where open churches are no longer available and the provision of public transport is poor. But the strikingly high decline in the number of religious life-cycle rites, particularly of baptisms, in most areas within a rather short timespan after the introduction of the new socialist rites leaves no doubt about the fact that the latter bear a large share of the responsibility for this decline.

Documenting the great popularity of the socialist wedding rite are the following figures. In most areas, between 70 and 95 per cent of all couples to be married now opt for the performance of the socialist rite (e.g. El'chenko 1977: 41; *Nauka i religiya* 1978, 7: 18), and of the remaining 5–30 per cent most have a simple registry office wedding without ritual. Exceptions to this rule are the low participation in this rite in Catholic Lithuania (*Radio Liberty Research Bulletin* 265/78) and in the Muslim Central Asian republics (Lobacheva 1975). Church weddings have become very exceptional in most areas. The following data for two geographical areas clearly show the impact of the socialist wedding rite on the traditional religious rite: in Leningrad the proportion of church weddings fell from between 2–3 per cent in 1959 (when the socialist rite was first introduced) to 0.8 per cent in 1966 (Rudnev 1974: 84); in Estonia the proportion of church weddings fell from 29.8 per cent to 2.5 per cent in the first decade since the introduction of the socialist wedding rite (Ranne 1972: 183).

Turning to the ritual marking the birth of a child, we find a more uneven picture. Generally speaking, the acceptance of this socialist rite is said not to have been nearly as wide as that of the wedding rite, and in most areas it is only a large minority of eligible couples who opt for the Solemn Registration of the New-Born Child or one of its variants. Such a claim is supported, at least for the traditionally Russian Orthodox areas, by statistics on baptisms (see Lane 1978: 60). In the literature

245

there are, however, statistics which show that in some areas of the Soviet Union the level of participation in this rite is much higher and is approaching that indicated for the wedding rite. Exceptionally high rates of participation (between 80–90 per cent) have been reported for some large towns in the Ukraine (El'chenko 1976: 43) and in Krasnodar region (Kikilo 1969: 155), for the Baltic, traditionally Lutheran, republics (Gerodnik 1970: 101), and for some rural areas of Moldavia (Gazhos 1967: 123). A more moderate rate of success (between 36–57 per cent of all new-born children) is claimed by reports on Leningrad town (Rudnev 1974: 96), the central Russian Voronezh region (Teplyakov 1972: 92n.), and the ethnically mixed area of East Kazakhstan (Sorokin 1970: 45). No figures are supplied for those geographical–religious areas in which the socialist birth ritual is said to have made very little impact, such as the Catholic and Muslim areas.

Reports which relate the success of the socialist birth rite to the falling rate of acceptance of church baptisms supply the following figures: in Estonia there has been a five-fold decline of baptisms during the first decade after the introduction of the new Soviet rite (*Voprosy nauchnogo ateizma* 1973, 14: 78); in Leningrad region the decline was 2.5 times during a twelve-year period (Rudnev 1974: 99); in Krasnodar region the number of baptisms was halved in the decade since the introduction of the socialist equivalent (Andrianov 1976: 3); and in the town of Sevastopol the proportion of baptized children declined from 20 per cent to 2.5 per cent during the same timespan (Fursin 1977: 44).

In most republics a socialist funeral rite is still only performed in exceptional cases (e.g. El'chenko 1976a: 45), and many Soviet studies of the development of the new system of rituals do not even mention this rite. The exceptions to this rule are given by the practice in Estonia and Latvia and, to a much lesser degree, in Leningrad. Thus in Latvia in 1967, 53 per cent of the deceased were buried (privately) by the Soviet funeral bureau, and another sizeable group had a socialist rite arranged for them by their work or political collective (Gerodnik 1970: 83). In Estonia's capital, Tallin, as many as 74 per cent of deceased received the socialist rite in 1970 (Ranne 1972: 186). In these two traditionally Lutheran republics, too, the impact of the socialist funeral rite on the performance of its religious equivalent has been significant. In Estonia there occurred a decline of 25.5 per cent over a fifteen-year period (*ibid.*: 187), while in Latvia the average share of church funerals was only 25 per cent in 1967 (Gerodnik 1970: 83).

There is little discussion in the Soviet literature of why the socialist funeral rite is still so infrequently performed in the other republics. Therefore, we do not know to what extent this state of affairs is due to its lack of acceptance by the Soviet people outside the two Baltic republics and to what extent its infrequent performance is due to the lack of an established and good organization. The figures from the two Baltic republics show that, given time and the right approach, it is possible to gain widespread acceptance even for a socialist funeral rite. McDowell's claim (1974: 278) that "only the funeral ceremony, because it does not promise eternal life to the individual, contains an intrinsic and insurmountable barrier to popular acceptance" is thus too simplistic, especially in view of the fact, reported by many surveys of religious attitudes, that only a minority of even the "believers" now accept the notion of eternal life.

How then can one explain the differential success of the three main life-cycle rites? There is no serious discussion of this question offered in the Soviet literature on the subject, and this study can do no more than offer a number of hypotheses. First, the lower rate of acceptance of the socialist funeral and birth rites, as compared with the wedding rite, must mean that the creation and cessation of life suggests existential problems which, for the majority of the Soviet population, still require religious answers. This response not only deters people from choosing a socialist rite, but it also makes ritual specialists more hesitant in providing such a rite. Yet the statistics above cited for the growing popularity of the socialist birth rite and the more selective acceptance of the funeral rite show that political religion, in principle, can usurp even the function of providing answers to existential dilemmas, usually only associated with conventional religion. Secondly, the discrepantly low acceptance of the funeral rite in relation to the other two may also be due to the fact that the main participant in the rite is usually an old person and so is more likely to have been a member of a religious organization, either due to socialization or because of freedom from social pressure against religious adherence. Participants in the other two rites, in contrast, are usually people just embarking on their career who are much more vulnerable to pressures against a conventional religious choice.

In addition to being influenced by factors given by the nature of the various rites and of the ritualized social relations, the impact of the new socialist rituals will also differ among the various social strata in Soviet society. To examine the relation between degree of acceptance and position in the Soviet system of social stratification, we have to look at rites which are aimed at the *whole* population and where participation is optional. This leaves us mainly with the rituals of the life cycle, some rites of initiation and the ritual of the holidays of the calendric cycle. Although it would seem vital for ritual specialists to know which social strata have responded to their efforts, there is not one published study analysing the social background of participants in these rituals. It is very common among Soviet social scientists to make such analyses with regard to religious practice, and the recording of personal data in Wedding and Baby Palaces would make such a task very easy as regards the life-cycle rites. Consequently, it is tempting to conclude that such analyses have not been made or, at least, have not been published, because the results would be embarrassing. Impressionistic information gathered by me during study visits to the Soviet Union, as well as some indirect indicators, would confirm such a conclusion. While questions on this matter to those professionally concerned with the new rituals received only evasive answers, more informal questioning of general contacts (who were all members of the intelligentsia) made it clear that the new rituals appeal to what the latter called the "ordinary people", namely manual and lower white-collar workers. The new rites were viewed by my intelligentsia contacts either with condescension or contempt. For some this negative evaluation focused on the quality of the ritual scenarios or on the *petit-bourgeois* festive trappings that tend to surround them (see also Bromlei 1977). For others the negative response was based on a clear recognition of the new ritual as a means to maintain social control. The impression that a large section of the intelligentsia is thus withholding itself from an acceptance of the new ritual is also supported by the fact, widely acknowledged by ritual specialists, that the creative intelligentsia has not come forward to assist ritual specialists in developing the aesthetic side of the new rituals.

From a discussion of the impact of the new socialist system of rituals in terms of the degree of acceptance of the various constituent rites among different populations and social groups, we must now turn to the effect of this ritual on participants' attitudes and behaviour. To establish whether the new ritual has, indeed, fulfilled the functions the ritual specialists attribute to it, or whether it has become accepted for other reasons, we need to ascertain both what meaning the various rites have for those who participate in them and whether changed behaviour after participation is the consequence of changed value orientations. Although the answers to such questions should be of

248

vital importance to ritual specialists, hardly any research has been conducted which would throw light on these problems. Consequently we are again forced to resolve them in a very piecemeal and impressionistic way.

Turning to the mass political holidays, we have no information on what meaning they have for those who participate in them. My observation of participants and remarks about the two main holidays made both by my contacts and, more importantly, by ritual specialists themselves (e.g. Timoshin 1966: 165; Aliev 1968: 160) indicate that people feel rather bored or disenchanted with them. They are therefore unlikely to be deeply moved by them, let alone be propelled into action.

As regards the rituals of initiation into social and political collectives, we have again extremely scanty information to draw on. When I observed the initiation of children into the Young Pioneers, their general demeanour and facial expressions suggested to me that they were deeply affected by the rite. Their behaviour during the conducted tour of the Lenin museum after the rite, in particular their seemingly spontaneous placing of flowers by figures or busts of Lenin, would have pleased those who devised this particular rite.

Turning to other rites of initiation, I can only quote some rather cryptic information about the impact on the behaviour of initiands of two specific rites in two geographical areas. In Leningrad, where the ritual of "Enlistment into the Army" is relatively well established, the political department and the command section of the local army unit found that those who were ritually initiated had a much higher degree of political maturity and discipline. Of particularly high quality were those recruits who came from a well-known Leningrad factory with a long tradition of patriotic education through ritual and other means (Rudnev 1974: 53, 54). In a Dnepropetrovsk enterprise, where the initiation of new workers and a system of patronship by older, experienced workers has been established for several years, a "growth of consciousness" among young workers has been discerned. This is seen as being expressed quantitatively in the following statistics: the turnover of cadres during a three-year period has declined from 10 to 7 per cent; the number of difficult youths has decreased by four times and that of "amoral deeds" by nearly one-half; there has been a steep rise in the proportion of young people who overfulfil production norms (Zots 1976: 31, 33). The question of whether these observed modes of behaviour were due to the impact of the rites, or whether

249

they were caused by a more general approach to training (especially by the system of "patronship") of young people by particular factories with above-average reputations is unfortunately not confronted by the two quoted authors.

A survey of the limited evidence on the impact of the life-cycle rituals on attitudes and behaviour suggests that in many cases participation does not signify any strong convictions or deep emotions about the socialist values embodied in the rites. The tendency of some people to participate consecutively both in a socialist and in a conventional religious rite (Brudnyi 1968: 161; Zuev *et al.* 1974: 55) or to insert traditional religious practice into a socialist rite, for example blessing the wedding couple in front of icons before their departure to the wedding palace, indicates that at best, an ambiguous and, at worst, a shallow ideological commitment is involved. Of the two Soviet surveys conducted on this problem, one confirms this impression. In this survey the great majority of respondents' answers to the question of what they liked about the new life-cycle rites pointed to factors other than the socialist essence of the rituals (Kampars and Zakovich 1967: 77). The majority regarded them merely as events which afford an occasion for social contact and create a solemn, festive mood. The second survey (*ibid.*: 224), posing the more clearly formulated question of "What reasons impelled you to observe the new holidays and rites?", in contrast, established that a large minority (38 per cent) had some awareness of the nature of the new ritual. They indicated that they wanted to observe significant events in personal and social life in a *new* way. But more, and less vague, survey data would be needed to come to a firmer conclusion as to what meaning the new rituals have for participants. Even that approach could not settle the question conclusively, as many people will not be fully conscious of their motivations and feelings on this matter.

While our lack of knowledge about the meaning the new life-cycle rites have for participants makes it impossible to draw any *general* conclusions about their impact on attitudes and behaviour, we can make a more limited deduction about their effect on one area of attitudes and behaviour, namely those oriented towards a supernatural power. As the figures on p. 246 show, the new rites have made a significant contribution towards decreasing their prevalence. Although it must be noted that, unlike conventional religious ritual, the socialist rites are not staged frequently enough to make a lasting impact. Whereas the churches involve their active members in ritual

acts at least once a week, the Soviet socialist system of ritual has as yet
no equivalent to the regular services of the churches. Also in contrast
to the priest, known and deferred to by his flock, the master of
(socialist) ceremonies is not usually a community figure and thus
cannot rely on natural authority to add impact to his celebration of the
rites.

To sum up, the data presented in this chapter show conclusively that
despite their numerous shortcomings the new socialist rituals have
made a significant impact on the Soviet population in that, at the least,
a very large minority has accepted them. The limited direct and indirect information available is insufficient, however, to investigate
whether this impact corresponds to what ritual specialists set out to
achieve. While some evidence points to a certain amount of success of
ritual specialists' political socialization efforts, other findings suggest
that functions other than the ideological one are the reason for the
acceptance of the new ritual. Thus it must remain an open question as
to whether participation in the new ritual does in any sense enhance
the "political religion" status of the official ideology, or whether the
rhetoric of Soviet Marxism–Leninism is regarded as no more than an
acceptable back-cloth to occasions that mark events in personal life in
an elevated form. Even if the latter is the case there must result a
diffuse kind of identification with the political system which made the
staging of these solemn occasions possible.

14

Conclusion: ritual in modern society – a comparative analysis

The foregoing discussion has made it clear that the Soviet system of rituals is an unusual phenomenon in modern society with respect to both its nature and scope. It is now appropriate to look at comparable ritual, that is ritual sacralizing the social order, in several other modern societies, both of the developed and the developing types. Such a comparison will highlight significant differences and similarities between them and examine how these reflect parallels and divergencies in the *actual* political relations of the societies concerned. It will also reveal the relationship in each society between the political ideology and the conventional religion and investigate in what circumstances this relationship becomes sufficiently formalized to lead to the creation of a civil religion or, if the relation is antagonistic, of a political religion.

Ritual in Soviet society (seen as a "total mobilization" type of society) will be contrasted with ritual in Western pluralist societies (Britain and the USA); in developing post-colonial societies (Mali and New Guinea); in a fascist society (Nazi Germany); and in an emerging post-feudal Western society (France after 1789). These are well-known and well-documented types of society and they by no means represent an exhaustive list: the most notable omission is probably Japan. Japan represents a particularly complex and intriguing case of a highly advanced industrial and politically pluralist society in which a feudal remnant – an intricate hierarchical ranking system – has facilitated the retention of a well-developed system of rituals sacralizing the Japanese societal and national entity. An analysis of Japanese ritual would require more space than can be given in one comparative chapter (for details on Japanese ritual see Nakane 1973; Maruyama 1963; Lebra 1976; Swyngedouw 1979).

The analysis of ritual in the above-mentioned societies will be based on a limited amount of secondary data. The scope of this book allows

252

no more than outline descriptions which, of necessity, cannot probe the depths of the various complexes of ritual. Many of the studies of comparable ritual in other societies have, not surprisingly, been made by functionalists. My utilization of their material in this book must not be interpreted as implying an acceptance of their fallacious conclusion that the existence of overarching social norms and values necessarily implies their general acceptance and transformation into obligation. Nor does my comparison of these different value systems imply that they necessarily have the same status in their respective societies. I chiefly reserve judgment on such important questions as to whether a value system is dominant or merely official, whether it is imposed or genuinely popular.

Instead my task will be to draw attention to certain systems of values and to explain why and how their perpetuation is being attempted. In other words, rather than presupposing a value consensus, I want to examine how strong an aspiration exists for the achievement of such consensus among political elites in different types of society, and to what extent ritual is utilized to move towards the realization of such an aspiration.

One of the clearest points emerging from the current debate among Western scholars on ritual in modern industrial society is the conclusion that ritual sacralizing the social system is on the wane in contemporary society. It is held that both the structure of that society and the dispositions of its citizens have contributed to its weakening appeal and militate against any further creation of such rites in the future. Versions of these arguments are put forward by many sociologists and anthropologists (e.g. Luckmann 1967; Shils 1969; V. Turner 1969b: 10; M. Wilson 1971; Martin 1978: 88). Even Bocock (1974), who sees ritual as being much more prevalent and important in modern industrial society than is usually thought, concedes that ritual relating the individual to the whole society has become difficult to sustain at the present time (*ibid.*: 16, 56). It is argued by these diverse authors that a general value system, the precondition for a system of rituals sacralizing a social system, can no longer be sustained by a modern industrial society. In such a society, it is said, values do not differ only between various functional sub-groups but even within them, and constant support for them from authoritative institutions is no longer available. It is suggested that the Durkheimian fusion of the political and the religious was only appropriate in the analysis of the simple "mechanical solidarity" types of society, but is no longer appropriate in relation to

253

complex modern societies. It is also pointed out that in addition to lack of structural support for the creation of *new* ritual, public opinion has turned against *existing* ritual, viewing it either as mere irrelevant spectacle from the past or approaching its cognitive and moral content with distrust. While most of these analyses focus only on the absence of a sacred cosmos in modern industrial societies of the West, Luckmann (1967: 101) considers attempts to transform what he calls "institutional ideologies" into encompassing world views in societies of both the pluralist and the Soviet type. He claims that attempts in the Soviet Union to provide such a world view have failed, because elites have been unable to transform a socially prefabricated world view into a subjectively meaningful system of "ultimate significance". The logical conclusion of his book is that sociologists should abandon the idea of a unified overarching sacred cosmos and instead assume the existence of an assortment of system of "ultimate significance". The basic assumption behind this is that, because Soviet attempts to create a new sacred cosmos have not been entirely successful up to now, sociologists need not concern themselves any longer with Soviet efforts in this area. What is not generally realized is the fact that Soviet elites have not conceded defeat and that they have, since the early sixties, adopted a new and more subtle means towards the desired end of creating a "new Soviet man".

To establish whether all these very general and abstract analyses are right in positing the demise of ritual in modern complex societies or whether, given certain conditions, ritual can be prominent even in this type of society it is necessary to undertake some empirical studies of this phenomenon in a variety of such societies. In the following, I shall therefore engage in such studies and then attempt to answer these basic questions (see pp. 281–2). Let us first consider the example of contemporary societies of the West. In European societies like France, Italy, Spain and Portugal, where Catholic religion once held a powerful monopoly position and then became challenged by an influential political ideology of protest, polarization between Catholic religion and left-wing political ideology has prevented the emergence of a general civil or political religion and/or of associated ritual, although ritual with a nationalist focus still exists. A different situation prevails in Western societies with a Protestant tradition of religious pluralism. Let us take the cases of the United States and Britain and examine to what extent there are still attempts in these societies to maintain a general value system, what its nature is, and in what way ritual is utilized to inculcate it. Here it will be necessary for comparative purposes to make some assumptions about the apparent pervasiveness and scope of such ritual without, however, implying any judgment about the degree of acceptance and effectiveness of the latter.

RITUAL IN BRITAIN AND THE USA

In the United States, the work of Bellah (1967) on civil religion and the lively debate engendered by it have drawn attention to the fact that such a value system is still extant there, and that ritual to gain people's commitment to it is by no means dying out, but is still a fairly prominent and constant feature of American society. It becomes most "visible" on such regularly recurring occasions like Independence Day, Memorial Day, Thanksgiving Day, the anniversaries of Lincoln's and Washington's birthdays, and in the cult of the American flag. It is also a part of more episodic and rarer events such as presidential inaugurations or deaths in office, the Kennedy assassination being a prime example (for details see Warner 1965; Bellah 1967; Verba 1965; J. F. Wilson 1971).

Although the term "civil religion" for a system of beliefs and practice of this type has been coined with reference to American society it can, with some reservations, also be applied to British society. Formally, the role of religion in the political realm in Britain is the traditional one assigned to it by an established Church, but in practice the established character of the Church of England is often ignored by participants in civil religious ritual. The report of the Archbishop's Commission on relations of Church and State in 1970 cited evidence showing that the linking of Crown and Church in the course of the coronation was accepted by many people outside the Church of England and that the religious element was general enough to have wide appeal (Bocock 1974: 101). In British society such a civil religion is much less prominent, salient and pervasive, and most of its ritual is performed episodically and/or mainly in the metropolis. British civil religion receives concrete expression chiefly in coronation ceremonies (Shils and Young 1953) and funerals of monarchs or, more exceptionally, of prominent political leaders (e.g. Churchill) and is less strongly and clearly articulated in such recurring events as the annual Trooping the Colour and Memorial Day and the many rites investing persons with the special authority of office. Civil religion and its ritual in Britain is more often regarded as a historical relic from past centuries, from the time when

England was being transformed into a modern nation state. It is very illuminating that the following observations by Bagehot on ritual, centred on the monarchy of his time, identify functions that are almost identical to those implied, though never stated blatantly, by some Soviet authors (see pp. 20 and 22) in relation to socialist ritual. Ritual around the monarchy "tamed the uncouth labourers . . . who, in their simplicity, needed a person to symbolize the State . . . The English Monarchy gives a vast strength to the entire constitution, by enlisting on its behalf the credulous obedience of enormous masses" (quoted by Shils and Young 1953: 35, 39 from Bagehot, *The English Constitution*).

When we examine the nature of these two civil religions we find that, as the name implies, they are a combination of conventional religious and political values and beliefs. In contrast to Soviet political religion these two Western civil religions do not completely fuse the political and the religious, but the two remain analytically distinct and are combined to reinforce each other. Whereas the Soviet belief system of Marxism–Leninism aims at the total individual and does not recognize a division between a public, macro-political sphere and a private moral one, civil religion in the West has more modest aims. It leaves individual morals and many areas of interpersonal relations to conventional religion or to a privatized "invisible" religion of the kind Luckmann (1967) has described. Consequently, the religious element in the Soviet belief system involves it in bitter conflict with "church" religion due to competing and mutually exclusive claims on "believers'" commitment. The religious element in civil religion, in contrast, does not compete with (church) religion but is supportive of it. This claim of Soviet political religion to have a monopoly on sacred values and the resulting demand for total commitment and exclusive allegiance have given rise to the notions of heretics (dissidents) and sacrilege (crime against the State). Civil religion in Western society, in contrast, although also laying claim to being a repository of sacred values, normally could not possibly make such demands, even less ask for a declaration of faith. (I say "normally" because there have been exceptions to this rule, particularly in the United States. The McCarthy period is one example which comes to mind.) Like conventional religion in these societies, civil religion is constrained by the content of its own doctrine to practise tolerance.

These differing claims and functions of the two kinds of belief system are naturally reflected in their structure and content. The

American and British civil religions are posed at a very high level of generality and lack internal differentiation, which renders them so vague as to become elusive. But attempts to define each have been made and, despite their vagueness, they reflect the different cultural and historical backgrounds of the two countries. In Britain Shils and Young described these values as being "generosity, charity, loyalty, justice in the distribution of opportunities and rewards, reasonable respect for authority, the dignity of the individual and his right to freedom" (Shils and Young 1953: 65). These values and the structure of authority that they support are sacralized in a general way by an association with God, and the monarchy is seen as a mediator between the sacred and the secular (Shils and Young 1953). In American civil religion, in contrast, the relation between American society and God is seen to be more specific and is described in Christian imagery. Talk is not merely about a sacralization of the social and political system, but claims are made for the American people to be a chosen people with a special mission and with a special responsibility to God for that mission (Bellah 1967). Sacred values to be upheld and defended are seen to be individual freedom, personal independence, human dignity, community responsibility and social and political democracy (J. F. Wilson 1971: 6).

The high level of generality and the lack of internal differentiation of these two belief systems reflect, of course, the function and goal of civil religion in a highly differentiated modern society. The high level of generality is dictated by the recognition that in complex class societies any more specific belief system would be divisive rather than integrative, but it is also determined by the more limited goal of civil religion. Trying to generate commitment to values relating only to the macro-political sphere the belief system does not need to be internally differentiated and to spell out more specific norms for various kinds of social relations. Soviet political religion, in contrast, has deduced a set of specific norms of conduct from a general body of doctrine. The Soviet Moral Code of the Builder of Communism can be seen as the socialist equivalent of the Christian Ten Commandments, stipulating norms of conduct in a large variety of social and political spheres.

The differences in the nature and content of the two contrasted belief systems are, of course, expressed in their ritual dimension. Whereas Soviet ritual is very pervasive, entering the life of every Soviet citizen during various stages of his life and of the calendric cycle, the ritual of Western civil religion intrudes to a much lesser extent into the daily lives of citizens, and it is easy to avoid participation completely. While the ritual system of civil religion includes rites expressing only very general and highly abstract values, the Soviet ritual system also contains rites modelling more concrete and specific social relations. It specifies how to be an exemplary political activist, manual worker, soldier, student or parent, always retaining, of course, a reference to more abstract values. These latter rites differ also in that they command active participation, whereas the former, although demanding it, often get only spectatorship.

This contrast of Western civil religion with Soviet political religion has served to make some theoretical points. In the process I have overdrawn both the similarities between American and British civil religion and the differences between the former and Soviet political religion. It is necessary to correct this impression and to emphasize once more that civil religion in Britain is only a shadow of its American counterpart and that the similarities between American and Soviet ritual are in some ways more striking than those between the two pluralist Western societies. The American civil religion, I said earlier, is more securely established and more pervasive than the British variant. This, I would argue, is due to a number of features favouring ritualization which American and Soviet society have in common. Both Soviet and American society are relatively young societies. After a bitter civil war they had to forge a national and political identity in conditions where social divisions were intensified by both geographical and, more importantly, ethnic/national-religious diversity. In the face of this lack of any *actual* unity, the creation of unity at the ideological level became compelling, and it was realized that only an ideology with a religious dimension would be equal to such a task. In this respect it is notable that both societies are said to have a special historical mission to liberate humanity, whereas in post-war Britain (in contrast to colonial Great Britain) the idea of a national political mission has become suspect and is now only envisaged by right-wing extremists.

For both the United States and the Soviet Union, their early formative period has become a "holy" period, and the political leaders of that time are worshipped like saints. In the same way as Soviet school children grow up with the name, life-story and portrait of Lenin constantly brought to mind, American school children are made to relate to Lincoln and Washington (Hammond 1969:.383). (It is not implied, though, that the scope and intensity of such a cult is at the same high level in the United States as it is in Soviet society.) In both societies the cult of dead saints and minor heroes focusses on national shrines, the American Gettysburg and Arlington cemeteries and the Lincoln Memorial being the equivalent of Lenin's mausoleum and several famous war memorials (see p. 148) in Soviet society. In Britain, in contrast, such cults of leaders and heroes is absent, and even the British Remembrance Day is only a shadow of the American Memorial Day (see Warner 1965: 249) and, even more so, of the Soviet Victory Day (see pp. 143ff). As well as sharing the idea of making a cult of dead political leaders, the two societies also have in common a notable tendency to worship their respective national flags. Lastly, it is interesting that the religious dimension in the ideologies of both societies was opposed by the founding fathers of either society and has gradually crept in as the years have gone by (for Soviet society see p. 215 and for America see Brogan 1969; Pfeffer 1969).

The preceding argument has shown that ritual, sacralizing the social and political order of a society, does still exist in modern industrial society, although it is more marginal and less obligatory in Western than in Soviet society. This is because political elites cannot provide a whole number of institutional supports throughout society for sacred values. Therefore they can do no more than diffuse them at a very high level of generality and make optional both belief in, and practice of, civil religion. As a result the fundamental normative orientations activated by ritual in Western society are often at odds with orientations evoked by other social relations, and the type of ritual under discussion is in danger of becoming an anachronism. In Soviet society, in contrast, institutional supports for the political religion exist in all spheres and at all levels of society, excepting only the family, some informal organizations based on friendship networks and the churches. (Some of the latter, however, are now also partially incorporated into the system; see Lane 1978: 33ff.) Cultural management through ritual supports, and is supported by, the inculcation of fundamental value orientations by other means (e.g. education, literature and art, mass communication, propaganda) and thus endows ritual with added authority. In Soviet society much better conditions are given for overcoming the obstacles against the creation of solidarity generated by modern industrial society, even if the means for achieving it differ radically from those Durkheim had in mind. Thus the theses on ritual in modern industrial society cited on p. 253 are apt as far as the analysis of Western society is concerned, but are inadequate in explaining the situation in the contemporary Soviet Union. In Britain and the USA the ritual of civil religion is now no more than an embellishment that is thought necessary only by a few. This is not to say, however, that there is little or no ideology in these Western societies, merely that the values propagated are more often instrumental rather than consummatory ones and that there is not one homogeneous value system but a number of conflicting ones. The ritual of Soviet political religion, in contrast, can be seen as an essential device of cultural management in a society where exclusive allegiance to the norms and values of Marxism–Leninism is a precondition of the continuation of the existing power structure and political elites.

One feature about the ritualization of social relations in the Soviet Union that is emphasized in other parts of this book, namely the element of conscious direction by a relatively easily definable group of ritual specialists from the lower levels of the political elites, is not very notable in the ritual dimension of civil religion in the West. Conscious creation of new, and adaptation or borrowing of old, ritual has been more common in other new societies which, like the Soviet Union, have been faced with the urgent problem of both forging a new and powerful national and/or political identity and of initiating modernization. Thus, in what follows I shall briefly turn my attention to post-revolutionary societies, considering such diverse types as a developing post-colonial society of the present time and such historical societies as France after the 1789 Revolution and Nazi Germany before the Second World War.

THE RITUAL OF POST-COLONIAL SOCIETIES

Many years after the Soviet Union was already well established as a new type of society and had made great progress in restructuring the outlook of its citizens in accordance with this new image, there emerged in the third world a number of new states with similar but incomparably more serious problems of forging new identities at both the social and the individual level. The political elites of these countries were faced with the problem of changing their countries from colonial, economically and socially underdeveloped, culturally backwards and ethnically and linguistically divided entities into politically independent, modern nation states. They therefore had little option but to try and create a powerful political religion which would unite tribal factions on the basis of a new loyalty and legitimate the new central authority. It would also attempt to change basic attitudes of all citizens in accordance with the new roles they would be required to play in the tremendous task of modernization. Typical examples of such new states, analysed in the work of Apter (1963) and Marriott (1963), are Ghana, Guinea and Mali. While the political elites of these states profess a kind of socialism, none has practised it consistently, and their overriding goal is not so much the achievement of full socialism but of modernization (Apter 1963: 58). In contrast to the beliefs and practice of Soviet Marxism–Leninism their political religion is not very co-herent, differentiated and systematized. It contains jumbled-together elements of socialist beliefs, ritual symbols (e.g. Ghana's Black Star and their Pioneer rites and symbols) and organizational practice (the one-party system) and of indigenous traditional communal and aesthetic culture (e.g. tribal robes and symbols). This conglomerate is held together by a leader cult, elevating the leader of the liberation period into a figure who is at one and the same time a man of the people and a superhuman prophet and saint. He is said to know the needs of the people, show them the new way and guide them towards an idyllic future. Identification with this leader provides both social and per-sonal meaning, facilitates the restructuring of basic attitudes and motiva-tions and justifies the privations and upheaval endured for the sake of a bright future. The extreme adulation extended to such leaders is well illustrated by the following extract from the book *A Portrait of Nkrumah* (quoted by Apter 1963: 298): ". . . to us, his people, Kwame Nkrumah is our father, teacher, our brother, our friend, indeed our very lives, for without him we would . . . not have lived; there would have been no hope of a cure for our souls, no taste of glorious victory after a life-time of suffering". An even more extreme example of the leader cult is a poem on Sekou Touré of Guinea, which takes the form of a political prayer (quoted in full by Apter 1963: 83).

Although the political religions of these new nations contain a cer-tain amount of ritual (a Mali wedding rite, described *ibid.*: 299, has many parallels with the Soviet version), none have a unified system of rituals comparable to the Soviet one. Instead they bear a great similar-ity to the system of beliefs and practice current in the Soviet Union during the thirties, at the height of Stalin's power. At that time, too, tenets of Marxist–Leninist belief became eclipsed by the more pragma-tic considerations dictated by the industrialization drive, nationalism triumphed over internationalism and the strong cult of Stalin served both to mobilize people to extreme effort and to legitimate the growth of centralized autocratic political power. Whereas African leaders recognized straight away that loyalties could be redirected only if the political religion amalgamated imported international and avowedly secular symbolism with indigenous tribal and religious elements, Soviet ritual specialists have come to this realization very late and have systematically fused elements of traditional popular culture with those of socialist origin only from the 1960s onwards, when the new system of rituals evolved.

To find a political or civil religion with a more elaborate complex of ritual activity we have to turn to two societies of the distant and more recent past respectively, namely to French society after the 1789 Revolution and German society under Hitler.

THE RITUAL OF THE FRENCH REVOLUTION

A comparison of Soviet socialist ritual with the civil ritual of the revolutionary festivals in post-revolutionary France between 1790–4 yields more striking parallels and reveals more obvious continuities than emerged from the comparison with ritual employed by post-colonial modernizing African new states. The political leaders of post-revolutionary France realized very soon that revolutionary–patriotic festivals were an ideal means to gain the loyalty of the illiterate and impressionable masses for the new regime. Robespierre in particular saw them as a tool to both control and create public opinion, and conscious attempts to exploit revolutionary spontaneity to this end were systematically made (Dowd 1948: 120).

What then were the changes in values and attitudes the new leaders hoped to bring about? First, they wanted to gain solid acceptance of the three revolutionary political values of liberty, equality and fraternity and of a political culture of mass involvement as against ascriptive elitism in government. Although the inculcation of new civic virtues was considered a part of the effort to consolidate political change, there was no attempt to introduce a comprehensive new philosophy of life to revolutionize the ethics of interpersonal relations. A second and equally important strand in this bundle of values was a patriotism anxious to preserve France in its old territorial borders. Thirdly, and only during the beginning of this period, both leaders and masses expressed strong anti-clerical and anti-religious sentiments, associating the Catholic clergy with the hated *ancien régime*. Some attempts were made to put a cult of reason in the place of Christian worship, but this proved too abstract an object of worship and did not engage the feelings of the masses. A more personalized cult of martyrs of the Revolution, in contrast, stirred the people deeply (Soboul 1974: 348). In the closing year of this period, however, the de-Christianization campaign lost its impetus, and some political leaders, notably Robespierre, wanted to introduce a state religion of patriotism to lend moral force to the attainment of the ideals of the Revolution (Dowd 1948: 120). The religious elements called into being were not Catholic but were very general notions of a God and of immortality in the deist tradition. The Festival of the Supreme Being in 1794 made a very promising beginning to this endeavour. But efforts were not continued in the same dedicated way under the new regime of the Directory, and the campaign for a state religion soon petered out. Last, but not least, the festivals were designed to identify the political leaders of the day, the Jacobins, with the achievements of the Revolution and to designate them as the natural leaders in the new epoch.

Turning from the content to the forms of the festivals, of their ritual and symbolism, as well as to the organization of all the festive events, the following general features are noteworthy. The main form of ritual was the massed procession, ending in a climactic gathering in one of the places closely associated with the Revolution. Often the procession would progress from station to station, halting in various symbolic places (e.g. the Mars Field). Here events were enlivened by ritual acts, such as the burning of effigies, the planting of a tree of fraternity, the honouring and mourning of dead heroes, swearing a mass patriotic oath to defend liberty, equality and the indivisibility of the Republic, blessing the banners of the national guard, military pantomimes, songs and dances of a revolutionary and/or patriotic nature and massed choirs of the people, giving expression to their newly acquired unity and power (Soboul 1974: 594).

The symbolism of the revolutionary–patriotic festivals consisted in part of elements borrowed from Greek and Roman antiquity and in part of more original elements created by the Revolution itself. The symbolism of the neo-classical monumental art was designed to bring back the pomp and grandeur of antiquity and also the idea of popular participation, of "irresistible might and timeless solidity" (Dowd 1948: 130). It had been introduced by the famous neo-classical artist David who was in charge of the overall artistic design of most of the festivals. He created such symbols as an amphitheatre on the Mars Field, where the procession filed past the political elites, an Altar of the Fatherland and numerous triumphal arches. These were combined with republican and revolutionary symbols, such as a statue of liberty, a table of the Rights of Man, the Banner of the Republic and the *bonnet rouge*, the symbol of enfranchisement and liberty (*ibid.*: 65). The overall impression of the processions is said to have been one of colourful splendour and revolutionary vigour, exciting the participant masses and elevating their mood.

These revolutionary festivals were the result of both spontaneous manifestations of revolutionary and patriotic enthusiasm and of conscious and systematic preparation, the latter probably outweighing the former. The realization that a new time needs new holidays and rituals was soon institutionalized in the introduction of a new revolutionary calendar, changing not only the main holidays but also the basic way of measuring the flow of time and the sub-division of the year into units. Although the festivals of 1790–4 were not institutionalized but have to be regarded as spontaneously evolved expressions of the mood of the moment on the part of the revolutionarily engaged population, in 1793 a list of fixed civic holidays was established. Some of the new holidays were consciously created in contradistinction to old ones and competed with them for popularity. Robespierre's new calendar envisaged four great republican holidays "as days of homage to the glorious revolutionary journées" (Soboul 1974: 398).

In the first four years of their existence these civic holidays were balanced between the elements of spontaneous popular participation and conscious planning and direction. Although participation was by no means universal it was wide. People took part not just under pressure from a collective but joined in as individuals. They actively participated in the planned rituals, as well as improvising their own contributions to the complex of festive activity (Dowd 1948: 61; Soboul 1974: 594). There were, of course, also a great many people who regarded these festivals with great scepticism or even hostility and who refused to become part of them. After the fall of the Jacobin regime, however, the new holidays gradually changed their character. Their organization became centralized in the hands of the state, and the people assumed walk-on parts. Under Bonaparte the holidays completely lost their popular appeal, and the people became mere spectators of the mainly military parades (Dowd 1948: 128; Soboul 1974: 595).

A comparison of these civil holidays and their ritual with the Soviet mass political holidays in the early post-revolutionary period reveals a number of striking parallels as well as a fundamental difference. It is, however, difficult to decide whether the many similarities or even identities in the details of ritual and of the organization of the whole complex of festivities are due to the functional requirements of similar political situations and corresponding popular moods, or whether they have been consciously copied from the French pattern by Soviet ritual specialists. It is well known that the latter were greatly influenced by the example of the French revolutionary holidays in general and that in some cases, for example the preponderance of massive monumental neo-classical symbolism in the first few years, straight copying was practised.

The study of both early post-revolutionary French and Soviet society reveals the anxiety of political leaders to consolidate social change and the legitimacy of their rule by transformations in the symbolic realm. This is accompanied and reinforced by widespread and urgent popular feelings that the far-reaching political and social transformations should find expression in new symbolic forms. The ritual of the early political holidays in both societies was well balanced in its development of both the "model of" and the "model for" aspects. The holidays were an expression of a prevalent political mood and the means to deepen and direct it. At the same time they were a tool for political leaders to widen the pool of loyal followers of the Revolution by drawing in those who were as yet uncommitted and wavering. This dual function of the ritual, given by the procession–demonstration, manifested itself in both societies in the widespread spontaneous individual, rather than organized group, participation in the ritual and in the scope that was then still given to popular revolutionary creativity. In both societies this well-balanced ritual activity could only be sustained for a limited number of years. Waning excitement, enthusiasm, idealism and popular involvement on the political scene became expressed in less well-balanced ritual activity, and centralized organization and direction from above gradually became the only way to keep these holidays alive.

Equally striking are the similarities when we look at the ritual forms and at the symbolism evolved by both the French and the Soviet holidays. Not only the basic medium of the French civic holidays – the procession–demonstration – but also its general character and the complex of ritual activities performed within its framework have nearly all been reproduced either as an occasional or as a permanent feature of the Soviet mass political holidays (for details see pp. 153ff). Many of these features have also become incorporated into the system of rituals evolved since the early sixties. Of the symbols of the French Revolution, those inspired by neo-classicism, as was pointed out above, were copied only for a very short time and were soon dropped as being inappropriate for the expression of the values of Soviet society. But their influence has lingered on in less obvious ways. The idea of the amphitheatre on Mars Field, from which the leaders received the salutes of the passing masses, has been perpetuated in the tribune on Red Square; the Altar to the Fatherland is recognizable in the Monument to the Fallen Soldier with its Eternal Flame by the Kremlin wall; and the proclivity to create monumental art of vast proportions and on a large scale is more developed in Soviet society than it was in post-revolutionary France, even if the style is no longer neo-classical. Of the more indigenous French revolutionary symbols, the revolutionary banner and the colour red also occupy an extremely important place in Soviet ritual symbolism, whereas symbols, such as the statue of liberty and the table of the Rights of Man, have rightly been thought to be incompatible with the more radical ideology of the Soviet Revolution.

The biggest difference between these two complexes of ritual lies in their content, in the nature of the norms and values expressed through ritual and in the ideologies of which they are a part. The ideology of the French Revolution, bourgeois democracy, was a political ideology structuring mainly socio-political relations as opposed to the whole of human existence. In the early years of the period under discussion it appeared as if it might widen its scope and, by replacing religion, become concerned with existential problems. But it soon became clear that the anti-religious strand in the revolutionary mood was motivated more by anti-clerical sentiments than by the thorough rejection of a conventional religious world view. Soviet ideology, in contrast, as pointed out above, has always aimed to offer a complete philosophy of life and has demanded exclusive allegiance. Although these differences between the two ideologies and their embodiment in ritual were not very pronounced in the early post-revolutionary years of the two societies, it became clearer in later years that the ritual of the French Revolution was the ritual of civil religion, while that of Soviet society was the behavioural dimension of political religion. In 1794, with the celebration of the Festival of the Supreme Being, French ritual moved considerably closer to the ritual of civil religion identified in the USA of the present than to the Soviet system of socialist rituals, which is the topic of this study.

Conclusion: ritual in modern society

RITUAL IN NATIONAL SOCIALIST GERMANY

To contrast Soviet socialist ritual with the ritual devised in Nazi Germany yields the most striking parallels of all the comparisons made. The similarities between the two systems of ritual do not lie merely in the forms of ritual and in the symbolism employed, but can also be detected in some of the content as well as in the underlying orientations and in the intentions pursued by political leaders. It is needless to stress that there are also a number of important divergencies between the two systems of ritual. Before proceeding to such a comparison, however, a compressed general description of the Nazi ideology and its system of rites and holidays is necessary.

Although the Third Reich lasted for only just over a decade, Hitler's ideological cadres managed to establish in this short time a very comprehensive and, as concerns scenarios and symbolism, well-developed system of rituals embodying the values of National Socialism. Some elements of it – the cult of the leader, of martyred heroes (of those Party members who died in the 1923 Putsch) and of the flag – were, of course, well established before Hitler came to power. Otherwise Nazi ritual specialists had no tradition to follow and no models to copy. But the content of the ritual, as many writers have shown (e.g. Hayes 1973; Glaser 1978), had been deeply embedded in German culture, particularly that of the nineteenth century, even if the particular combination of elements and their extreme interpretation was peculiar to National Socialism. In addition, some general inspiration was also gained from a very remote and nebulous Germanic past.

The sacred values of National Socialism were the notions of the nation, the people (*das Volk*) and the Führer. The value orientations to be encouraged were the development of a sense of national confidence and mission which, allied to the notion of race, became a chauvinistic and militaristic nationalism; the idea of an elite of supermen, who would heroically sacrifice themselves for the nation, was linked to the idea that the state was supreme and that individual interests were to be subordinated to it; and lastly, there was the notion that the interest of the nation was expressed by the Führer, who could demand unswerving and unquestioning loyalty. The ideology promised that when the ideal end-state, the new millennium, was reached, all the sacrifices of the individual would be rewarded. He would partake in the greatness of the great German people and empire.

Dedication to the pursuit of these goals was further strengthened by

267

a strong element of confused mysticism in National Socialist ideology which romanticized the more prosaic facts and obscured their less savoury aspects. Beliefs about racial superiority and the destiny of the German people were linked to ideas of a blood myth, a blood will and the notion of the clan, forming the link between present generations and mythical Germanic forefathers. The ideology promised that the attainment of an ideal future, peopled by racially pure people, would again restore the state that was once enjoyed in a mythical heroic Germanic past, before the German race and blood had been contaminated by the Jews and other undesirable racial elements. This new value system was meant to oust not only old political values, like those of liberal democracy or revolutionary socialism, but also religious world views. It intended to replace religious soul-searching and other-worldly orientations with a secular and activist orientation to the world. This secularism led an uneasy co-existence with a leaning towards paganism.

One important means of inculcating these new values and mobilizing the population to the pursuit of the new goals was a system of National Socialist holidays and rituals and a leader cult, used either separately or in combination. In particular, the more mystical and obscurantist elements of the new belief system were instilled in this way. This is well brought out in the official definition of that ritual by one of the chief ritual specialists. (The Germans preferred the word *"Brauchtum"*, translatable as "usages and customs", or "traditions", to "ritual", because of the latter's religious associations, but it emerges from the context that they use the word in the sense of "ritual".) The following extract is quoted in German by Soehngen 1950:61:

Ritual, in its symbols and symbolic actions, is the expression of a world view and a racially determined belief in destiny. In ritual, man of our kind acknowledges a predestined order of the world and consequently of all life, he actively integrates his life and that of his clan and community into a great order so as to fulfil the meaning of life, its continual renewal and rebirth.

Whereas the cult of Hitler had evolved in part spontaneously and in part as a consequence of sponsorship by the Party propaganda machine, the system of rituals was consciously devised and instituted by the Party. It was organized mainly by the *Hauptkulturamt* under the Party's propaganda department but also by the *Volkskulturwerk*. The influence of the Party in all areas of German life ensured that the new rituals were soon widely dispersed. A large number of significant transitions in the individual, social and natural cycle became ritualized.

Besides rites to mark the three main transitions of the life cycle – birth, marriage and death – there existed initiation rituals into the political youth organizations and into the Party and its related organizations. The most important holidays of the natural cycle were a Spring Holiday (to replace Easter), a summer solstice, a Harvest Festival, a winter solstice and Christmas (in its pagan aspects). There was also a secularized Mothers' Day and a Holiday of Labour on 1 May. Besides the general labour holiday, there were many rites and holidays celebrated on a factory or an enterprise basis to unite the work force into a cohesive community (Gamm 1962: 100). Mass political holidays, marking significant transitions in the life of the whole society, included the Anniversary of the Assumption of Power, a Heroes' Memorial Day and Hitler's Birthday. In addition there were two holidays dedicated to the Party and the National Socialist movement – the Nürnberg Party rally and a Day for the Blood Witnesses of the Movement. On the eve of the latter, rites of initiation into the Party and the *Schutzstaffel* were customarily performed (*ibid.*: 157).

All these rites were replete with symbolism. Most of the symbols had grown directly out of the National Socialist ideology and movement, but some were derived from a mystical and distant Germanic past. The key indigenous symbols were "blood" and the "flag", the two being fused in the idea of the "blood flag", the flag carried by those who fell as victims of the Putsch of 1923 and which later became used to consecrate new flags. The blood myth of Nazi ideology posited historical continuity based on a blood relationship between ancient Germanic heroes and the German people, and claimed that the purity of that blood had been contaminated by Jewish blood. To restore the racially pure and heroic Nordic type which would lead the German people to greatness, this myth decreed that the blood of Jews had to be spilled. The symbolism of the flag – its red and white colour and the swastika – was carefully worked out. The colour red stood for socialism (and for blood), white indicated the nationalist element and the swastika symbolized struggle for the victory of Aryan man and, at the same time, the victory of the idea of creative labour. It was also, according to Reich (1972: 100ff), a sexual symbol, known in many ancient cultures. Among the symbols derived from a Germanic pagan past were light and fire, the idea of struggle and of the Germanic hall (*Halle*).

Besides such well-known symbols, the symbolism of mass formations of people – in demonstration, procession, rally, gymnastic and
dance displays and flag waving – was also of great importance. Combined with the symbols of light, fire and flag, they were employed to
create highly dramatic spectacles of a ritual kind, the impressiveness of
which is widely attested to even by those who were very hostile to the
ideas embodied in the ritual.

Concerning the music and poetry of the various rites, it is notable
that poets and composers contributed extensively to this side of ritual.
According to Soehngen (1950: 29, 30), the artistic design, particularly
of the life-cycle rites, was often "astonishingly successful" and the art
of such a high quality that it could easily rival that of the Church. Many
of the ritual songs became widely known, and participants in ritual
performances would usually render songs communally.

Little that is conclusive can be said about the impact of this system of
National Socialist ritual on the German people and about the degree of
acceptance gained in this short period. While we know from historical
descriptions that the public holidays and rituals attracted a large and
enthusiastic following, which often became involved to the point of
ecstasy, we have no reliable information on the impact of the familial
rites. Unger (1974: 181) states that Party confidential reports, measuring the success of the National Socialist life-cycle rites in relation to the
traditional religious *rites de passage*, speak both of growing appreciation
of the new rites by the German people and of failure, depending on the
geographical–religious (Lutheran or Catholic) region under scrutiny.
On the whole, however, Party ritual specialists were convinced that
they had found an effective "means of access to the German soul"
(*ibid.*). The fact that the National Socialists managed to involve in the
work on ritual a large number of members of the creative intelligentsia
and even to inspire them with it would support their conclusion and
make Unger's own rather more sceptical evaluation (*ibid.*: 178ff) seem
unwarranted.

The preceding review of the National Socialist system of rituals and
holidays has shown that, although it differs in important ways from
the Soviet ritual system, the parallels between the two are in fact the
more striking. This overlap is due to the fact that, despite great differences between the ideologies of the two social systems, they have in
fact some general underlying political orientations, methods and in-
termediate goals in common. These have become expressed in both the
forms and, to a slightly lesser extent, the content of their political

ritual. A study of the ritual of these two political systems, I hope to show, is more revealing about actual political goals and methods than is a study of their respective ideologies.

In both societies political elites were not only faced with the necessity of immediate radical social and political transformation but were also committed to achieving an ideal end-state, a secular millennium. The pursuit of these far-reaching short- and long-term goals under initially very unfavourable conditions required not only the creation of a certain political structure (a one-party system and a strong centralized state); it also demanded fundamental changes in the value orientations of all citizens and their total mobilization in pursuit of these goals. In both cases this reorientation has entailed above all a changed relation of the self to the collective, a willingness to exalt the State above all and to subordinate and even sacrifice the interests of the individual to those of the large collective. This exaltation of the State has entailed not only material sacrifice but also the abdication of individual political initiative and responsibility. The rather abstract notion of "the State" has been made more appealing by the substitution of emotionally more satisfying collectives, such as the nation, the people and the father- or mother-land, as well as having all these collectives personified by a strong leader.

Of the means to inculcate new value orientations ideological indoctrination has been of unprecedented importance in both Nazi Germany and Soviet Russia and has been one of the most vital tasks of their respective political parties. A decisive difference between the two political systems may be found in their approach to political socialization, conditioned directly by the nature of their respective ideologies. In Nazi Germany, political persuasion from the beginning entailed the use of methods appealing to the emotions and even to the primitive instincts of men. In the Soviet Union, in contrast, rational argument and an appeal to the intellect and moral sentiments were uppermost in the early years (up to the early thirties) and have remained important even in later years. Consequently, a system of ritual which, after all, appeals to emotions and instincts has quite naturally grown out of National Socialist ideology and has been an integral part of Nazi political socialization from very early on. In the Soviet Union, in contrast, such a system of rituals could not easily be reconciled with an ideology devised to create a more rational society and to emancipate man to a higher level of social existence. It could not take root until the ideology had been diluted with alien elements (patriotism, a leader

271

cult, the preservation of the existing power structure as an end in itself) and had lost its emancipatory potential. Even then it has been difficult to achieve congruity between the ideology, as made explicit in the 1961 Party Programme, and the values expressed in the symbolism of the new rites, particularly those of the life cycle and calendric cycle (see the discussion of this point in chapters 11 and 12). Also, a number of Soviet communists, as the literature on ritual shows, still find it difficult to reconcile the notion of ritual with their conception of Marxism–Leninism as a revolutionary ideology (e.g. *Leninizm* . . . 1970: 328ff).

As already indicated, in both political systems leaders needed the exclusive allegiance of their citizens and put forward an ideology which aimed not only at the ordering of political relations but at the totality of social life. This necessity consequently also became expressed in the ritual system of both societies. Both systems include rites which try to regulate both public and private, collective and individual, life. Also both systems entered into competition with the alternative ideology, conventional religion, and tried to replace it with a political religion.

Of the two political ideologies, National Socialism had a much less clearly elaborated relation to conventional religion. Although the National Socialist regime was not a militantly atheist one it went even further than Soviet political elites in trying to weaken religion by the creation of substitute rites. In addition to the rites of the life cycle and the calendric cycle, the National Socialists also created the so-called Morning Celebration (*Morgenfeier*), designed to displace the ordinary Sunday service of the churches. Also the Führer assumed a much stronger and more explicit God-like role than did either Lenin or Stalin in the Soviet Union. National Socialism saw in conventional religion a rival ideology which sapped the strength of the German people by inducing them to engage in the inner-directed, individualistic soul-searching that prevented the development of the political activism needed by the regime. But at the same time individual political leaders would often refer to God and other supra-empirical notions in their speeches. The more mystical side of religion even seemed to have an attraction for men reared on the irrational ideology of National Socialism and was unscrupulously utilized by them if propaganda purposes required it. Their opposition to conventional religion was thus based on pragmatic considerations rather than on ideological principles that were irreconcilable with a conventional religious world view.

Thus, to sum up, the political religion of National Socialism could not tolerate a rival belief system and would doubtless have destroyed

Christian religion as an *independent* force if the regime had persisted. Nevertheless, there are affinities between the two which are totally absent in the Soviet case. These affinities might have resulted in a fusion which would have been radically different from the one termed "civil religion", where conventional religion remained independent from politics. In contrast, Christian religion in Germany would have been totally subjected to the goals of National Socialism.

Having highlighted the similarity in general political orientations and goals underlying the creation of the two systems of ritual, it is now appropriate to investigate which areas of social relations have become ritualized in both social systems, and why. Looking at the ritual calendar of both societies, it is striking to find a large overlap between the two. It comes as a surprise that a supposedly socialist society should ritualize very much the same social relations as a fascist one. Let us consider which areas of social relations have been ritualized in both societies and what are the implications of such ritualizations. The first area consists of the important transitions in the lives of individuals as members of a family. This concern, as pointed out above, reflects the efforts of a total ideology to penetrate *all* spheres of social existence and to eliminate the idea of a private sphere. The preoccupation with familial life-cycle rites also reflects the fact that a "mobilization" society depends on a strong and stable family, either for an industrial army or for a military army, or for both. (This is, of course, where the "mother heroines", first created during Stalinist industrialization and later on adopted in Nazi Germany, are also relevant.)

The similarity in general intent in this respect is well illustrated by the following extract from the Nazi literature on life-cycle rites, which could have come just as easily from a Soviet source: "Life-cycle rites (*Lebensfeiern*) are a decisive part of the ideological struggle, of the great spiritual controversy . . . They are the last decisive touchstone for the implementation and realization of the total political–ideological leadership of the movement" (extract from *Lebensfeiern*: 5, translated and quoted by Unger 1974: 176).

The efforts to gain access to family life and to regulate family relations and socialization of children were developed further in the Nazi ideology and ritual system than in its Soviet equivalents. This was probably due to the Nazi preoccupation with race and blood and the necessity to control procreation arising from it. National Socialist ideology included the notion of the clan as an agency of control, mediating between the State and the nuclear family. Ritual specialists addressed themselves to the clan elder (*Sippenältester*), supplying him with instructions on how to conduct *all* family celebrations and not merely the semi-public life-cycle rites (Unger 1974: 173).

The second area of social relations extensively ritualized in both societies concerns the important transitions in the life of young people, particularly those that incorporate them into various social and political collectives. The political socialization of the young is an important objective for all types of society, but it becomes an overriding concern in those social systems that are trying to establish total ideological domination. Ritual, as I have repeatedly pointed out, is an ideal means for political socialization. Besides being important for political socialization of the young in general, each initiation rite also indicates which collectives or complexes of social relations are particularly important to the functioning of a society. Both Nazi Germany and the Soviet Union put high priority on political and military collectives. The Soviet Union alone has had to ritualize incorporation into educational collectives and into the manual working class. Ritualization of the former is probably due to the fact that the Soviet Union has long had an undereducated and underqualified labour force, while the second rite of incorporation has arisen in response to the problem of a shortage of *manual* labour.

The third area of social relations selected for ritualization are certain changes in the life of the society, which can be turned into occasions legitimating or even sacralizing that order. Here, anniversaries of the birth both of the political order and of its first and/or current leader have been considered particularly suitable. In Nazi Germany, in addition, the important transitions in the life of the Party and the individual's relation to the Party have also been ritualized. In Soviet society, in contrast, Party members are deemed ideologically mature and not in need of ritual. Both societies also have ritual occasions explicitly or implicitly devoted to a complex of patriotic–military values which concentrate the citizens' attention on the more emotionally charged notions of the nation or father- mother-land. The notions of heroism and sacrifice on behalf of the nation, and symbolic acts of a military kind, pervade most ritual acts. Such a strong emphasis on these values is very much in keeping with the openly nationalistic and aggressively militaristic ideology of National Socialist Germany. It is, however, more difficult to reconcile with the complete verbal repudiation of military aggression in official Soviet ideology and with its claims to be one of the foremost forces for the promotion of world peace.

The fourth complex of social relations selected for ritualization in both societies revolves around labour. These ritual performances are presented as occasions which glorify labour and speak of "the nobility of manual labour". More importantly, labour ritual is meant to inspire further effort on behalf of the collective, as well as to transform labour collectives into cohesive communities which can direct and control a wide range of members' social relationships in the interest of the collective. Whereas in Nazi Germany the latter goal was pursued by making the working collective the base for many ritual occasions not directly associated with labour (Gamm 1962: 100ff), in the Soviet Union a wide range of specific labour rites and the development of Brigades of Communist Labour (see p. 117) fulfils this function.

Both ideologies have, of course, a concern with labour as a major focus, albeit interpreting it in very different ways. This radical difference *cannot* be discerned in the labour ritual of the two systems. In both complexes of labour ritual, it is the individual's labour contribution to the collective, rather than his self-realization and emancipation through labour, which is being ritualized. Labour ritual, it must be noted, occurs far more frequently in the Soviet ritual system than in the Nazi system. This perhaps reflects the fact that a general work ethic and labour discipline were much less strongly developed in the new Soviet society than in the transformed German society.

Lastly, both societies have a number of holidays marking the important seasonal transitions. In both cases they were mainly old popular holidays with pagan associations that were revived to replace the main religious holidays. Whereas this is consistent with National Socialism's identification with an ancient Germanic festive tradition, there is nothing in the ideology of Soviet Marxism–Leninism to suggest such celebrations, and a socialist value orientation consequently had to be superimposed on their ancient rites.

Not only did ritual specialists in the two societies ritualize almost identical social relations but there are great similarities also in the form, content and symbolism of the ritual created. This similarity is particularly developed in some of the life-cycle rites. Thus the Nazi, like the Soviet, funeral rite tries to develop, through ritual formulae and actions, a life-affirming focus that draws the attention away from death to life and replaces an indulgence in the grief of parting with an activist orientation towards the continuance of the work of the departed. Both rites also stress the contribution of the deceased to the collective ("society" in the Soviet and "people" in the German case) and try to

275

create a secular interpretation of immortality. Turning to the birth rite, both the National Socialist and some of the Soviet variants of this rite have at their centre the symbolic act (of pagan origin) of lighting a candle, a light of life. Despite these similarities in details, the overall impression conveyed by the rites of the life cycle in the two systems differs. The National Socialist rites are both more heavily politicized and more mystic than their Soviet equivalents.

Turning to the symbolism of the two systems of rituals, we find the most striking common features. Both systems have widely adopted the symbolism of fire and light. (Not only is it present in much of the newly devised ritual, but it also explains the revival and continued popularity in both systems of the ancient pagan holidays of the summer solstice.) The torch is a key symbol in both systems. Soviet ritual specialists stress the secular meaning of this group of symbols, while National Socialists emphasized its pagan origins and associations (see Soehngen 1950: 76, 77; Gamm 1962: 179).

Another key symbol of both National Socialist and Soviet socialist ritual is the flag. Although a "sea of red flags" is quite a common picture on Soviet mass political holidays, the symbolism of massed flags has been used neither as extensively nor in the sinister and threatening manner in which it was utilized in Nazi mass rallies. Whereas in the Soviet context the symbol of the flag has retained its socialist association, in Nazi Germany it was meant to evoke aspirations to national grandeur, chauvinistic conquest and subjugation of other nations and ethnic groups. In Nazi ritual it was utilized also to express the irrational, mystical element as, for example, in the idea of the "blood flag", used by Hitler to consecrate new flags.

The impression of the overwhelming power of "mass" in both systems was also applied to people. Massed formations of people – marching, parading, flag swinging, performing gymnastics – have been common to festive occasions in both societies. Photographs of massed gymnastic displays or massed dancing by girls in national costume, taken on festive occasions in either society, could easily be exchanged one for the other. The use of this kind of symbolism indicates the political leaders' concern with mass mobilization and with the integration of the individual into the collective. Although only in Nazi Germany were attempts made to manipulate the emotions of these massed groups of people and to whip up mass exaltation through the use of rousing music, speeches, singing and flag waving. Hitler himself was particularly adept at this practice.

There is one other type of symbolism that pervades the ritual of both societies: the notion of the hero in general and the cult of the leader in particular. In the Soviet Union these "symbols" developed, in spite of the values of Marxism–Leninism at a time when political practice could no longer effectively be legitimated by reference to them. In Germany, in contrast, the notions of heroism and of an idolized leader were built into the ideology of National Socialism from the beginning and were, indeed, part of the basic elements. In a society which saw itself as "a nation of heroes and supermen" (Glaser 1978: 193ff), and which traced its origins directly back to ancient Germanic heroes, hero-worship and a leader cult flourished quite naturally. Consequently, a leader cult was a permanent element in Nazi Germany, but has arisen only episodically in the Soviet Union. Also, the notion of the hero was interpreted more physically in Nazi Germany. The hero had a strong physique and was militarily aggressive and daring, and the idea of the hero was closely connected to the notions of race and blood. In Soviet society heroism is built more on social achievement, although propaganda is not adverse to extolling military prowess and sacrifice. Indeed, the hero fallen in battle is one of the most powerful symbols in both societies. Hitler had already planned before the war that if Germany was victorious, he would erect the most splendid memorial complexes all over Europe (*ibid.*: 199). I have highlighted the key status of such memorials in the context of present Soviet society.

Consequently, although there are numerous parallels between the leader cults of the two political systems there are also important divergencies, particularly when we contrast the cult of Hitler only with that of Lenin. I am thinking of parallels such as the wide scope of the cults, their function to mobilize the population to greater achievement and sacrifice, the identification of the leader with the social system in order to legitimate the latter and its sometimes unscrupulous exploitation for inhuman ends, though the latter was rarely the case in the adulation which developed around Lenin. While the devotion to leaders in Soviet society certainly has a religious dimension to it, never, as in the Hitler cult, does it encourage an obscurantist mystical relation that endows the object of worship with near-magical powers. Hitler adulation reached a much higher pitch and was more consistently performed than either the cults of Lenin or of Stalin. Although Stalin in particular was occasionally raised to nearly a god-like status, there was nothing in his cult comparable to either the ubiquitous German salute

"Heil Hitler!" or to the "Hymn to the Führer", which became a staple component of most ritual occasions (Unger 1974: 173).

Lenin-worship, the most persistent leader cult in Soviet society, developed, as I stated previously, against Lenin's wishes and after his death. Also, unlike the Hitler cult, it has never been performed for the aggrandizement of the leader as an end in itself. Although the Soviet system, like the Nazi one, fosters the development of a subject citizen, the adulation of Lenin has never degenerated into encouraging mindless submission, the readiness to "do anything" in the name of the leader which resulted from the Hitler cult. The cult of Stalin, in contrast, came much nearer to that description.

To sum up, the comparison of the system of rituals developed in National Socialist Germany with that of the contemporary Soviet Union has yielded by far the most striking similarities in both general underlying orientations of ritual specialists and political leaders, in the scope of the ritual system and in the details of the particular rites comprised in the system. The number of features which the two systems of ritual hold in common indicates that, despite very fundamental differences in the ideology of the two societies, many basic orientations and goals of their political leaders do, in fact, overlap. The greatest degree of similarity lies in the utilization of ritual by both societies to induce the individual to serve the collective in a very one-sided way, often to the point of sacrifice, for the sake of an ideal future which comes no nearer with the passage of time.

Whereas in the case of Nazi Germany there was found to be a close correspondence between official ideology and the norms and values embodied in the system of rituals, in Soviet society considerable divergencies between the two have been revealed, and the ritual system was found to give a more truthful statement of actual political goals and strategies.

But the analysis also revealed very fundamental discrepancies between the two systems of ritual that were due to important differences in their underlying ideologies. To use the words of Glaser (1978: 97), in National Socialist ideology *logos* has capitulated before a degenerate kind of *mythos*, in which confusion, illogicality and anti-rationality prevail, whereas in classical Marxism–Leninism *logos* has been paramount. This basic characteristic of Soviet ideology still conditions actual political action, including the creation of a system of rituals. Thus while National Socialist ritual revels in embodying the degenerate and confused myth-like notions of its ideology, the rational thrust of Marxism–Leninism puts limits on such a practice and allows only the occasional aberration in this direction. While the symbolism of National Socialist ritual makes an appeal to physical urges and base instincts, Soviet ritual symbolism is extremely restrained in the use of body symbolism and the arousal of lower instincts. Lastly, whereas Nazi ritual consistently and openly evokes the romanticism of heroic heathendom, Soviet ritual turns to paganism more hesitantly and inadvertently.

It is necessary to consider what general conclusions can be derived from this comparative analysis of ritual in modern society. Such conclusions will be about the interrelationship between ideology and ritual at the level of the whole society; about the nature and role of this ritual; about the conditions which enable it to exist in modern societies; and about the nature of the different social orders involved, as revealed by ritual.

There is an aspiration for the maintenance of some common value system among the political elites of all modern societies, albeit of varying degrees. The values remain few, abstract and vague in Western pluralist societies (although there are also significant differences between the latter) and plentiful, detailed and concrete in "total mobilization" societies. Despite a general sociological post-mortem on ritual as a means to inculcate such value systems, ritual is by no means dead. It lingers on in Western pluralist society, where it chiefly models relations of the individual to his society at a high level of abstraction and tends to be fairly unco-ordinated and haphazardly developed. Recent events (May 1980) in West Germany vividly demonstrate what happens when leaders in Western pluralist societies try to ignore these unwritten rules and attempt to introduce more explicit rituals of the Soviet type. A ceremony was staged to commemorate Germany's twenty-fifth year of membership of the NATO alliance, during which the President heard 1000 soldiers swear allegiance to West Germany. Outside the stadium, 7000 demonstrators staged a violent protest against this attempt to sacralize the German political system and its military policy (see *The Guardian*, 7 May 1980).

Ritual has a sudden resurgence in societies which have undergone a drastic transformation in socio-political relations. In such societies it serves both the ends of political elites, who need to instil the new values on which the changed socio-political relations are based, and the wishes of many social groups, who want to express their affirmation of the changed socio-political circumstances. Ritual in such

279

societies is not very systematically developed and consists usually of mass ritual, like that developed around political holidays and a leader cult. A fully developed and systematically devised system of rituals is usually created only when the new society is already well established and the initial revolutionary *élan* has been lost. Whereas in Soviet society there was a forty-year gap between the first and the second stage, in Nazi Germany the two stages were almost telescoped into one. The latter may have been due to the much higher cultural standards in Germany of both the general population and of the ideological cadres, which must be regarded as a necessary precondition for the creation of a system of ritual.

The creation of ritual sacralizing the social order is paralleled by a fusion of political and religious elements in the society's ideology. In pluralist society there occurs borrowing from conventional religion. The resulting civil religion is formulated at such a high level of generality that it does not usually conflict with conventional religion. Furthermore, civil religion and its rites remain as optional as conventional religion. Except for occasions commemorating certain important transitions in the life of society, they do not impinge very much on the lives of those for whom they were devised.

In societies aspiring to total ideological control, in strong contrast, the political ideology assumes many features of conventional religion. It turns itself into a political religion which enters into sharp conflict with conventional religion. Belief in the tenets of this political religion is considered obligatory. A system of ritual is devised in order to close the gap between the political elites' aspiration for total value consensus and the actual extent of belief in this political religion. Although performance of its rites is in theory not obligatory, the great proliferation of the rites and the severe restrictions on alternatives do not render them completely optional either. In contrast to the ritual of civil religion, it is impossible to ignore completely the rites of political religion.

In new developing societies of the post-colonial type the political elites steer a middle course between adopting a civil religion and a political religion when presenting their ideology and ritual. Although these societies possess many features of the "total mobilization" type of society their ideology is not yet sufficiently clearly articulated to become a political religion. Also, the control of political elites over their society is not securely established. Consequently, reliance on traditional tribal religions to aid realignment of popular loyalties is still great during the transition period. Such reliance brings their ideology closer to civil religion. Their ritual is neither as systematically developed nor is it as wide in scope as the ritual of political religion.

The substantial, though varying, degree of overlap in the role played by ritual in various societies, as revealed by this comparative study, is duplicated in the form, content and general symbolism of ritual, as well as in the choice of social relations that are selected for ritualization. Certain important transitions in the life of society, relating to the legitimacy of the present social order, particularly its foundation and its involvement in military confrontation with other societies, have become ritualized in all the societies under review here. Other social relations, affecting only certain social groups or institutions vital to the survival of the whole society, have become ritualized only in those societies that have the aim of total ideological control. Similarly, some ritual acts, such as the cult of a dead or living leader or worship of the flag, are common to the ritual of every society discussed in this study, although they may differ in content and form. In contrast, other symbolic acts or objects, such as those connected with light and fire (having a pagan or secular meaning), or those involving mass formations of people, are features only of the societies that are aiming at total ideological control (hostility to conventional religion) and at mass mobilization.

What conclusions can be drawn about the structure of ritual, sacralizing the social order, in modern society? What is the balance, in such ritual, between the "model for" and the "model of" aspect in the rendering of social relations in ritual form? This structure, it was found, differs not only between societies (and the exact degree of difference is impossible to determine) but also within societies over time. It can be said that the nearer a society is to its foundation or radical transformation, the better maintained is the balance between these two aspects of ritual. Ritual is shaped both by the direction of ritual specialists (who emphasize the "model for" aspect) and by spontaneous popular contribution (which favours the "model of" aspect). As the new political elites become more securely established and more able to assert their definition of social relationships, spontaneous popular creativity in relation to ritual falls by the wayside. At this stage, ritual can only be created and maintained by a discrepantly strong development of its "model for" aspect.

To return to the points made at the beginning of this chapter (see p. 254) it is necessary to explore the question of what conditions need to prevail before ritual can exist in modern industrial society. Whether or not a system of rituals can survive or take root (in the sense of not being an obvious failure) in a modern, highly differentiated society depends not only on the merits of the system itself but also on the structural and ideological support that is given to the values embodied in that ritual by various means at all levels of society. Such support requires, amongst other things, the availability of a group of ritual specialists who, in the absence of a genuine community, take over the creative and organizational tasks usually performed by members of the community. This group of ritual specialists must, of course, be close to, and under the control of, the political elites. Such a group evolves quite easily out of the ideological cadres in a one-party system, but cannot be sustained by a pluralist society. The survival of a system of ritual in a modern society depends also on the degree of success with which political elites contain the translation of increasing social differentiation into political differentiation and thus can suppress the articulation of group interests that threaten the value consensus implied by the dominant ideology. Contrary to the expectations of most sociologists and anthropologists, it has been shown by this study that if these two basic conditions are fulfilled, as they certainly are in the case of Soviet society, a system of ritual can take root and develop in a modern industrial, highly differentiated society, although the process of implantation and growth is a highly directed one. Such a system could never be created in a pluralist society, although a less systematic and comprehensive complex of ritual manages to linger on in even this type of society.

Lastly, it is necessary to address ourselves more systematically to the question of what a society's system of ritual tells us about actual political relations in that society. A system of ritual in modern society, I pointed out in chapter 1, arises to obscure the gap between the ideologically determined definition of social and political relations and the relations as they actually affect actors in a social system.

A wide-ranging and systematically elaborated complex of ritual at the societal level therefore suggests a society where:

(a) there exists a comprehensive, detailed and clearly articulated ideology
(b) political elites are united in a strong commitment to the creation of a value consensus on the basis of this ideology
(c) there exists a large gap between ideological definitions of relations and their actual state

(*d*) *political* differentiation is narrowly circumscribed by the political elites and the resulting lack of permanent political interest groups keeps the large majority of citizens unaware of these gaps.

A loosely elaborated complex of ritual with a relatively narrow range of application indicates a society where:

(*a*) ideology is general, vaguely articulated and poorly elaborated, and remuneration tends to be the more important means of getting compliance

(*b*) political elites are not united and put forward conflicting ideologies

(*c*) the gap between ideological definitions of relations and their actual state is less pronounced or non-existent, either because the ideology does not aim for a perfect end-state or because the ideological definition of a given social relation is too vague or non-existent

(*d*) there exists a high degree of both social and political differentiation and a large proportion of the population is consequently well aware of conflictual social relations and presses for the *actual* resolution of conflict rather than for its *apparent* overcoming through ritual.

A loosely elaborated complex of ritual with a medium range of application points towards a society where:

(*a*) ideology is still in the process of being elaborated and political elites rely as much on coercion as on persuasion to gain compliance

(*b*) political elites still have to make concessions to groups representing the old value system

(*c*) and (*d*) are the same as in the first example

Of the three types of political system outlined above the first obviously depicts Soviet society. Both this particular outline of basic political features and the argument throughout this book imply a view of Soviet society which, to avoid misunderstandings, needs to be made explicit. The focus of this study on ritual as an embodiment of ideology, of some of the fundamentals of the system, and on the utilization of ritual as a means to preserve these fundamentals entails a preoccupation with the most conservative part of the Soviet system. This aspect of Soviet society also yields the most striking contrasts to Western pluralist societies. Consequently the theoretical approach most consistent with the empirical facts of this study underlines the following elements:

(*a*) the conservative character of the Soviet system which, as far as fundamentals are concerned, comes close to petrification

(*b*) the unified nature of the political elite and a dichotomization of society into elite and masses

283

(*c*) the manipulation of the masses by the elite in its attempt to manage conflict

(*d*) the mobilization of the masses to greater effort in order to ensure the future viability of the social and political system.

This conception of Soviet society comes close to Brzezinski's theory (1970) of Oligarchic Petrification but also maintains the focus on mobilization stressed in his earlier theory of totalitarianism (Friedrich and Brzezinski 1966).

Such a theoretical approach does not coincide with those adopted by scholars who emphasize the great changes in Soviet society and the growing similarity of its political process to that of Western pluralist societies. My theoretical orientation has to a large extent been determined by the nature of the book's subject-matter and is consonant with the facts presented here. Had I concentrated on other aspects of Soviet society, such as, say, the process of the distribution of resources between different sectors of industry or the interrelationship between the Party secretariat and the Presidium of the Council of Ministers (i.e. with inter-elite decision-making on more instrumental issues) then no doubt the theoretical orientation outlined above would be inadequate. My approach is based on only a partial view of Soviet society and does not claim to offer a paradigm for the understanding of all aspects of Soviet society. Rather than studying general power relations in Soviet society I focus on one crucial aspect of such relations: the utilization of ideology and ritual to maintain and perpetuate power relations between political elites and the masses. I would contend that, despite many changes in the political process of Soviet society, in this respect power relations in Soviet society remain quite distinct from those of other contemporary advanced societies.

Appendix A

vvvvvvvvvvvvvvvvvvvvvvvvvvvvvvvvvvvvvvvvvvvvvvvvvvvvvvvvvvvvvvvvvvvvvvvvvvvvvvvvvv

Ritual songs and verse

Note: the translations are my own.

<table>
<tr><td>

Pust' Vsegda Budet Sol'ntse

Sol'nechny krug, nebo vokrug –
Eto risunok mal'chishki.
Narisoval on na listke
I napisal v ugol'ke:
Khor
Pust' vsegda budet sol'ntse,
Pust' vsegda budet nebo
Pust' vsegda budet mama,
Pust' vsegda budu ya.

</td><td>

Let There Always be Sunshine

The sun's circle, sky around –
This is the drawing of a little boy.
He drew it on a piece of paper
And wrote in the corner:
Chorus
Let there always be sunshine
Let there always be sky,
Let there always be mummy,
Let there always be me.

</td></tr>
<tr><td>

Milyi moi drug,
Dobryi moi drug
Lyudyam tak khochetsya mira!
I v tridtsat' pyat'
Serdtse opyat
Ne ustaet povtoryat':
Khor

</td><td>

My dear friend,
My good friend
People do so want peace!
And at 35
The heart again
Does not tire to repeat:
Chorus

</td></tr>
<tr><td>

Tishe, soldat,
Slyshish soldat –
Lyudi pugayutsya vzryvov.
Tysyachi glaz
V nebo glyadyat,
Guby upryamo tverdyat:
Khor

</td><td>

Be still, soldier,
Do you hear soldier –
People are afraid of explosions.
A thousand eyes
Look into the sky,
Lips insistently repeat:
Chorus

</td></tr>
<tr><td>

Protiv bedy,
Protiv voiny
Vstanem za nashikh mal'chishek
Sol'ntse navek! Schast'e navek! –
Tak povelel chelovek:
Khor

</td><td>

Against trouble,
Against war
Let us stand up for our little boy.
Sun for ever! Happiness for ever! –
Thus man commanded:
Chorus

</td></tr>
</table>

Appendix A: Ritual songs and verse

Molodaya Gvardiya	*The Young Guard*
Chtoby sdelat' zemnoi shar schastlivym	To make the earth a happy one
My klyanemsya Partii rodnoi.	We dedicate ouselves to the native Party.
My, molodaya gvardiya	We, the young guard
Rabochikh i krestyan.	Of workers and peasants.

S Chego Nachinaetsya Rodina?

S chego nachinaetsya Rodina?
S kartinke v tvoem bukvare,
S khoroshikh i vernikh tovarishchei
Zhivushchikh v sosednem dvore?
A mozhet, ona nachinaetsya
S toi pesni, chto pela nam mat',
So togo, chto v lyubykh ispytaniyakh
U nas nikomy ne otnyat'.

S chego nachinaetsya Rodina?
S zavetnoi skamy u vorot.
S toi samoi berezki, chto vo pole,
Pod vetrom sklonyayas', rastet.
A mozhet, ona nachinaetsya
S vesennei zapevki skvortsa
I s etoi dorogi proselochnoi,
Kotoroi ne vidno kontsa.

S chego nachinaetsya Rodina?
S okoshek, goryashchikh vdali,
So staroi ottsovskoi budenovki,
Chto gde-to v shkafu my nashli.
A mozhet, ona nachinaetsya
So stuka vagonnykh koles
I s klyatvy, kotoruyu v yunosti
Ty ei v svoem serdtse prines.
S chego nachinaetsya Rodina?

With What Does the Motherland Begin?

With what does the Motherland begin?
With a picture in your first ABC book,
With good and loyal friends
Living in the neighbouring yard?
But, may be, it begins
With that song which Mother sang to us,
With that which no ordeal
Can ever take away from us.

With what does the Motherland begin?
With the cherished bench by the gate.
With the very same birch tree which in the field,
Bending down in the wind, grows.
But may be, it begins
With the spring song of the starling
And with this dear country road
Of which there is no end in sight.

With what does the Motherland begin?
With the little windows shining from afar,
With father's old little soldier's cap
Which we found somewhere in the cupboard.
And maybe, it begins
With the rumble of wagon wheels
And with the oath which in your youth
You gave to it in your heart.
With what does the Motherland begin?

Rekviem
[R. Rozhdestvenskii]

Pomnite!
Cherez veka,
cherez goda –
Pomnite!
O tekh
Kto uzhe ne pridet nikogda –
Pomnite!

Ne plach'te!
V gorle
sderzhite stony,
gor'kie stony.
Pamyati
pavshikh
bud'te dostoiny!

Vechno
Dostoiny!
Khlebom i pesnei
mechtoi i stikhami,
Zhizn'yu
prostornoi
Kazhdoi sekundoi
Kazhdym dykhan'iem
bud'te dostoiny!

Requiem
[R. Rozhdestvenskii]

Remember!
Across the centuries,
Across the years –
Remember!
About those
Who will never come again –
Remember!

Do not cry!
In your throat hold the groans,
The bitter groans
Of the memory
Of the fallen
Be worthy!

Eternally worthy!
With bread and with song
With a dream and with verses,
With your free life
With every second,
Every breath
Be worthy!

Lyudi!
Pokuda serdtsa stuchatsya –
Pomnite!
pesnyu svoyu otpravlyaya v polem –
Pomnite!
O tekh
kto uzhe nikogda ne spoet –
Pomnite!

Detyam svoim rasskazhite o nikh,
chtob zapomnili!
Detyam detei rasskazhite o nikh,
chtoby tozhe zapomnili!
Vo vse vremena bessmertnoi
zemli
Pomnite!

Mechty pronesite cherez goda
I zhizn'yu napolnite! . . .
No o tekh,
Kto uzhe ne pridet nikogda –
Zaklinayu –
Pomnite!

People!
As long as your hearts are beating –
Remember!
Sending your song flying –
Remember!
About those
Who already will sing no more –
Remember!

Tell your children about them,
so that they remember!
Tell your children's children about
them, so that they, too, remember!
Through all the ages of the immortal
world
Remember!

Carry your dream through the years
and live life to the full ! . . .
But about those,
Who will not be there any more –
I implore –
Remember!

Appendix B

vvvvvvvvvvvvvvvvvvvvvvvvvvvvvvvvvvvvvvvvvvvvvvvvvvvvvvvvvvvvvvvvvvvvvvvvvvvvvvvv

The Soviet ritual calendar

Note: based on *Nashi prazdniki* (1977), appendix.
Figures in brackets after the holiday denote the year of its establishment.

January	
1	New Year's Day (1919)
February	
23	Day of the Soviet Army and Navy
March	
8	International Woman's Day (1913) [Mother's Day]
18	Day of the Paris Commune (1918)
Third Sunday	Day of Workers in Housing and Communal Services (1977)
27	International Day of the Theatre (1961)
April	
First Sunday	Day of the Geologist (1966)
7	All-World Day of Health (1948)
Second Sunday	Day of the Forces of Anti-Aircraft Defence (1975)
12	Day of Astronautics
22	Anniversary of Lenin's Birthday
24	International Day of Solidarity of Youth (1955)
May	
1	Day of International Workers' Solidarity [May Day] (1918)
5	Day of the Press (1922)
7	Day of the Radio (1967)
9	Victory Day (1945)
19	Birthday of the Pioneer Organization in the Name of Lenin
25	Day of the Liberation of Africa (1963)
28	Day of the Frontier Guard
Last Sunday	Day of the Worker in the Chemical Industry (1965)
June	
1	International Day for the Protection of Children (1950)
First Sunday	Day of the Land Reclamation Worker (1976)
Second Sunday	Day of the Worker in Light Industry (1966)
Third Sunday	Day of the Worker in the Medical Services (1963)

289

Last Sunday	Day of Soviet Youth (1958)

July

First Sunday	Day of International Co-operation (1923)
First Sunday	Day of the Worker of the Sea and River Fleet [Merchant Navy] (1976)
Second Sunday	Day of the Fisherman (1965)
Third Sunday	Day of the Metallurgist (1957)
Fourth Sunday	Day of the Worker in Trade (1966)
Last Sunday	Day of the Navy of the USSR (1939)

August

First Sunday	All-Union Day of the Railway Worker (1936)
Second Sunday	All-Union Day of the Athlete and Gymnast (1939)
Second Sunday	Day of the Construction Worker (1955)
Third Sunday	Day of the Air Force of the USSR (1933)
Last Sunday	Day of the Miner (1947)

September

First Sunday	All-Union Day of Workers in the Oil and Gas Industry (1965)
8	International Day of Solidarity of Journalists (1958)
Second Sunday	Day of the Tank Soldier (*tankist*) (1946)
Third Sunday	Day of the Forestry Worker (1966)
Last Sunday	Day of the Worker in Heavy Engineering (1966)

October

First Sunday	Day of the Teacher (1965)
Second Sunday	All-Union Day of Workers in Agriculture (1966)
Third Sunday	Day of Workers in the Food Processing Industry (1966)
24	International Day of the United Nations Organization (1945)
29	Birthday of the *Komsomol* (1919)
Last Sunday	Day of Drivers (1976)

November

7	Anniversary of the Great October Socialist Revolution (1918)
10	Day of Soviet Police (1962)
10	All-World Day of Youth (1945)
17	International Students' Day (1941)
19	Day of the Rocket Forces (1964) and of the Artillery (1944)

December

22	Day of the Worker in Power Engineering (1966)

Bibliography

Abramov, A. (1969) *Mavzolei Lenina*. Moscow.

Abramyan, A. (1966) *Massovye gimnasticheskie vystupleniya*. Moscow.

Agitatsionno-massovoe iskusstvo pervykh let Oktyabrya (1971). Moscow.

Alekseev, N. P. (1970) Prichiny sokhraneniya religioznosti v psikhologii kol-
khoznogo krestyanstva i puti ee preodoleniya, in *Kollektiv kolkhoznikov*.
Moscow.

Aliev, A. K. (1968) *Narodnye traditsii, obychai i ikh rol' v formirovanii novogo
cheloveka*. Makhachkala.

Andrianov, N. (1976) Sovetskomu cheloveku – novye obryady. *Pravda* 28 May:
3.

Apter, D. E. (1963) Political religion in the new nations, in C. Geertz (ed.), *Old
Societies and New States*. New York–London.

Aspaturian, V. V. (1968) The non-Russian nationalities, in A. Kassof (ed.),
Prospects for Soviet Society. London.

Avdeev, A. D. (1926) Oktyabr', 1924 g., in *Massovye prazdnestva*. Leningrad.

Balashov, D. (1965) Traditsionnoe i sovremennoe. *Nauka i religiya*, 12.

Barghoorn, F. (1972) *Politics in the USSR* (2nd edn). Yale University Press.

Barth, F. (1975) *Ritual and Knowledge among the Baktiman of New Guinea*. Oslo.

Barthes, R. (1967) *Elements of Semiology*. New York.

Basilov, V. N. (1967) Etnograficheskoe issledovanie religioznykh verovanii
sel'skogo naseleniya, in *Konkretyne izucheniya sovremennykh religioznykh
verovanii*. Moscow.

Baturin, I. (1967) Novye sovetskie traditsii – vazhnoe sredstvo kommunis-
ticheskogo vospitaniya molodezhi. *Voprosy nauchnogo ateizma*, 3.

Baturin, I. (1976) Letnie dni molodezhi, in *Prazdniki, obryady, traditsii*. Moscow.

Bellah, R. N. (1967) Civil religion in America. *Daedalus*, 96: 1–21.

Bellah, R. N. (1969) Civil religion in America, in D. R. Cutler (ed.), *The World
Year Book of Religion*, vol. i. London.

Bellah, R. N. (1975) *The Broken Covenant. American Civil Religion in Time of Trial*.
New York.

Belousov, Ya. (1972) Genezis, sotsial'naya sushchnost' i funktsii bezreligioz-
nykh form prazdnovaniya. Unpublished dissertation summary. Alma-
Ata.

Belousov, Ya. P. (1973) *Dorogami novykh traditsii*. Alma-Ata.

Belousov, Ya. (1974) *Prazdniki starye i novye*. Alma-Ata.

Bibliography

Benkliev, S. N. (1971) *Sovetskomu bytu – novye obryady*. Voronezh.

Berestovskaya, L. E. (1968) *V prazdniki i v budni*. Stavropol'.

Binns, C. (1979) Sowjetische Feste und Rituale, I and II. *Osteuropa*, Jan.: 12–21; Feb: 110–22.

Birnbaum, N. (1955) Monarchs and sociologists: a reply to Prof. Shils and Mr. Young. *Sociological Review*, 3: 5ff.

Blinova, G. P. (1968) K voprosy klassifikatsii novykh Sovetskikh obryadov. *Uchenye zapiski Moskovskogo Gosudarstvennogo Instituta Kul'tury*, 15: 341–357.

Bocock, R. (1974) *Ritual in Industrial Society: A Sociological Analysis of Ritualism in Modern England*. London.

Brodskii, V. Ya. (1926). Vneshnii byt massovogo prazdnika, in *Massovye prazdnestva*, pp. 200–5. Moscow.

Brogan, D. W. (1969) Commentaries on R. N. Bellah's article "Civil religion in America", in D. R. Cutler (ed.), *The World Year Book of Religion*, vol. I, pp. 356ff. London.

Bromlei, Yu. (1977) *Literaturnaya Gazeta* 31 August: 12.

Brown, A. (1978) Political developments, in A. Brown and M. Kaser (eds), *The Soviet Union Since the Fall of Khrushchev*. London.

Brown, E. J. (1963) *Russian Literature since the Revolution*. New York.

Brown, E. J. (1973) *Mayakovskii. A Poet in the Revolution*. Princeton University Press.

Brudnyi, V. I. (1968) *Obryady vchera i sevodnya*. Moscow.

Brzezinski, Z. K. (1967) *Ideology and Power in Soviet Politics* (2nd edn). New York–London.

Brzezinski, Z. (1970) *Between Two Ages*. New York.

Budd, S. (1977) *Varieties of Unbelief*. London.

Charlton, D. (1963) *Secular Religions in France*. Oxford University Press.

Chotonov, Ya. (1971) Mesto traditsii v sovremennoi sotsialisticheskoi kul'ture narodov SSSR, in *Leninizm i razvitie sotsialisticheskoi kul'tury*. Moscow–Tashkent.

Churchward, L. G. (1973) *The Soviet Intelligentsia*. London.

Cohen, A. (1969) Political anthropology: the analysis of the symbolism of power relations. *Man* 4(2): 217–35.

Cohen, A. (1974) *Two-Dimensional Man. An Essay on the Anthropology of Power and Symbolism in Complex Society*. London.

Coles, W. A. and Hammond, P. E. (1974) Religious pluralism, legal development, and societal complexity: rudimentary forms of civil religion. *Journal for the Scientific Study of Religion*, 13: 177ff.

Da Matta, R. (1974) Constraint and license: a preliminary study of two Brazilian rituals, in Secular rituals considered: prolegomena toward a theory of ritual, ceremony and formality. Unpublished paper in Burg Wartenstein Symposium no. 64.

Den' yunogo geroya-antifashista (1975). Moscow.

Deutscher, T. (ed.) (1973) *Not By Politics Alone. The Other Lenin*. London.

Dolgova, V. (1970) Novye obryady privivayutsya. *Nauka i religiya*, 3: 29–31.

Douglas, M. (1970) *Natural Symbols: Explorations in Cosmology*. London.

Bibliography

Dowd, D. L. (1948) *Pageant-Master of the Republic (Jacques-Louis David and the French Revolution)*. University of Nebraska Studies, series 3.

Drazheva, R. D. (1973) Obryady, svyazannye s okhranoi zdorov'ya v prazdnike letnego solntsestoyaniya u vostochnykh i yuzhnykh slavyan. *Sovetskaya etnografiya*, 6: 109–19.

Duncan-Jones, A. S. (1959) The burial of the dead, in *Liturgy and Worship*, pp. 616–26. London.

Dunham, V. (1976) *In Stalin's Time. Middleclass Values in Soviet Fiction*. Cambridge University Press.

Dunn, S. P. (1971) Structure and functions of the Soviet rural family, in J. R. Millar (ed.), *The Soviet Rural Community*. London.

Durkheim, E. (1968) *The Elementary Forms of the Religious Life*. London.

Dushbamirov, S. G. (1967) Mesto obychaev i traditsii v sisteme sotsialisticheskikh sotsial'nykh norm. *Uchenye zapiski* (Azerb. Universiteta), ser. istoricheskikh i filosofskikh nauk, 1.

Eberpi, A. (1969) Salam Bakhar! Zdravstvui Vesna! *Nauka i religiya*, 4: 72–5.

Eisenstadt, S. N. and Curelaru, M. (1976) *The Form of Sociology: Paradigms and Crises*. New York.

Eisenstadt, B. W. (1970) *Lenin and Leninism*. London.

El'chenko, Yu. N. (1976a) *Novomu cheloveku – novye obryady*. Moscow.

El'chenko, Yu. (1976b) Sovetskie prazdniki. *Kommunist*, 13: 71–9.

El'chenko, Yu. (1977) *Novye traditsii i obryady*. Moscow.

Erikson, E. H. (1969) The development of ritualization, in D. Cutler (ed.), *The World Year Book of Religion*, vol. i. London.

Etzioni, A. (1968) *A Comparative Analysis of Complex Organizations*. New York.

Filatov, A. (1967) *O novykh i starykh obryadakh*. Moscow.

Fitzpatrick, S. (1978) Cultural revolution as class war, in S. Fitzpatrick (ed.), *Cultural Revolution in Russia 1928–31*. Indiana University Press.

French, R. (1959) The services of the eastern Orthodox Church, in *Liturgy and Worship*. London.

Friedrich, C. J. and Brzezinski, Z. K. (1966) *Totalitarian Dictatorship and Autocracy* (rev. edn). New York.

Fursin, I. I. (1972) O prirode i sotsial'nykh funktsiyakh obryadnosti v sotsialisticheskom obshchestve. *Voprosy nauchnogo ateizma*, 13: 158–98.

Fursin, I. I. (1973) Obryadnost' i ee rol' v formirovanii mirovozzreniya, in *Esli ateisty aktivny*. Simferopol'.

Fursin, I. I. (1977) *Obryadnost' i ee mesto v sotsialisticheskom obraze zhizni*. Moscow.

Gamm, H. J. (1962) *Der braune Kult*. Hamburg.

Gavriel'yan, N. K. (1974) *Partkom i sorevnovanie*. Leningrad.

Gazhos, V. F. (1967) Vnedrenie novykh semeino-bytovykh obryadov – sostavnaya chast' ateisticheskogo vospitaniya na sovremennom etape, in *Trud i kommunisticheskaya soznatel'nost'*. Kishinev.

Geertz, C. (1957–8) Ethos, world-view and the analysis of sacred symbols. *Antioch Review*.

Geertz, C. (1964) Ideology as a cultural system, in D. Apter (ed.), *Ideology of Discontent*. New York.

Geertz, C. (1968) Religion as a cultural system, in M. Banton (ed.), *Anthropological Approaches to the Study of Religion*. London.

Geertz, C. (1973) *The Interpretation of Cultures*. New York.

Geertz, C. (ed.) (1963) *Old Societies and New States*. London.

Gegeshidze, D. (1976) Mtskhetoba ili shotoba, in *Prazdniki, obryady, traditsii*. Moscow.

Genkin, D. M. (1975) *Massovye prazdniki*. Moscow.

Gerandokov, M. Kh. (1970) *O novykh Sovetskykh traditsiyakh i obryadakh*. Nal'chik.

Gerasimov, S. (1957) Pervoe prazdnestvo Oktyabr'skoi revolyutsii. *Iskusstvo*, 7.

Gerodnik, G. (1970) *O parkakh dobrykh vospominanii*. Tallin.

Gerodnik, G. (1976) Eto nado zhivym, in *Prazdniki, obryady, traditsii*. Moscow.

Glaser, H. (1978) *The Cultural Roots of National Socialism*. London.

Gluckman, M. (1962) Les rites de passage, in *Essays on the Ritual of Social Relations*. Manchester.

Gluckman, M. and Gluckman, M. (1974) On drama and games and athletic contests, in Secular rituals considered: prolegomena toward a theory of ritual, ceremony and formality. Unpublished paper in Burg Wartenstein Symposium, no. 64.

Glyaser, S. (1938) *Narodnye prazdnestva* (V pomoshch' organizatoru i oformitelyu pervomaiskogo prazdnika). Moscow.

Godelier, N. (1977) *Perspectives in Marxist Anthropology*. Cambridge University Press.

Goncharov, N. F. (1972) *Kommunisticheskoe vospitanie rabochikh promyslennykh predpriyatii*. Voronezh.

Goodin, R. E. (1978) Rites of rulers. *The British Journal of Sociology*, 3.

Goody, J. (1961) Religion and ritual: the definitional problem. *The British Journal of Sociology*, 2.

Goody, J. (1974) Against ritual: loosely structured thoughts on a loosely defined topic, in Secular rituals considered: prolegomena toward a theory of ritual, ceremony, and formality. Unpublished paper in Burg Wartenstein Symposium, no. 64.

Grishchenko, P. S. and Kakonin, V. (1974) *Trudovye prazdniki i traditsii*. Moscow.

Gushchin, A. S. (1930) *Izo-iskusstvo v massovykh prazdnestvakh i demonstratsiakh*. Moscow.

Gvozdev, A. A. (1926) Massovye prazdnestva na Zapade, in *Massovye prazdnestva*. Leningrad.

Haimson, L. (1970) The solitary hero, in R. Pipes (ed.), *The Russian Intelligentsia*. Columbia University Press.

Hammond, P. E. (1969) Commentaries on R. N. Bellah's article "Civil religion in America", in D. R. Cutler (ed.), *The World Year Book of Religion*, vol. I, pp. 356ff. London.

Harper, S. N. (1929) *Civic Training in Soviet Russia*. Chicago.

Hayes, P. (1973) *Fascism*. London.

Hollander, P. (1973) *Soviet and American Society*. Oxford University Press.

Hook, S. (1945) *The Hero in History*. London.
Hough, J. (1977) *The Soviet Union and Social Science Theory*. Harvard University Press.
Huxley, J. (1969) Ritual in human societies, in D. Cutler (ed.), *World Year Book of Religion*. vol. I, pp. 696–711. London.
Inkeles, A. (1961) Mobilizing public opinion, in A. Inkeles and K. Geiger (eds), *Soviet Society*. London.
Ivanov, V. M. (1968) *Novoe vremya – novaya zhizn'*. Minsk.
Izvekov, N. E. (1926) Massovye prazdnestva Leningrada 1924–5 g. Predislovie. *Massovye prazdnestva*. Leningrad.
Izvekov, N. P. (1926) "1 Maya" 1925 g., in *Massovye prazdnestva*. Leningrad.
Izvestiya (1959) 5 December.
Izvestiya (1964) 20 December.
Izvestiya (*CDSP*) (1971) 23 November.
Izvestiya (1973) 22 September.
Izvestiya (1978) 22 October.
Kak provesti torzhestvenno vruchenie pervogo pasporta (1966). Minsk.
Kampars, P. P. (1969) Nekotorye problemy grazhdanskoi obryadnosti, in Z. Balevits (ed.), *Ateizm i religiya*. Riga.
Kampars, P. P. and Zakovich, N. M. (1967) *Sovetskaya grazhdanskaya obryadnost*. Moscow.
Khachirov, A. K.; Orlova, V.; Kesaev, V. (1973) *Novye traditsii i bor''ba s perezhitkami v soznanii lyudei*. Ordzhonikidze.
Khasanova, Kh. (1976) Nachalo bol'shoi raboty, in *Prazdniki, obryady, traditsii*. Moscow.
Khashimov, A. Kh. (1972) *Formirovanie novykh semeino–bytovykh otnoshenii u narodov Srednei Azii*. Dushanbe.
Kikilo, I. P. (1969) *Novoe vremya – novye traditsii*. Moscow.
Klapp, O. E. (1948) The creation of popular heroes. *American Journal of Sociology*, 54: 135–41.
Klimov, E. (1965) *Prazdnik prishel v tvoi dom*. Perm.
Kobetskii, V. D. (1978) *Sotsiologicheskoe izuchenie religioznosti i ateizma*. Leningrad.
Kolarz, W. (1952) *Russia and Her Colonies*. London.
Kommunist Estonii (1968) 7: 29–34.
Kommunist Estonii (1969) 6: 50–6.
Kop'ev N. Ya. (1966) *Daetsya grazhdanstvo Sovetskoe*. Petrozavodsk.
Korchagina, V. B. (1970a) O sotsial'noi sushchnosti i funktsiyakh obryada. *Vestnik Moskovskogo Universiteta*, seriya VIII, filosofiya, 3: 72–80.
Korchagina, V. B. (1970b) Spetsifika obrayda kak sotsial'nogo yavleniya. *Voprosy sotsiologii i obshchestvennoi psikhologii*, 1: 161–71.
Kryvelev, I. A. (1977) Sovremennye obryady i rol' etnograficheskoi nauki v ikh izuchenii, formirovanii i vnedrenii. *Sovetskaya etnografiya*, 5: 36–45.
Kuchiev, A. G. (1974) Formirovanie novoi grazhdanskoi obryadnosti v Severnoi Osetii. *Voprosy nauchnogo ateizma*, 16: 60–8.
Kulagin, G. A. (1974) *Trudovye resursy i voprosy vospitaniya*. Moscow.
La Fontaine, J. S. (1972) *The Interpretation of Ritual*. London.

Bibliography

Lane, C. O. (1976) The impact of communist ideology and soviet order on christian religion in the contemporary USSR (1959–74). Unpublished Ph.D. thesis, University of London.

Lane, C. O. (1978) Christian Religion in the Soviet Union. London.

Lapidus, G. (1978) *Women in Soviet Society*. University of California Press.

Laskina, L. (1976) "Alym Parusam" – plyt, in *Prazdniki, obryady, traditsii*. Moscow.

Lastochkin, N. A. (1926) Khudozhestvennoe oformlenie prazdnika, in *Massovye prazdnestva*. Leningrad.

Leach, E. R. (1954) *Political Systems of Highland Burma*. London.

Leach, E. R. (1968) Ritual, in *International Encyclopedia of the Social Sciences*, vol. 13: 521–3.

Leach, E. R. (1976) *Culture and Communication*. Cambridge University Press.

Lebra, T. S. (1976) *Japanese Patterns of Behaviour*. University Press of Hawaii.

Lenin, V. I. (1976) A great beginning, in *Selected Works*, vol. 3. Moscow.

Lenin, V. I. (1976) On proletarian culture, in *Selected Works*, vol. 3. Moscow.

Leninizm i dialektiya obshchestvennogo razvitiya (1970), chapter 10. Moscow.

Lepeshinskii, P. (1925) *Proletarskii klassovyi prazdnik*. Kharkov.

Levkovich, V. P. (1970) Obychai i obryady i ikh rol' v sovershenstvovanii semeinykh otnoshenii. *Sotsial'nye issledovaniya*, 4: 115–21. Moscow.

Lisavtsev, E. I. (1966) *Novye sovetskie traditsii*. Moscow.

Lobacheva, N. P. (1972) O protsesse formirovanii novoi semeinoi obryadnosti. *Sovetskaya etnografiya* 1: 3–13.

Lobacheva, N. P. (1973) O formirovanii novoi obryadnosti u narodov SSSR. *Sovetskaya etnografiya*, 4: 14–24.

Lobacheva, N. P. (1975) *Formirovanie novoi obryadnosti Uzbekov*. Moscow.

Lobacheva, N. P. and Tul'tseva, L. A. (1977) Traditsii v sovremennoi obryadnosti u Uzbekov. *Sovetskaya etnografiya*, 6: 32–44.

Luckmann, T. (1967) *The Invisible Religion*. London.

Lukacher, V. (1971) Deyatel'nost KPSS po kommunisticheskomu pereustroistvu byta i utverzhdenie novykh traditsii i obychaev. *Trudy Samarkandskogo Universiteta*, 196: 103–6.

Lukes, S. (1973) *Emile Durkheim. His Life and Work*. London.

Lukes, S. (1975) Political ritual and social integration. *Sociology*, 2: 289–308.

Lunacharskii, A. (1924) *Teatr i revolyutsiya*. Moscow.

Lynch, W. F. (1969) Commentary on ritual and liturgy, in D. Cutler (ed.), *The World Year Book of Religion*, vol. i, London.

McAuley, M. (1977) *Politics and the Soviet Union*. Harmondsworth.

McDowell, J. (1974) Soviet civil ceremonies. *Journal for the Scientific Study of Religion*, xiii, 3: 265–79.

MacRae, D. G. (1954) The Bolshevik ideology. *The Cambridge Journal*, 3: 164ff.

Magdeev, M. (1976) Sabantui, in *Prazdniki, obryady, traditsii*. Moscow.

Makrushenko, P. (1963) "Pervomai" (1917). *Kul'turno-prosvetitel'naya rabota*, 4.

Malkonduev, A. M. (1969) *Rol' sotsialisticheskikh traditsii i obychaev v formirovanii novogo cheloveka*. Nal'chik.

Marriott, McK. (1963) Cultural policy in the new states, in C. Geertz (ed.), *Old Societies and New States*. New York–London.

Bibliography

Marshall, H. (1945) *Mayakovsky and His Poetry*. London.

Martin, D. (1978) *A General Theory of Secularization*. Oxford University Press.

Maruyama, M. (1963) *Thought and Behaviour in Modern Japanese Politics*. Oxford University Press.

Massovoe deistvo (1932) (Pervomaiskii prazdnik 1932g.) Sbornik. Moscow–Leningrad.

Massovye prazdniki i zrelshcha (1961). Moscow.

Meleshko, A. A. (1973) *Sovremennye Sovetskie prazdniki i grazhdanskie obryady*. Minsk.

Mel'nikova, T. (1976) Priglashayutsya vse, in *Prazdniki, obryady, traditsii*. Moscow.

Michaelsen, R. (1971) Is the public school religious or secular?, in E. A. Smith (ed.), *The Religion of the Republic*. Philadelphia.

Momylev, A. S. (1975) *Moral'nye stimuly k trudu*. Moscow.

Moore, S. F. (1974) Political meetings and the simulation of unanimity. Kilimanjaro 1973, in Secular rituals considered: prolegomena towards a theory of ritual, ceremony and formality. Unpublished paper in Burg Wartenstein Symposium no. 64.

Munn, N. (1973) Symbolism in a ritual context, in J. Honigman (ed.), *A Handbook of Social and Cultural Anthropology*.

Myerhoff, B. (1974) We don't wrap herring in a printed page: linkage, claims and fictions in secular ritual, in Secular rituals considered: prolegomena towards a theory of ritual, ceremony and formality. Unpublished paper in Burg Wartenstein Symposium no. 64.

Mytskyula, P. (1968) O sovremennykh obychayakh. *Kommunist Estonii*, 4: 48–58.

My zhivem na Prospekte Sovetskom. Prazdnik Ulitsy (1967). Alma-Ata.

Nagirnyak, E. V., Petrova, V. Ya, Rauzen, M. V. (1970) *Novye obryady i prazdniki* (2nd edn). Sovetskaya Rossiya.

Nakane, C. (1973) *Japanese Society*. Harmondsworth.

Nashi prazdniki (1977) ed. V. G. Sinitsyn. Moscow.

Nauka i religiya (1964) 8: 86ff.

Nauka i religiya (1971) 5: 16–18.

Nauka i religiya (1972) 2: 7–13.

Nauka i religiya (1972) 4: 34–5.

Nauka i religiya (1973) 4: 30–43.

Nauka i religiya (1974) 4: 33.

Nauka i religiya (1975) 12: 32–3.

Nauka i religiya (1977) 7: 43–5.

Nauka i religiya (1978) 7: 17–24.

Nedelya (1978) 48: 21.

Nemiro, O. (1969) Lenin i revolyutsionnye prazdniki. *Iskusstvo*, 10 (5).

Nemiro, O. (1973) *V gorod prikhodit prazdnik*. Leningrad.

Nemiro, O. (1977) Ob etom mechtali v ssylkakh. *Nauka i religiya*, 11: 5–7.

Nosova, G. A. (1972) Sozdanie novykh grazhdanskikh obryadov i prazdnikov. *Voprosy nauchnogo ateizma*, 13: 404–8.

Novopistsev, I. (1970) Traditsii dobra i krasoty. *Nauka i religiya* 3: 48–50.

Bibliography

O'Dell, F. (1978) *Socialisation through Children's Literature*. Cambridge University Press.

Ortner, S. B. (1973) On key symbols. *American Anthropologist* 75 (5): 1338–46.

Ortner, S. B. (1975) Gods, bodies, gods' food: a symbolic analysis of Sherpa ritual, in R. Willis (ed.), *The Interpretation of Symbolism*. London.

Panteleev, I. (1939) *Pervoe Maya*. Sverdlovsk.

Partiinaya Zhizn' (1964) 2: 22–6.

Peacock, J. L. (1968) *The Rites of Modernisation: Symbolic and Social Aspects of Indonesian Proletarian Drama*. Chicago.

Pervomai (1974). Moscow.

Petukhov, A. (1969) Bumazhnye tsvety. *Novy Mir*, 6: 272ff.

Pfeffer, L. (1969) Commentaries on R. N. Bellah's article "Civil religion in America", in D. R. Cutler (ed.), *The World Year Book of Religion*, vol. I, pp. 356ff. London.

Piotrovskii, A. I. (1926) Khronika Leningradskikh prazdnestv 1919–22 g., in *Massovye prazdnestva*. Leningrad.

Pisarevskii, D. S. (1940) *Parki kul'tury i otdykha*. Moscow.

Pivovarov, V. G. (1975) Sotsiologicheskoe issledovanie problem byta, kul'tury, natsional'nykh traditsii i verovanii v Checheno-Ingushskoi ASSR. *Voprosy nauchnogo ateizma*, 17: 310–19.

Powell, D. E. (1975) *Antireligious Propaganda in the Soviet Union*. Cambridge, Mass. and London.

Pravda (1971) 18 September.

Prazdniki, obryady, torzhestva (Sbornik stsenariev) (1975). Moscow.

Prazdniki, obryady, traditsii (1976). Moscow.

Prokhanov, A. (1970) Nuzhny li svad'by? *Literaturnaya Gazeta*, 19 August.

Radcliffe-Brown, A. R. (1952) *Structure and Function in Primitive Society*. London.

Radio Liberty Research Bulletin (1978). Munich.

Ranne, V. Ya. (1972) Novye obryady i ikh mesto v dukhovnoi zhizni Sovetskikh ludei. *Voprosy nauchnogo ateizma* 13: 181–97.

Reich, W. (1972) *The Mass Psychology of Fascism*. London.

Rezhissura i organizatsiya massovykh zrelishch (1973). Khar'kov.

Riordan, J. (1977) *Sport in Soviet Society*. Cambridge University Press.

Robertson, R. (1978) *Meaning and Change*. London.

Rogozina, E. N. (1973) *Novye grazhdanskie obryady*. Leningrad.

Rudnev, V. A. (1966) Kommunisticheskomy bytu novye Sovetskie traditsii, in N. P. Krasnikov (ed.), *Voprosy preodoleniya religioznykh perezhitkov v SSSR*. Moscow.

Rudnev, V. A. (1967) Deyatel'nost' KPSS po kommunisticheskomy pereustroistvu byta i utverzhdeniyu novykh traditsii i obychaev 1961–66. Unpublished dissertation summary. Moscow.

Rudnev, V. A. (1974) *Sovietskie obychai i obryady*. Leningrad.

Rudnev, V. A. (1979) *Sovetskie prazdniki, obryady, ritualy*. Leningrad.

Sarsenbaev, N. S. (1974) *Obychai, traditsii i obshchestvennaya zhizn'*. Alma-Ata.

Schlesinger, R. (1956) *Changing Attitudes in Soviet Russia: The Nationalities Problem and Soviet Administration*. London.

Bibliography

Shchukin, Yu. and Magidson, A. (1932) *Oformlenie massovogo prazdnestva i demonstratsii*. Moscow–Leningrad.

Shepetis, L. (1978) V nogu so vremenem. *Nauka i religiya*, 9: 4–7.

Shevelev, V. (1976) Vysota, in *Prazdniki, obryady, traditsii*. Moscow.

Shils, E. (1969) Ritual and crisis, in D. Cutler (ed.), *The World Year Book of Religion*, vol. I. London.

Shils, E. and Young, M. (1953) The meaning of the coronation. *Sociological Review*, I: 63–81.

Shiryaeva, P. G. (1975) Iz istorii razvitiya nekotorykh revolyutsionnykh traditsii. *Sovetskaya etnografiya*, 6: 63–70.

Shneidere, B. (1969) Sovetskie obryady – partiinoe delo. *Nauka i religiya*, 2: 36–7.

Slonim, M. (1977) *Soviet Russian Literature (Writers and Problems. 1917–1977)*. Oxford – New York.

Smith, H. (1976) *The Russians*. London.

Soboul, A. (1974) *The French Revolution. 1787–1799*. London.

Soehngen, O. (1950) *Säkulasierter Kultus*. Gütersloh.

Sorokin, P. (1970) Delo slozhnoe, tonkoe, kropotlivoe. *Nauka i religiya*, 3: 44–5.

Sovetskaya etnografiya (1977) 5: 36–45.

Sperber, D. (1975) *Rethinking Symbolism*. Cambridge University Press.

Stetsenko, S. (1975) Novaya zhizn' – novye prazdniki. *Nauka i religiya*, 4: 13–19.

Stroitel'stvo kommunizma i dukhovny mir cheloveka (1966). Moscow.

Struve, N. (1969) Pseudo-religious rites in the USSR, in D. R. Cutler (ed.), *World Year Book of Religion*, vol. I. London.

Stsenarii teatralizovannykh massovykh prazdnikov (1967). Moscow.

Sukhanov, I. V. (1973) *Obychai, traditsii, obryady kak sotsial'nye yavleniya*. Gorkii.

Sukhanov, I. V. (1976) *Obychai, traditsii i preemstvennost' pokolenii*. Moscow.

Sukhov, Yu. (1976) Primer molodym, in *Prazdniki, obryady, traditsii*. Moscow.

Sushkov, I. M. (1969) *Geroizm i geroicheskie traditsii*. Rostov on Don.

Swyngedouw, J. (1979) A few sociological notes on sacredness and Japan. *Japanese Religions*, 1: 17–38.

Teplyakov, M. K. (1972) *Problemy ateisticheskogo vospitaniya v praktike parti i noi raboty*. Voronezh.

Timoshin, I. R. (1966) Rol' revolyutsionnykh prazdnikov, razvitie i obogoshchenie revolyutsionnykh traditsii nashego naroda. *Uchenye zapiski Moskovskogo Instituta Kul'tury*, 13, pp. 143–68.

Tonkonogov, M. (1975) *Metodicheskie rekomendatsii po vnedreniyu novykh obryadov i ritualov v byt Sovetskikh lyudei*. Tashkent.

Torzhestvennaya registratsiya rozhdenii v organakh ZAGSA Latviiskoi SSR (1974). Riga.

Torzhestvenno, krasivo, pamyatno (1966). Moscow.

Trotsky, L. (1960) *Literature and Revolution*. University of Michigan.

Trotsky, L. (1973) *Problems of Everyday Life*. New York.

Tsekhnovitser, O. V. (1931) *Prazdnestva revolyutsii*. Leningrad.

Tucker, R. C. (1977) Stalinism as revolution from above, in R. C. Tucker (ed.), *Stalinism*. New York.

Bibliography

Tumanov, I. M. (1974) *Rezhissura massovogo prazdnika i teatralizovannogo kontserta*. Leningrad.

Turner, T. (1974) Groping for the elephant; ritual as process, as model, and as hierarchical system, in Secular rituals considered: prolegomena towards a theory of ritual, ceremony and formality. Unpublished paper in Burg Wartenstein Symposium no. 64.

Turner, V. W. (1966) Ndembu circumcision ritual, in M. Gluckman (ed.), *Essays on The Ritual of Social Relations*. Manchester.

Turner, V. W. (1967) Symbols in Ndembu ritual, in M. Gluckman (ed.), *Closed Systems and Open Minds*. Chicago.

Turner, V. W. (1967) *The Forest of Symbols*. New York.

Turner, V. W. (1969a) *The Ritual Process: Structure and Anti-structure*. London.

Turner, V. W. (1969b) Forms of symbolic action, in R. Spencer (ed.), *Forms of Symbolic Action*. Seattle.

Ugrinovich, D. M. (1975) *Obryady. Za i protiv*. Moscow.

Umurzakova, O. P. (1971) Rol' novykh traditsii v kommunisticheskom vospitanii trudyashchikhsya, in *Leninizm, i razvitie sotsialisticheskoi kul'tury*. Moscow–Tashkent.

Unger, A. L. (1974) *The Totalitarian Party*. Cambridge University Press.

Urazmanova, P. K. (1977) Narodnyi prazdnik Sabantui u Tatar. *Sovetskaya etnografiya*, 1: 94–100.

Utechin, S. V. (1961) *Everyman's Concise Encyclopaedia of Russia*. London–New York.

Van Gennep, A. (1960) *The Rites of Passage*. London.

Vavilova, I. A. and Filippov, G. G. (1967) Problema trebuet dal'neishego issledovaniya. *Filosofskie nauka*, 1: 150–2.

Verba, S. (1965) The Kennedy assassination and the nature of political commitment, in B. S. Greenberg and E. B. Parker (eds.), *The Kennedy Assassination and the American Public*. Stanford University Press.

Veresaev, V. V. (1926) *Ob obryadakh starykh i novykh*. Moscow.

Veselev, P. Ya. (1973) Novye obryady vkhodyat v zhizn', in *Esli ateisty aktivny*. Simferopol'.

Vestnikov, A. (1964) Narod sozdaet traditsii. *Nauka i religiya*, 1: 60–1.

Voina, V. (1976) Novye uzory po staroi kanve, in *Prazdniki, obryady, traditsii*. Moscow.

Voprosy nauchnogo ateizma (1973).

Voronitsyn, S. (1969) The Lenin cult and Soviet youth. *Studies on the Soviet Union*, NS, vol. IX, 1: 31–6. Munich.

Vorotnikova, A. (1971) Novye obryady i ritualy vkhodyat v zhizn'. *Partiinaya zhizn'*, 10: 79–82.

Vries, de A. (1974) *Dictionary of Symbols and Images*. Amsterdam.

Warner, L. (1965) *The Living and the Dead*. Yale University Press.

White, S. (1977) The USSR: patterns of autocracy and industrialism, in A. Brown and J. Gray (eds.), *Political Culture and Political Change in Communist States*. London.

White, S. (1979) *Political Culture and Soviet Politics*. London.

Bibliography

Whittick, A. (1971) *Symbols, Signs and their Meaning and Uses in Design* (2nd edn). London.

Whyte, H. K. (1975) *Small Groups and Political Rituals in China.* University of California Press.

Wilson, J. F. (1971) The status of civil religion in America, in E. A. Smith (ed.), *The Religion of the Republic.* Philadelphia.

Wilson, M. (1971) *Religion and the Transformation of Society.* Cambridge University Press.

Wimberley, R. C., Clelland, D. A., Hood, T. C., Lipsey, C. M. (1976) The civil religious dimension: is it there? *Social Forces,* 54, 4: 890–900.

Wolfe, T. W. (1968) The military, in A. Kassof (ed.), *Prospects for Soviet Society.* London.

Yablokov, I. N. (1969) Transformatsiya religioznoi morali v soznanii veruyushchikh v usloviyakh sotsializma, in *Konkretno-sotsiologicheskoe izuchenie sostoyaniya religioznosti i opyta ateisticheskogo vospitaniya.* Moscow.

Yudin, B. V. *et al.* (1935) *Massovye prazdnestva.* Moscow.

Zakharina, N. (1971) Novye prazdniki, novye traditsii. *Partiinaya zhizn',* 1: 69–75.

Zav'yalov, A. (1973) *Novaya zhizn' obryadov, prazdnikov, traditsii.* Askhabad.

Zeldin, M. B. (1969) The religious nature of Russian Marxism. *Journal for the Scientific Study of Religion,* viii, 1: 100–11.

Zelenchuk, V. and Popovich, Yu. (1972) Novye obychai i obryady – sostavnaya chast' dukhovnoi kul'tury sotsializma. *Kommunist Moldavii,* 1: 17–25.

Zhemchuzhnyi, V. (1927) *Kak organizovat' oktyabr'skuyu demonstratsiyu.*

Zhirnova, G. V. (1971) O sovremennom gorodskom svadebnom obryade. *Sovetskaya etnografiya,* 3: 68–78.

Zots, V. A. (1976) Vospitanie ubezhdennosti, in *Prazdniki, obryady traditsii.* Moscow.

Zots, V. A. (1978) *Dukhovnaya kul'tura i ateisticheskoe vospitanie.* Moscow.

Zots, V. A. and Poluk, I. V. (1978) Traditsii, rozhdennye sotsializmom. *Voprosy nauchnogo ateizma* 22: 85–94.

Zuev, Yu. P., Lopatkin, P. A., Fursin, I. I. (1974) Nekotorye teoreticheskie i prakticheskie problemy sotsialisticheskoi obryadnosti. *Voprosy nauchnogo ateizma,* 16: 43ff.

Index

Abramov 211, 216
Abramyan 124, 226
Alekseev 83
Alekseeva 244
Aliev 47, 48, 51, 81, 114, 117, 185, 209, 233, 249
ambiguity of social relations 12, 13
Andrianov 246
Anniversary: of the Assumption of Power in Nazi Germany 269; of Bloody Sunday 154; of the February Revolution 154; of the October Revolution 4, 153–4; of the Second International 154
Apter 42, 43, 261
armed forces 4, *see also* ritual: and the armed forces; Induction into, 105–8
Aspaturian 143
Avdeev 169

Bagehot 256
Basilov 83
Baturin 56, 103, 104, 105
Bellah 41, 42, 255, 257
Berestovskaya 50, 56, 74, 113
Binns 4, 22
birth ritual 68–74, 201, 221, 232, 245–6
Bocock 43, 44, 253, 255
body symbolism *see* symbolism
Bonaparte 264
Brezhnev 185, 187, 188; cult of 220
Brigade of Communist Labour 114
Brogan 259
Bromlei 248
Brown, A. 220
Brown, E. J. 208
Brudnyi 23, 35, 60, 62, 84, 97, 104, 108, 110, 123, 130, 133, 162, 193, 194, 204, 235, 250

Brzezinski 284

ceremony, definitions of 14–15
Christmas 137
Churchward 219
civil religion 41, 43, 44, 255–8, 266, 280–1; in America 41, 44, 52; and (church) religion 256
collective farm peasantry and ritual, the 120, 127–8
colour symbolism *see* symbolism
coming-of-age ritual 102–5
Communist Party 26, 46, 47, 48, 49, 54, 216, 274; initiation into 94; Programme of 24, 35
conflict and ritual 11, 12, 13, 16, 33, 284
cult: of the leader *see* leader cult; of Hitler *see* Hitler cult; of Lenin *see* Lenin cult; of Stalin *see* Stalin cult
cultural management 1, 2, 3, 13, 16, 25, 27–31, 259
cultural revolution 1, 2, 3, 28, 32
cultural revolution, Chinese 2

David 263
Day: for the Blood Witnesses (in Nazi Germany) 269; of the Constitution 100, 154; of Maturity 103–5
Demonstration *see* mass political holidays
Douglas 224
Down 262, 263, 264
Dozhinki 124
Drazheva 135
Dunham 34
Dunn 79
Durkheim 14, 153, 259

Eberpi 137
El'chenko 47, 49, 51, 60, 80, 145, 230, 246

Index

Engels 185, 187, 188, 220
escape ritual 23
expressive activity 11, 222

festival: definition of 15
Festival of the Supreme Being 263, 266
Festive Registration of the New-Born Child 4; *see also* birth ritual
Festive Session 158–9
Filatov 57, 75, 120, 123, 193, 204
Fitzpatrick 2, 202
Founder's Day 113
Friedrich 284
functionalism *see* ritual, functionalist approach to
funeral rite 4, 38, 82–6, 246–7
Fursin 20, 21, 23, 49, 57, 90, 108, 119, 159, 193, 223, 240, 246

Gagarin 211
Gamm 269, 275, 276
Gazhos 245, 246
Geertz 12, 17, 39, 152
Genkin 51, 110, 114, 153, 156, 185, 207
Gerandokov 47, 50, 74, 82, 90, 91, 107, 112, 113, 114, 121, 123
Gerodnik 83, 84, 85, 87, 88, 147, 246
Glaser 267, 277, 278
Gluckman 14, 15, 23
Glyaser 178
Goodin 16, 43, 44
Goody 239
Gorky 203
Grishchenko 54, 105, 107, 111, 115, 117, 223, 243
Gushchin 163, 164, 167, 171, 174, 175, 178

Haimson 207
Hammond 258
Harper 122
Harvest Day 122–3
Harvest Festival 4; in Nazi Germany 269
Hawthorn 214
Hayes 267
hero: definition of 205–6; of labour 208–9; military 107, 277; Soviet definition of 206; in Soviet culture 205, 207–8; as symbol 207–10, 214; worship of 36, 277
'hero' towns 146, 223

Heroes' Memorial Day (in Nazi Germany) 269
Hitler 268, 269, 276, 277; cult of 277–8
Holiday: definition of 15; of the Birch 134–5; of Hammer and Sickle 127–8; of the First Furrow 126–7; of the First Sheaf 126–7; of *Ivan Kupala* 136, 234–5; of the New Year *see* New Year; of Spring *see* Novruz; of Spring (in Nazi Germany) 269; of the Street 150–2
holidays: of the calendric cycle 54, 56, 64, 130–9, 193; acceptance of 243; of occupations 114
Hollander 3, 220
Human Rights Day 16
Human Rights groups 16

iconicity of ritual 17
ideology 12, 18, 30, 266, 271–2, 275, 282–3, 284; definition of 39, 40
Induction into the Armed Forces 105–8
initiation ritual: acceptance of 243–4
Initiation: as cultivators 121–2; as grain collectors 121–2; into the Komsomol 90–1; as students 98–9; into Oktyabryata 90; into the working class 110–12, 243; into the Young Pioneers 90–3
instrumental activity 11, 12, 221
intelligentsia and Soviet ritual 26, 34, 143, 194, 203, 248
International Women's Day 154
Islam *see* ritual and Islam
Izvekov, N. P. 167

Kakonin 54, 105, 107, 111, 115, 117, 223, 243
Kampars 23, 36, 37, 51, 52, 53, 69, 83, 111, 114, 120, 124, 131, 132, 133, 139, 141, 146, 149, 155, 193, 229, 230, 231, 237
key scenario 195, 222, 227
key symbol 195, 198, 202
Khachirov 74
Khasanova 50
Khrushchev 29, 30, 31, 217, 219, 220
Kikilo 139, 149, 151, 246
Knowledge Society 46
Kolarz 177
Komsomol: initiation into 90–1
Korchagina 18
Kryvelev 58
Kuchiev 112, 113, 120, 123, 127

Index

305

Index

Robertson 44

Robespierre 262, 263

Rogozina 51, 75, 76, 82, 98, 100, 101, 107

Rousseau 41

Rudnev 36, 37, 46, 70, 71, 75, 80, 84, 85, 89, 90, 91, 97, 99, 100, 106, 110, 113, 114, 115, 119, 120, 123, 132, 147, 149, 162, 185, 202, 243, 244, 245, 246, 249

Russian Orthodox religion and ritual 88, 130–1, 236, 237

Sabantui 124–6, 234

Sarsenbaev 233

Scarlet Sails ritual 97

school-leaving ritual 60

secular ritual 11, 37, 38, 39; definition of 35, 36

Seeing-off of Winter see Maslenitsa

Sekou Touré 261

Semik 134

Shchukin 179

Shevelev 36, 37

Shils 3, 21, 239, 253, 255, 256, 257

Shiryaeva 153

Shneidere 52, 240

Smith 105, 140, 141, 197, 210, 213

Soboul 263, 264

social control 19, 22, 25, 27, 28, 31

socialist internationalism 140, 141, 142, 143

Socialist Labour Competition 116, 117, 118, 221

Soehngen 270, 276

Solemn Registration of the New-Born Child see birth ritual

Solzhenytsin 219

Sorokin 246

Soviet Marxism–Leninism 20, 24, 25, 26, 28, 31, 34, 35, 36, 37, 38, 40, 41, 210, 212, 225, 251, 260, 272, 278–9

Spring Days for Children 94

Stakhanovite Movement 116, 221

Stalin 154, 176, 182, 214, 261; cult of 29, 217–18, 219, 277–8

Struve 57, 241

Subbotnik 116, 118, 119, 162–3, 212, 221

Sukhanov 20, 21, 31, 131

Sukhov 115, 116

Summer Days of Youth 103–5

summer solstice 4; in Nazi Germany 269

Sushkov 206, 208

Swyngedouw 252

symbol: of the Blazing Torch 96–7, 276; of the Birch 134, 199; elaborating 194–5, 202, 212–13; of the Eternal Flame 37, 145, 196–7; of fire 199–200, 276; of the flag 276; of the hero see hero; key 195, 198, 202; of Lenin see Lenin; of the lighted candle 198; of the relay race 202; summarizing 194–5, 198, 212–13; see also symbolism, sacred; of young tree 198

symbolism 11, 17, 37, 191–227; body 178, 224–7; of colour red 200–1; of the French Revolution 263–4, 265–6; historical 222; history of Soviet 191–2; of holidays of calendric cycle 193; of life-cycle ritual 193; of light 199, 276; of the massed choir 225; of massed gymnastic displays 226, 276; of the mass political holidays 153, 164, 168, 171, 174, 175, 177, 181, 182–3, 185, 187; military 117, 181, 202, 224; musical 214; of Nazi ritual 269–70; of poetry 203; of rites of initiation 193; sacred 197, 199, 213, 223, 227; see also symbols, summarizing; secular 197, 200, 202, 227, 275–6; sexual 224; Ortner's typology of 194; Soviet approaches to 34; of swearing an oath 202–3

syncretism 229–38

Teplyakov 53, 148, 246

Timoshin 154, 160, 161, 166, 172, 180, 182, 185, 188, 249

Trotsky 2, 58

Tsekhnovitser 158, 164, 168, 171, 174, 179, 180, 225

Tucker 2

Tul'tseva 81, 230

Turner, T. 12, 17, 21, 35, 36

Turner, V. 17, 23, 45, 61, 191, 195, 200, 253

Ugrinovich 18, 20, 21, 57, 68, 70, 104, 114, 115, 193, 229, 240, 243

Unger 4, 64, 241, 270, 273, 278

Urazmanova 125

Utechin 177

value consensus see ritual: and value consensus